What people say about this *Complete Idiot's Guide* book:

"Thom Lisk knows speakers. He knows how they think, he knows how they work and he knows how they succeed. In this book, Thom shares his years of experience to help new and experienced speakers take their business to the next level."

—**Dr. Tim Ursiny,** author, *The Top Performer's Guide to Presentations*

"The genius of this book is that it takes years and years of accumulated wisdom, knowledge and skill that he boils down to the core, to the absolute essentials you must know to thrive and build a satisfying, lucrative career with unlimited potential. If you only have time to read a single book in this field, this is the one to read."

—**Peter Reilly, Esquire,** law professor and professional speaker and trainer

"A powerful collection of tools that will take your speaker career to the next level. Reading and applying these ideas will save you years and speed up your success."

—**Bill McGrane,** The McGrane Center for Personal Transformation

"Dr. Thom Lisk knows of what he writes and speaks. He is an expert in the fields of leadership and public speaking. This is a very thorough and excellent guide to the 'in's and out's' of being in the business of professional speaking."

—**Charles Smyser,** Global Executive Development Services, LLC

"Written with lively stories and examples, you'll learn more about running your speaking business than you can from any other books. I just loved the stories because they made it so easy to learn what I should do to take my speaking business to the next level! We speakers use the medium of storytelling ourselves—and it's said people 'teach like they learn'—Thom you're brilliant!"

—**Carolyn B. Thompson,** Training Systems, Inc.

"Marketing and branding THEMSELVES are vitally important for speakers so I am glad that Dr. Lisk covers this in an excellent, useable way. These guidelines work."

—**Bill Hoke,** Small Business Marketing Partners and 90 Minute Branding and Marketing Plan workshops

"Thom Lisk writes from his extensive real world experience coaching, promoting and booking speakers. By applying just a few of his practical ideas, you are guaranteed to increase your bookings!"

—**Michael Bergdahl,** international keynote speaker and author

"I am a world traveler and have heard speakers for 50 years. I would have become a pro speaker years ago had I a guideline like this great book. It helps you eliminate trial and error. Use his guidance and succeed!"

—**Kenneth Pearce,** fellow of the Royal Society of Health

"This is a hard way to make an easy living. Be so-o glad you have Dr. Thom's *Idiot's Guide...* to help make it all more DO-able."

—**Nanci McGraw,** "Life Rewards the DO-ers!"™ keynoter, author, and winner of 100+ broadcasting awards

"I have been in speaking business for 25 years and it took me a long time to learn what is in this book. Don't waste years on your own, follow this book."

—**Paul Clayton,** PE Clayton & Associates, Inc.

"A wonderful step by step approach for anyone planning a truly successful career as a speaker. The author is a successful speaker of many, many years in an industry that is lucrative but difficult to penetrate. His experienced guidance in this book is priceless!"

—**Dr. Susan Flowers,** CEO of Manifesting Success Network, Speaker & Consultants

"Very practical, down-to-earth tips that can help anyone wanting to market themselves as a professional speaker. All of the author's advice is based on years of experience in the field. A *must read*."

—**Dr. Marilyn Manning,** CEO, The Consulting Team, LLC, international speaker, author, and consultant

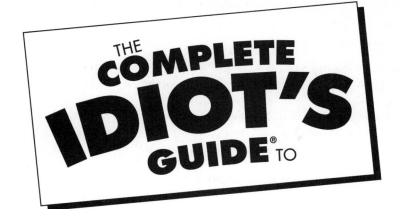

THE COMPLETE IDIOT'S GUIDE® TO

Success as a Professional Speaker

by Thomas (Thom) A. Lisk, LHD

A member of Penguin Group (USA) Inc.

I dedicate this book to our grandchildren—growing speakers.

ALPHA BOOKS

Published by the Penguin Group

Penguin Group (USA) Inc., 375 Hudson Street, New York, New York 10014, USA

Penguin Group (Canada), 90 Eglinton Avenue East, Suite 700, Toronto, Ontario M4P 2Y3, Canada (a division of Pearson Penguin Canada Inc.)

Penguin Books Ltd., 80 Strand, London WC2R 0RL, England

Penguin Ireland, 25 St. Stephen's Green, Dublin 2, Ireland (a division of Penguin Books Ltd.)

Penguin Group (Australia), 250 Camberwell Road, Camberwell, Victoria 3124, Australia (a division of Pearson Australia Group Pty. Ltd.)

Penguin Books India Pvt. Ltd., 11 Community Centre, Panchsheel Park, New Delhi—110 017, India

Penguin Group (NZ), 67 Apollo Drive, Rosedale, North Shore, Auckland 1311, New Zealand (a division of Pearson New Zealand Ltd.)

Penguin Books (South Africa) (Pty.) Ltd., 24 Sturdee Avenue, Rosebank, Johannesburg 2196, South Africa

Penguin Books Ltd., Registered Offices: 80 Strand, London WC2R 0RL, England

International Standard Book Number: 978-1-59257-744-6
Library of Congress Catalog Card Number: 2008920833

10   09   08   8   7   6   5   4   3   2

Interpretation of the printing code: The rightmost number of the first series of numbers is the year of the book's printing; the rightmost number of the second series of numbers is the number of the book's printing. For example, a printing code of 08-1 shows that the first printing occurred in 2008.

Printed in the United States of America

Note: This publication contains the opinions and ideas of its author. It is intended to provide helpful and informative material on the subject matter covered. It is sold with the understanding that the author and publisher are not engaged in rendering professional services in the book. If the reader requires personal assistance or advice, a competent professional should be consulted.

The author and publisher specifically disclaim any responsibility for any liability, loss, or risk, personal or otherwise, which is incurred as a consequence, directly or indirectly, of the use and application of any of the contents of this book.

Most Alpha books are available at special quantity discounts for bulk purchases for sales promotions, premiums, fund-raising, or educational use. Special books, or book excerpts, can also be created to fit specific needs.

For details, write: Special Markets, Alpha Books, 375 Hudson Street, New York, NY 10014.

Publisher: *Marie Butler-Knight*
Editorial Director: *Mike Sanders*
Senior Managing Editor: *Billy Fields*
Senior Acquisitions Editor: *Paul Dinas*
Development Editor: *Nancy D. Lewis*
Production Editor: *Kayla Dugger*
Copy Editor: *Jan Zoya*

Cartoonist: *Steve Barr*
Cover Designer: *Bill Thomas*
Book Designer: *Trina Wurst*
Indexer: *Celia McCoy*
Layout: *Brian Massey*
Proofreader: *Mary Hunt*

Contents at a Glance

Contents

Introduction

What does it take to succeed in the world of paid professional speaking? A sense of humor and a solid plan. I can help motivate you toward a positive mental attitude (it's something that you must work on developing, if you don't already have PMA). In this book, I lay out before you all the necessary steps that you must take if you are to take your speaking career to its optimum level.

All professional speakers have a passion for their message or topic; they feel compelled to share what they know with people who can learn from their experience, knowledge, and wisdom. All professional speakers must also be business-minded people. Ideally you love your audience. Those who take the time to learn the ins and outs of this great business usually go as far as they want to; but in order to do so, you need to stay focused and motivated. Those who believe that their message and/or their unique delivery of that message will automatically take them into the stratosphere of the speaker world are simply naïve. This is the exact reason why so many aspiring speakers do not find consistent and well-paying bookings and why they hang up their speaker hats after only a year or two. Please don't let this be you—go for it long term!

Routine is essential to the professional speaker's long-term success. You must view speaking as a full-time (eventually at least) profession, even if you are not speaking full time at the moment. Most part-timers who are uncommitted just do not make it long term in any kind of profession—you know that. Be prepared to invest at least 15 hours per week at first, researching and contacting your best potential clients while also developing your presentation content. Keep track of the time invested, and don't cut corners. You will never move up to the top of the ladder of success if you try to skip steps.

Above all, I urge you to keep your life in balance. Professional success means nothing if you've lost your loved ones, your health, and your dignity along the way. Good luck and God bless you in your professional speaking ventures.

How to Use This Book

This book is divided into five parts.

In **Part 1, "A Professional Speaker's Primer,"** you'll learn that professional speakers who sustain themselves tend to have several characteristics in common, including a real knack for the business end of the profession. This part describes some of the other personality traits professional speakers tend to share and also gives you a peek into the lives of several typical speakers.

In **Part 2, "In Pursuit of the Profession,"** you'll read everything you need to know about developing your best topics and much more. As an example, you'll learn why it's important to open your message up to different clients and audiences. This is the difference between having a small audience (or only a few clients) and having a career that's ever-expanding!

Part 3, "Cultivating Your Speaking Career," includes tips for marketing and "branding" yourself as a unique and totally unforgettable speaker. When people remember you, they are more likely to seek you out and refer you to others. Clients want to book you, audience members look to purchase your books and/or other materials, and your career can take off in a new and unstoppable direction toward big-time success!

Part 4, "Financial Fundamentals," teaches you about pricing your services, billing clients, and collecting on your debts, among other important issues. You'll read about how to find the highest-paying clients in your field, how to land them, and the best ways to keep them, along with other success ideas.

Part 5, "Career Advancement," talks about how to use your positive speaking experiences as a springboard for future success. You'll also read about some ethically challenging speaker situations and how to avoid getting caught in the middle of them. Your continued upward success depends as much on your off-the-center-stage behavior as on your speaking skill. Sometimes, knowing what *not* to do is an important part of this business!

Sidebars

As you read the text, you'll notice the occasional sidebar. There are three types.

Success Shortcuts

Advice on which corners can be cut on the road to success as a professional speaker.

Words to the Wise

Warnings to help aspiring speakers prevent wasting time and money.

def•i•ni•tion

Clear, concise explanations of the lingo used by professional speakers.

Acknowledgments

Special thanks to my staff in my company, Professional Speakers' Bureau Int'l and TerrificSpeakers.com, who covered for me while I worked on this book; and thanks to our clients and my speaker friends over the past 30-plus years, so many of whom have taught me so much. Thanks to Paul Dinas, my wonderful acquisitions editor who encouraged me and believed that I was/am the perfect person to write this book. Thanks to Shelly Hagen, who assisted me in many ways in writing the book—she was a great help along the way. Thanks to everyone at the publisher for their attention to detail. Thanks to my parents, one an award-winning teacher, the other an award-winning journalist; what great examples! Thanks to my wife, Lorna M. Lisk, a great gift from God, and an aspiring speaker herself. Thanks to our five married children and their spouses for their love and respect.

Trademarks

All terms mentioned in this book that are known to be or are suspected of being trademarks or service marks have been appropriately capitalized. Alpha Books and Penguin Group (USA) Inc. cannot attest to the accuracy of this information. Use of a term in this book should not be regarded as affecting the validity of any trademark or service mark.

Part 1

A Professional Speaker's Primer

So you want to earn money for speaking your mind ... sounds like a pretty good way to make a living, especially for someone who enjoys communicating and loves to have an audience. But did you ever stop to think about the characteristics of professional speakers and the things that inspire them, or what a day in their life might be like? Here you'll learn what it takes to become (and remain) a successful professional speaker.

Chapter 1

Professionally Speaking ...

In This Chapter

- ◆ The difference between amateur and professional speakers
- ◆ What can speakers earn?
- ◆ Every topic is fair game for speakers!
- ◆ How speaking for free benefits you

Empowering yourself to start and continue your speaking career is every bit as important as learning all of the A-to-Z facts about the business of speaking. I have invested over 30 years as a speaker and as someone who books other speakers. During those 30 years, I have wanted to quit many times. Although I have had some great successes, I have often felt under-valued, not fully appreciated, and as though I were on my way out (when I didn't have as many upcoming bookings for speeches, seminars, or work-shops as I would have liked, for example). At those times, I could have used some guidance, and that's what I intend to provide you with in this book. I don't want you to have to learn by trial or error, the way I did.

When my business career was hitting on all cylinders, I found this business exhilarating and rewarding. The hours invested in research paid off when one of the speakers I worked with, or perhaps a letter from a client, would say, "Congratulations on a great program!" (and include a healthy check).

In this chapter, I'll give you an overview of who goes into the field of professional speaking, some of the routes they take along the way, and the likelihood of success.

Who Becomes a Professional Speaker?

Perhaps you've heard that next to death (and taxes), the fear of speaking in front of a group in public is the biggest fear of all. Although it's true that some people seem to be born with a gift for gab and entertaining while others simply aren't, almost anyone can become a terrific speaker, because professional speaking is a skill that can be developed like most other skills.

Speakers can start at any age, and many keep going and going and going—I actually know a few who have spoken for fees after age 90! Most begin in their 30s or 40s, though some may begin after retirement. There's no "perfect" age to jump into this career. Whenever you feel the need to share your knowledge with others, that's the time to make your move. And there's really no topic that you can't speak on. On the other hand, there are some professions that provide on-the-job training, so to speak, toward becoming a professional speaker. Other careers don't provide such an easy shift, but there are plenty of ways to prepare you to transition from Point A (your work or hobby) to Point B (teaching others about that line of work or hobby).

Are there inborn characteristics that a personal speaker has? Consider this: my mother, Betty, was a wonderful school teacher for 35 years and my father, Harold, was a journalist and bureau chief for an international news service. Was speaking and communication in my genetic makeup? Was I destined to be a speaker? Both my grandparents were part-time politicians. Now my environment certainly influenced me, but I believe that I made my own choices regarding my career. In short, I would not have followed this path had I not felt it were the right one for me. Now I ask you to examine the people who may be influencing your decision to become a speaker. Above all else, you have to know that this is what you want. And if it is what you want, you need to have the courage to move forward and develop your career.

Keep in mind, if you want to become a professional speaker, you are setting yourself up to be scrutinized and compared to greater and lesser speakers. Get ready for that! People who become terrific speakers are willing to overcome all kinds of obstacles and objections. So the second "skill" that must be in place before you begin your career is a belief in yourself and the need to share your message in spite of opposition, criticism, and unanticipated setbacks.

Inspiration is another important facet of a successful speaking career. Find an emotional reason to become a speaker and don't forget it. It could be that you want to prove your first wife or husband's mother wrong: you really are super-terrific! Or maybe you want to be more and do more than anyone else in your family tree has ever done. I know speakers who've felt they were called to the profession by God, and I am not specifically talking about ordained ministers.

Inspiration, belief in yourself, and courage aside, there are some professions that give aspiring speakers on-the-job training. We'll talk about who those folks might be in the following section.

Success Shortcuts _____

"Passion is the master key to success," or so I've been told by many established speakers. Leaders are passionate about saying to themselves, "My effort and actions are making a difference." Can you believe that? If your answer is a resounding "Yes!" then you are on your way to success as a speaker.

Careers That Translate Easily to Public Speaking

Professional speakers do two things: they inform and they keep their audiences interested. It stands to reason, then, that educators and entertainers would make outstanding public speakers.

Many educators, whether from primary, secondary, or advanced education, make an attempt at becoming professional speakers. There are dozens of reasons why; it is not always about money or attempting to move from an amateur to a professional status. Some educators simply burn out in the classroom, and some think they can make a bigger difference in the world by appealing to a wider audience.

How about entertainers? Years ago, I came to realize that most people would rather be entertained than educated. Look at how much Oprah Winfrey and David Letterman are paid, and compare that to the president of the largest university in your area. The entertainers make at least 20 times more than the educators, right? Some entertainers become professional speakers (Oprah Winfrey, for example, has been known to speak at commencements and for various good causes). But more often, speakers who educate decide that they must become entertaining in order to appeal to their audiences.

Success Shortcuts _____

Experts sometimes think they are above or beyond making people laugh or adding some entertaining element to their seminars or speeches. However, even a PowerPoint presentation can be made entertaining, so consider all the options and ask yourself what you're willing to do to receive rave reviews, keep people tuned in, and get invited back!

Speaking on Your Area of Expertise

Perhaps you've thought about becoming a speaker, but don't know where to begin. Maybe you question your abilities or your credentials. Maybe you have the misguided notion that professional speakers lucked out somewhere along the way—they either have unbelievable personal or professional connections or they possess a charisma that you feel you just don't have.

The truth is, professional speakers are some of the most interesting and interested people in society, people just like you! Every industry and every area of interest needs professional speakers. The question is, how passionate are you about your topic? How dedicated are you to the possibility of creating a full-time speaking career?

The greatest speakers throughout history—those who have changed society with their ideas—have been passionate about their mission to serve others. In fact, some speakers don't really start as speakers at all, but as common people with a deep love for their work or hobby that drives them to become experts in a particular topic area.

A man who loves working in his garden, for example, may be asked by others, "How do you grow such gigantic roses?" He becomes a consultant and expert to his friends and neighbors before joining a local horticulture group. Here, he learns even more about his favorite pastime, attends community events sponsored by his organization, speaks to the media, and ends up having his own spot on the noon news where he talks about the wonders of gardening. After some time, a national fertilizer company sponsors this man on a nationwide speaking tour.

The woman who turns her efforts to providing her terminally ill son's wish to be a fireman eventually puts her all into helping other families grant wishes to their dying children. A local newspaper covers the story, and the woman becomes a speaker/spokesperson for the rights of the terminally ill. This eventually leads her to a career as a professional speaker, addressing medical organizations, large corporations (in search of donations), and the like.

Many ex-Olympians turn their passion and expertise concerning their sport into a passion for speaking, turning life lessons into paid gigs. Sometimes it's more difficult for these folks to sustain a long-term career, however, especially if they do not have a mission and vision to serve others. In other words, once their notoriety wears off, they are no longer able to sell themselves as speakers—that is, if they're only in this business for the money.

Ex-athletes who really want to make a contribution to society by speaking about perseverance, hope, and courage, for example, often realize they can continue sharing their experiences with audiences for decades. Take Bob Richards, for example.

He adorned the Cheerios Cereal Box after he won the Decathlon in the 1956 Olympics and was hailed as the world's greatest athlete. Bob then went on to a 40-year career as a professional speaker. He wasn't sustaining his career on a past achievement; his life experiences and his passion for helping his audience are what sustained his career.

Some careers—or at least the topics that grow out of certain career fields—may not transition easily into professional speaking. A rocket scientist, for example, may not seem to be a natural for the professional speaking circuit, mostly because his area of expertise may be limited to highly complex and industry-specific information. Other scientists would enjoy hearing about his technical prowess, but the average corporate worker (the most common type of audiences that professional speakers address) wouldn't. Also because in-depth technical presentations are far less in demand than, say, business leadership messages, the pay tends to be much less.

If you find yourself in this position, don't lose hope. There's a silver lining if you can market and repackage your message to various organizations. To begin, think about how your expertise might be helpful to various groups of people and then format your expertise around a topic that will appeal to those groups. Let's say, for example, that you are a rocket scientist. Aside from other professionals in your field, who might benefit from hearing about your professional and personal achievements? High school seniors? Science majors at the local university? A science club? No matter what topic you're an expert in, you can mold your message to appeal to different audiences. In Part 3 of this book, we will discuss some test marketing of your material.

 Words to the Wise

If your colleagues have no interest in becoming professional speakers, you may feel isolated on the way to your goal. Learn how to encourage and motivate yourself. You can join groups of like-minded pioneers or aspiring entrepreneurs, an association like Toastmasters, or a community or church group to bounce ideas off of.

Establishing Yourself as a Public Speaker

Establishing yourself as a public speaker is not easy, but the good news is it can be a lot of fun. The challenge is easier if you like dealing with people and don't mind a little bit of criticism.

We all grow and improve when we have people giving us feedback and critiques of our efforts. Many public speakers start by giving free speeches or short talks at local libraries, service or community groups, special interest groups, or at their church, synagogue, or mosque. Many speakers have started out as volunteers, only to realize that speaking was their true calling!

I established my career at the age of 25, after attending a required work seminar. The speakers at this seminar changed my life for the better and I will never forget them. (Such can be the impact of terrific speakers.)

While attending that seminar, I was so moved by the speakers' passion and intelligence, I set some goals for myself, one of which included becoming a great speaker myself someday. I was very impressed with the positive communication the two speakers delivered and I was thankful to my employer for enabling me to receive this inspirational education. The speakers brilliantly delivered their generic material in a customized way that all attendees could understand and later apply. As a result of what I learned at that seminar, I became the number-one Branch Profit Center Manager at my workplace, outperforming people who had 20-plus years' experience on me.

When I was 27, after seeing that I had taken his words to heart and put them into action, one of those speakers recruited me into the business of full-time professional speaking and helped me to establish my career. What a great mentor!

You can establish yourself as a speaker by giving speeches anywhere and everywhere you can. When you are established (you've presented your material to various audiences and have been well received and/or invited back), you can begin charging a small fee for your programs. (You don't need a mentor; you have this book!) Keep your day job, of course, until you perfect your messages, study the market for your type of presentation, and are ready to commit to this line of work.

Defining the Professional Speaker

You may have been heard dozens of speakers in your life, but have you stopped to consider the difference between an amateur and *professional speaker?* Is the amateur any less intelligent? Is he less dedicated to the topic or the field of speaking? Is the professional humorless and committed only to earning as much money as she can? No, no, and no. In this section, you'll learn the difference between amateur and professional speakers … and you'll find that they actually have quite a few things in common.

def•i•ni•tion

Professional speakers are experts in their field and are paid for their presentations.

Professional vs. Amateur Ambitions

Generally speaking, the professional speaker attempts to make a living from sharing her information with others. She charges for presentations, spends 80 percent of her time marketing herself, and is constantly updating and customizing her material for her next speaking engagement. Amateurs, on the other hand, are content to speak here and there, aren't looking to make a full-time commitment to speaking, and aren't expecting to make their livelihood in this manner (at least not yet).

In most cases, you have to be the amateur before you become the professional. Does that mean that you aren't making a pledge to be your best, or that you'll never earn a living by speaking? No. It simply means that you have to sharpen your skills before you can command the big bucks. How are you going to do that, you wonder? Keep reading ...

Free Speech

Speakers who don't charge for their presentation are sometimes given a free meal and little else. But don't feel too sorry for these men and women: sometimes these free speakers have an ulterior motive (they want to sell copies of their book in the lobby, for example) or a vested interest in the goings-on of the group they're speaking to. (A civil engineer speaking about the impact of traffic signals at a town meeting may be interested in the safety of his hometown roads.) Thousands of such free speeches go on every day all over America and around the world.

Now I know the title of this book is *The Complete Idiot's Guide to Success as a Professional Speaker*, which implies that you'll be paid for your appearances. However, most experts in this field agree that giving free speeches is a good way to begin a speaking career. You can hone your skills, make contacts, and show people what you're made of before you start charging them!

As Chairman for Programs for Rotary International (Hilliard, Ohio chapter) for three consecutive years, I personally arranged 80 percent of the (free) speakers for the weekly meetings. We held 48 meetings a year; multiply that by three years, and I figure that I scheduled about 144 free speakers during that time. One of the best perks of being a Rotary member is that you can meet many of the movers and shakers, so to speak, in your home town, state, and nation. Can you envision some of the benefits of having these contacts? How could they help your speaking career?

Success Shortcuts

Rotary International claims to be the largest community service club organization in the world. Each club needs free speakers each week. The benefits of membership include developing skills as a speaker, making contacts, creating leadership opportunities, and much more. Other great and similar community service clubs include Kiwanis, Lions, and Sierra Clubs—all need speakers but don't pay for them.

You can also speak for free at local colleges or universities as a guest lecturer in your area of expertise. Business and sales managers in many industries or market niches have weekly management or sales meetings in-house, and they often welcome outside speakers who can share some valued ideas, and especially motivation, to make the meeting more meaningful. In these cases, it is expected that the speaker has some kind of not-so-hidden agenda. For example, I've known speakers who have made millions from giving what seemed to be free in-house speeches to companies—but the hook involved selling seats to seminars. This is just one masterful example of how some well-known speakers have gotten started in the speaking business, going on to become high-priced paid speakers.

Fee Speech

As a speaker, I have been paid anywhere from $25 to $5,000 for a speech, and more for seminars. I know speakers who have been paid $50,000 to give a 60-minute keynote speech. Is it the big-buck potential that attracts you to speaking? I hope not; I hope you have a great message burning within you that you must share with others. Established, well-paid speakers have a passion for their topics and their audiences. The passion is there first, you see, and the money is just icing on the cake.

Every day of the week, speakers are paid to give seminars or workshops, facilitate group meetings on all kinds of topics, lead training sessions that may last from three hours to five days in duration, and so on.

Now I have to address the misconception that you're going to earn millions of dollars in your first few years of speaking. Celebrity speakers can earn hundreds of thousands of dollars for one appearance; most "regular" speakers are not up in that price range, so you'll have to be more realistic about your career in speaking, especially when you're starting out. Speakers who are looking to make a living with their presentations definitely charge what they're worth, though.

Start-up speakers often report feeling exhilarated when receiving positive reviews from audience members—almost as though they are celebrities for the moment. This is natural and wonderful; however, don't jeopardize your financial and/or family's future in the pursuit of good feelings that enhance your self-esteem. Speaking is a business, and full-time speakers charge what they're worth. As a speaker, you'll invest time traveling, preparing or customizing materials, and marketing, so you have to take all of that into consideration when calculating your fee and deciding which route to take. Think about this: you could give 25 speeches a year at $2,000 to $4,000 each, or give 12 seminars during that same time period at $5,000 each. Both will provide you with great earnings, and both can be done as part-time ventures—but only if you're charging what your presentation is worth!

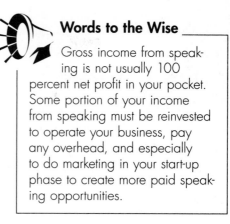

Words to the Wise

Gross income from speaking is not usually 100 percent net profit in your pocket. Some portion of your income from speaking must be reinvested to operate your business, pay any overhead, and especially to do marketing in your start-up phase to create more paid speaking opportunities.

Unfortunately, speakers often undervalue and underprice their programs—this is one thing you want to avoid. On the other hand, you don't want to overprice yourself as a speaker. We'll talk a lot more about pricing in Chapter 17.

Pros Earn the Most

Everyone knows who Tiger Woods is, right? The world's greatest golfer is paid far more than the men he competes against. Why? He's the best in his field, he's recognized as a major talent, and just as important, he's marketable. People like him. He has major endorsement deals because folks see him as a trustworthy, intelligent guy who isn't going to steer them wrong.

So how does Tiger Woods set an example for professional speakers? Professional speakers must strive to make themselves marketable (appealing to some niche of society and/or corporate America); then they have to get out there and market themselves, which is something Mr. Woods can afford to hire someone else to do for him. (We'll talk about tips for getting your name out there in Chapter 12.) Like Woods, you can earn more than other speakers who offer services similar to yours, but you have to know your markets and how to compete in them.

Strive to be the best, and success will invariably follow.

I admit to you that I lost track of this goal at times in my 30-year career as a speaker and as someone who books speakers. I want to challenge you to not allow all the distractions of life to compromise your intention to become the very best speaker you can become.

What do you have to lose? If you shoot for the moon and miss, you will end up among the stars, and that is a great place to be, too.

Industry Speakers

Industry speakers are experts in a given field who give presentations to their colleagues. For example, real estate speakers address other realtors. Within one industry, there can be different types of industry speakers. For example, the first type of real estate speaker is one who gives continuing-education classes for the 1 million or more realtors in America, state by state. (These speakers are lucky to scratch out a living, as many people can earn continuing-education credits online.)

def•i•ni•tion

> **Industry speakers** are experts who often have worked in a particular industry or type of business classification for many years. They know the buzzwords in that industry. They are well respected by top leaders in the specific industry.

The second type of industry speaker makes far more than the first. He speaks at big conferences and gives very specific educational and motivational seminars about how to be a successful realtor. This expert speaker has a very strong background in real estate sales. This also holds true in other industries, where the best of the best often become speakers later in their careers.

Most industries have at least one or two speakers who have reached an extreme level of success; in fact, some of these people approach becoming celebrities in that particular industry! Know anyone like that? Could you become a highly paid industry-expert speaker? That may be great way to start out. Just keep in mind that many industries offer scant pay to even the most expert speakers, so before you invest too much time in this venture, do your homework.

In any event, whether you're being paid a pittance or a fortune to speak to your colleagues, speaking is great exposure and a terrific way to make yourself known to people in your career field. Plus, word-of-mouth is a powerful tool. Deliver a winning presentation, and you may get a good-paying offer or two in return. And the experience of speaking in front of a large group is always invaluable. So use this opportunity to practice and upgrade your skills and perfect your message. There's no better way to do it!

The Least You Need to Know

◆ Familiarize yourself with various kinds of speaking, and determine which types are best suited for you.

◆ Speaking for free can be an effective way to gain experience, improve your skills, and start your business.

◆ Speaking for income on a consistent basis requires dedication to creating great programs and marketing.

◆ Earning significant income as a professional speaker takes time, effort, and patience.

Do You Have What It Takes?

In This Chapter

- ◆ Breaking down your personality
- ◆ Using your expertise and personal experience in your presentation
- ◆ Running your own business
- ◆ Watching the company you keep

What does it take to become a successful professional speaker? Time? Money? Intelligence? Well, it takes all of these to some extent … but there are also other contributing factors. Your personality, your home life, and your natural abilities all play into your achievements as a speaker.

In this chapter, we'll take a look at the foundational pillars for success, and consider the bedrock upon which the pillars stand. The world's greatest pro speakers are some of the world's most highly principled, intelligent, caring, and hard-working people … and their success was no accident. They've structured their personal lives as carefully as they've crafted their work.

Your Public Persona Pillar

We tend to think of public speakers as entertainers—boisterous, gregarious, rather loud people. Having worked with thousands of speakers, as well as thousands of audiences, I can assure you that terrific speakers come in all personality profiles. No matter what their personality, successful speakers find a way to show their audiences that they care about them.

Profiling Your Personality

Because I'm asserting that you can be a successful professional speaker regardless of your personality type, I won't bother listing individual character traits of speakers. If, however, you are the analytical type, you may want some more insight into your own personality.

Success Shortcuts

There are other personality tests, too. Find one that seems most helpful to you in first understanding yourself, and then in understanding and serving your audiences. These tools are especially helpful if you are focused on training or facilitation-type work as a speaker.

You can find out more about yourself with just the click of the mouse. Do a simple Google search for Myers-Briggs Type (MBT) Inventory or the Birkman Profile, two standard personality-deciphering tests. These tests may be available online, but for a deeper understanding of what makes you tick (and what makes you run for cover), you may want to find a consultant who specializes in this type of testing.

As I said, you can become a great speaker regardless of your personality profile—as long as you have a burning desire to share your knowledge with others. I don't care if you're as quiet as a church mouse. I don't care if others listen to you and look at you as though you're a little nutty. You can impart your love of your topic to others. Profiling your personality helps you to understand where you might need some help in appealing to the masses. For example, if your profile says that you aren't a great listener, then stop and consider how that could affect a speaking career:

- If you don't listen to your clients' needs, you can't provide them with the services they want.

- If you don't listen to audience members in a Q&A forum, you'll sound as though you're providing scripted responses.

- If you don't listen to audience feedback, you'll never be able to improve in the areas where you need it most.

This list could go on and on. Take a look at your personality profile and decide how your strengths and weaknesses could help or hurt your career. Then think of strategies to put your strong points to work and to overcome any obstacles your lesser points may present.

How Well Do You Relate to Others?

The MBT Inventory breaks people down into four basic behavioral categories. They are as follows:

- ◆ The E-I Scale: Extrovert to Introvert
- ◆ The S-N Scale: Sensing to Nurturing
- ◆ The T-F Scale: Thinking to Feeling
- ◆ The J-P Scale: Judging to Perceiving

Visualize four lines with the first letters above on a line to the extreme left of this page and the second letter to the extreme right of the page. The questions given in the MBT Inventory plot you on each line somewhere. For example, a very shy person (an introvert) would score over to the right of the line in the first category. The final tally of who you are is comprised of four letters, one from each category. You could be an INFP (introvert, nurturing, feeling, and perceiving) type; or you might be an ESFJ, an ISTJ, or any other number of combinations.

Basically, the questions are meant to answer the following questions:

- ◆ Where do you focus your attention and get your energy?
- ◆ How do you take in information and/or find things?
- ◆ How do you prefer to make a decision?
- ◆ What is your orientation toward the outer world?

If, as Socrates said, "Knowledge is power," then knowing yourself makes you more powerful, especially when it comes to understanding (and appealing to) others. If you've never thought about all the extremes of personality types out there, these personality profile tests will open your eyes to the way others think, feel, and judge. Hopefully, you'll keep this information in mind when you plan your presentations.

Pillar Doors

The doors on your pillars are the ways in and out of your speaking career. Although I would say that most professional speakers have a calling to enter this business, some of the most famous speakers don't—or at least they don't have a calling in the purest sense. No matter which way you enter this career, you'll find that hard work, intelligence, and marketing are a necessity for success!

Success Shortcuts _____

I find it helpful to label your central pillar Spirituality. This is important for many reasons, regardless of your religious affiliation or lack thereof. Spirituality provides many speakers with a sense of peacefulness and being grounded.

The doors on the pillar aren't really that important in terms of career success. The windows are. In this section, you'll read about the "Four E's" of the pillar windows and why they're so important to your audience.

Front Door and Back Door

Let's label the front door, the one you enter through, the "teacher's door." It's not a door reserved for certified educators—but it is a nod to those who helped you become who you are today (and thus helped you enter this door). Great teachers inspire minds and help people of all ages reach their potential. Regardless of your profession, no matter how high up on the corporate ladder you've risen, no matter how successful you become as a speaker, there was no doubt you had a wonderful teacher in your life who opened your eyes to the possibility of becoming a speaker somewhere along the way. He or she may have been an actual educator, but this person might also have been a friend or relative who helped you learn important lessons about yourself.

Success Shortcuts _____

Great speakers are often motivated by a need for positive feedback, applause, recognition, appreciation, or gratitude for their efforts. Give more to your audiences and you'll get more in return.

The back door is reserved for people who have become speakers not primarily because speaking was something they always wanted to do, but because the circumstances of their lives brought them to the speaking world. Top Gun pilot Bill Driscoll found his second calling when he became a trainer of Top Gun pilots. He found that he really enjoyed helping other pilots prepare for dog fights and battle. Shoot them down, or be shot down!

Well, "Willy," as his friends call him, discovered that he could use his Navy experience to teach civilians about coping with stressful situations. "Peak Performance Under Pressure" is the primary PowerPoint keynote presentation Willy tailors expertly for each client. His fee nearly doubled in the first five years of his speaking career, and so did his bookings for paid engagements.

You could say Willy entered into speaking from the back door because, like many currently high-paid presenters, he never set out to be a full-time speaker. However, also like many speakers, Willy leveraged his prior experiences and successes and worked them into a message that has universal appeal.

Who are some other back-door speakers?

- ◆ Colonel Oliver North shared his experiences as a convicted felon during a speaking tour and is now a radio talk-show host.

- ◆ Cindy Sheehan became a spokeswoman for the anti-war movement in 2006 after her son, Casey, an Army private, perished in the Middle East.

- ◆ Magic Johnson embarked on a speaking tour in 2003 to educate people about HIV medications.

Note that none of these people set out to become professional speakers. Col. North was a career military man; Cindy Sheehan was a housewife; Magic Johnson was a basketball star. When extraordinary things happened to them, they were inspired to reach out to others. Can you think of experiences in your life that might help you to relate to others and effect change in their lives?

Windows to Success

Windows allow the light of day to enter the room and they also let you see outside to reality. Every audience (even in a highly technical conference) wants to go away from that event encouraged, empowered to do something with the information received, educated, and enlightened. Those are what we call the Four E's. Don't keep them inside yourself—share them with those who are seeking out the information!

How will the messages or services you deliver bring the Four E's to your clients? Always ask yourself these questions:

- ◆ Does my message and my presentation of it encourage people in significant ways? If not, how must I improve?

- ◆ How do I provide empowerment to implement the ideas and information I provide in my presentation?

- ◆ Is the educational value of my message long-lasting? If not, what can I do to change my message (or handout materials) to make it memorable and truly educational?

◆ Am I truly enlightening audiences, or are they leaving the presentation somewhat confused? Do they actually understand the advanced message of my topic, or do I need to spend more time on the basic information?

Administrative and Management Pillar

Speakers may not be naturally inclined to want to manage their business effectively, especially if they're working on this career part time and maintaining another full-time job.

You may think that being skilled at administration is a gift, and indeed it is. Use it or lose it. In a speaking career, you keep track of your office, your speaking contracts, marketing materials, correspondence with clients and prospective clients, and so on. A great deal of your time can be spent (or invested) in your office, attending to the details of your business such as creating and organizing your presentations.

Success Shortcuts

Your answers to two questions can save you time and money, and keep you committed and motivated: What am I willing to give up to create what I want as a speaker? Will it be worth it?

Don't neglect the important aspects of your business. Some speakers are up very early even on holidays in their home offices attending to business before family or party time later in the day. Be your own hard-nosed boss!

Your Knowledge Pillar

It's not enough to know your topic inside and out—that's the bare-minimum requirement of all professional speakers. If you want to succeed in the long run, knowledge about how to run your business is every bit as important as delivering a great speech or seminar. Your presentation may be filled with important information and cutting-edge advice, but if you don't know how to sell it, no one's ever going to benefit from it (including you).

Here's a good analogy: when you're hungry, you can pull up to McDonald's or to a fancy restaurant. If you leave both places with your hunger sated, then are there really any fundamental differences between the two?

Of course there are! The fancy place has unique food, fine linens, exquisite décor, and well-dressed, polite servers. You're made to feel as though your dinner has been tailored to your exact needs. It's an entire experience, and for that reason, you feel as though the extra prices are justified. People come to this place for very specific reasons, whether it's the food, the ambience, the wine—the restaurant has something to offer that you simply can't get anywhere else. (To be fair, McDonald's has its secret sauce, which keeps people coming back for more!)

That's what you must aim to be in your professional speaking career. Ask yourself, "What am I doing to make myself unique and appealing? What is it about my presentation that no one else can duplicate?" If you don't know, find out! Educate yourself on unique marketing and presentation strategies and then put them into action!

Your Skill Pillar

When you're thinking about foundational pillars, ask yourself, "Who are the most skillful speakers I have heard?" Observe them carefully, either in person or by watching them on DVD, and note what works for them. Do they use hand movements? Do they use repetition? Do they use humor? I don't want you to mimic anyone else's presentation style; I want you to realize that there are all sorts of skills—physical, emotional, intellectual—that go into an appealing presentation. And it's not as easy as it looks.

Success Shortcuts

Great speakers are always learning and looking to improve their knowledge base by staying ahead of the competition and knowing the latest research relevant to their topics.

For over 30 years I have heard other speaking experts say, "If you want to get paid to speak, you must add some humor to your presentation." Delivering appropriate humor is a definite skill; it's not something that can be thrown together at the last minute. Of course, you can develop humor-delivering skills by watching TV sitcoms, going to comedy clubs, or reading tips on the Internet or in books. Practice your delivery in a mirror at home, along with your other delivery skills.

The skilled use of your voice may include the use of dramatic pauses, raising and/or lowering your voice to emphasize certain points, and the proper use of a microphone.

Speakers must be skilled (but not necessarily certified) teachers. Great teachers help their students find and ask the best and right questions; they do not simply impart solutions. Unless a person can adopt a question as her own, the solution may not be recognized as significant. To this end, speakers use the Socratic method of instruction, which is simply asking a lot of well-crafted questions. Are you aware of this technique? Sometimes a teacher (or speaker) is so effective at engaging the learner (or audience) to discover solutions, the learner thinks that the question and the answer came from himself, but indeed it was planted by a masterful teacher—the best kind of speaker.

Although successful speaking is a skill, sometimes it's what you don't say that sends the loudest message. I have seen studies over the years that claim 60 to 90 percent of communication is nonverbal in nature. Every movement you make can either underscore or contradict your spoken message, so it's a good idea to have a handle on body language. (I've listed a couple of helpful books for developing this skill in Appendix C.)

Environmental Pillars

The environmental pillar can make or break any speaker. This includes the people in your life, your office setting, the food you eat, and anything else that has the potential to either inspire or drain you.

We have to acknowledge that we become like the people we associate with most of the time, consciously or unconsciously; and our home as well as office environment can shape our responses to life. Look at your life and surroundings. Is your office neat and tidy? Are your personal relationships intact? Are you eating well and getting plenty of sleep? Take the time to examine what must go, what must improve, and what you have no control to change.

Home Environment and Office

Look around the office you intend to use for operating your speaker business and ask yourself these questions:

Words to the Wise

Don't shoot yourself in the foot or participate in self-defeating behavior by neglecting your environment. Loud noises, papers in disarray, and general clutter do not contribute to a productive work environment.

♦ "What kind of person operates from this space? Is that really who I want to be?"

♦ "How would I be judged if my best client prospect were to unexpectedly visit this office?"

♦ "What can I afford to do now to equip my office for efficient and inspiring work?"

Some speakers find it helpful to play their favorite inspirational music in the background 24/7 to keep themselves focused and motivated. If you have children, do they know to leave you alone when you are in your home office? What impression does it give a client when they can hear crying or bickering children or a barking dog in the background while you are on the phone?

Other Environments

Other negative environments can destroy any momentum you may gain from implementing the success methods in this book if you are not careful.

Mike was one of the best speakers in America. He had worked for a national seminar and personal development training company before going out on his own, and he was the kind of person everyone loved—and he loved them right back. He loved them so much that he couldn't make himself go home at night. He was always seen at networking events, and after that at bars where he would network some more. This lifestyle started to hurt his career. It wasn't that he was a drinker; it was that the wild nightlife wasn't the kind of uplifting, inspirational environment that Mike desperately needed.

Mike, like other speakers who work for themselves, lost the discipline to get up at 6 A.M. as he had when he was employed as one of the top seminar instructors in America. His career unwound, slowly but surely.

On the other hand, engaging in some activity that you find comforting or inspirational can have a marked positive improvement on your performance. Vince Lombardi Jr., the son of the legendary football coach, is a terrific speaker. However, in his initial years, he was rather tough in his delivery of his message. You can understand how growing up with a football coach for a dad might make a young man rough around the edges.

When Vince began to have more empathy for his audiences and got down into the audience rather than standing behind a podium, he received better reviews. So what changed? Like his father before him, Vince tries to attend Catholic Mass every morning. This environment helps him right his mistakes from the prior day so that he can serve with patience during the new day.

Emotional Pillars

Speaking is an emotional experience in many ways, even if you have a very pragmatic topic and style of presentation. In order to be effective in your presentation, you have to have a genuine passion for your topic, and you have to let your audience see it. Now I know there are some speakers who present very emotional issues—parents of children killed in violent high school situations, for example, or 9/11 survivors who must relive their personal tragedy every time they take the stage. Some are very careful about keeping their emotions in check; and while I certainly agree this is necessary to a point (no one can hear a speaker who's sobbing, after all), I also think that expressing true emotion is one of the most beneficial things you can do for your audience; it lets them know who you are and it drives home your point.

There are other emotional issues involved in professional speaking, and most are attached to criticism. No speaker likes to see evaluations where they are not well rated by everyone in attendance. But in this business, you're going to win some and you're going to lose some. That's just the way it is.

In any event, it is not the bad evaluations that do a speaker in, it is how speakers respond or react to the evaluations. Responding implies that you think about your response without overreacting. Too often speakers react to receiving "average" ratings on evaluations by becoming defensive rather than looking at how they can do better next time. And they react to poor evaluations by becoming angry and blaming the audience for not understanding them, or by resolving to quit the business altogether.

Words to the Wise

You have a choice at certain crossroads in your life. Will you decide to get better … or get bitter?

You need to develop thick skin to be a great speaker. No matter how skilled and how hard you work and how many extra bells and whistles you add to your presentations, face it: you cannot please all the people all the time! Don't let a lack of appreciation for your effort or bad or average evaluations affect your commitment to professional speaking.

The Least You Need to Know

- Personality as a speaker is not nearly as important as your desire to excel and understand other people.

- Your prior experiences, along with your expertise, can add to your speaking success.

- Managing your knowledge and skill takes daily commitment.

- Because speaking can be an emotional experience, do not allow negative or average evaluations to discourage you.

Chapter 3

A Day in the Life of a Professional Speaker

In This Chapter

- ◆ Booking a presentation
- ◆ Don't miss your flight!
- ◆ Tips for getting your point across
- ◆ Keeping your clients close

Most people like to have a routine or an ideal day spelled out for them. Without the ability to supervise themselves, few people can make it full time and/or long term in any kind of entrepreneurial. Speaking, whether part time or full time, is an effort at managing your own small business. The U.S. Department of Labor once did a survey and found the following statistics:

- ◆ Only 3 percent of people in the United States can survive and succeed long term in an unsupervised and unstructured job.

- ◆ Only 14 percent of Americans (true elsewhere, too) can succeed without supervision if they have a structured job.

- ◆ Eighty-three percent of Americans need ongoing supervision and reminders about how to stay structured on the job to succeed.

In this chapter, we'll take a day in the life of three speakers who come from varied backgrounds and who are dealing with varied tasks on this day in question. Regardless of your background or industry type, you will learn a lot from these examples.

Booking an Event

We'll begin with Scott, an expert in construction and part-time speaker. Scott rises around 6 A.M., and has his breakfast while reading something inspirational. He reads the newspaper, then showers, and then heads into his home office around 8 A.M. He checks his e-mail first thing to see if any of his construction clients are looking for him. After answering e-mails and finishing his focus on his full-time work, the first task he's faced with is attempting to *book* a speaking engagement for himself.

def•i•ni•tion

A **booking** refers to the act of scheduling a speaking engagement.

Because Scott is a part-time speaker, he knows he's going to have to wrap up his day in regard to speaking at around noon; he'll have to be at his construction job at 1 P.M. This may change if he has an evening speech or seminar to give. So how does he balance two careers? How much and how often does he concentrate on his speaking? Read on and you'll see ….

Booking Yourself

Scott has made a list of 17 potential speaking clients he intends to call this morning. Because he's an expert in construction, his potential clients include the Home Builders Association, several Boards of Realtors, a company that builds patio enclosures, a large home building company, a large commercial contracting company, a consulting engineering firm, and an association for architects.

With each phone call, Scott has the same objective: to unearth the needs of these prospective clients, and then to inform the decision-maker of how Scott can help address and solve those needs, all at a price the client will find acceptable.

Scott starts out by asking questions like …

♦ "Tell me about your business and your objectives."

♦ "Do you feel that the company is meeting those goals?"

♦ "Would you say that your workforce is focused and enthused?"

- "How is the relationship between your management and your employees?"

- "Does any department or division of your workplace need continuing education credits for relicensing?"

Once Scott has zeroed in on the company's greatest area of need, he asks the all-important question: "Has your organization ever hired an outside professional speaker?" He follows that up with an explanation of how he can best assist the company—in this case, the company has been talking about downsizing, and the employees are restless and agitated. Scott informs the client that he's certified in labor relations before asking whether he can send a packet with his information directly to the decision-maker. This is then backed up with a written e-mail proposal including a "Thanks for your time" message and/or link to his speaker website.

It can take three hours to make 17 phone calls if you get decision-makers on the phone. But usually for every 17 phone calls you make, at least 50 percent are simply leaving an effective voicemail message. Some of the calls Scott is making this morning are callbacks to people who were kind enough to return his earlier calls.

This morning, Scott was "lucky." He actually booked himself to speak twice. But scheduling a speech is more involved than simply writing something on a calendar or entering it into your computer so that you don't forget. The first thing Scott needs to do is to write a confirmation letter outlining the agreement he's made with his client. It may look something like this:

Dear Joe Bigshot,

Thank you for sharing your challenges and problems, which included the current difficulties you're experiencing between your labor force and your management team.

You and I discussed some ideas to help ease this issue, specifically my seminar that presents workable solutions to your staff. We agreed verbally to give this seminar four weeks from today on February 12, from 9:00 A.M. to noon in your conference room. You looked at my website, which gave you material about the seminar as well as references of others I have served.

The fee includes all of my preparation and a follow-up report to you, too. This fee is payable at 50 percent now, with the other 50 percent due the day of the seminar. Make checks payable to my speaking company (listed below).

Look for my faxed agreement for your signature. Please realize that as with your time, my time is of great value and I will turn down other opportunities for that same day; therefore, deposits paid are not refundable should you cancel or have to reschedule. If I must cancel, I will cheerfully return the deposit. However, I've never once canceled a seminar or speaking engagement. I plan on arriving at your office at 8 A.M. on February 12 to prepare on-site.

Best regard for your success,

Scott Speaker

SPEAKER FOR YOUR SUCCESS
Phone: 910-000-0000
E-mail:ScottSpeaker@ScottSpeaker.com
Website: www.scottspeaks.com

Working with a Speakers' Bureau

Scott has also been mulling over the idea of working with a speakers' bureau in order to beef up his speaking calendar and cut down on the amount of time he spends marketing himself. This morning he has a phone interview set up with the president of an international bureau.

He gets the bureau owner on the phone, and wisely first thanks this man for his valuable time before asking, "Tell me how I can earn the right to work with you?" The bureau owner says something like, "We have reviewed what you have sent to us so far and we see some possibilities in offering you paid bookings on an ongoing basis. First, we need you to do more than just e-mail us material and a link to your website. We need material mailed to us, along with a demo DVD tape if you have one; if not, send it to us when you create one. Scott, share with us some references and a complete press kit. As a bureau, we can become your biggest and best client. We will evaluate you after receiving these materials, and we will call you to discuss our clients past and present to whom we could present you; or you can call us, but give us a week or two."

So here's what Scott has learned this morning: he will have to pull together his marketing materials and, ideally, make sure that his contact information isn't visible anywhere. If he is currently pursuing any clients that work with the bureau, he may need to document each prior contact with the bureau to offer them as his clients; otherwise, if the client books him through the bureau, Scott will earn 30 percent less due to the bureau's commission fee.

He has further learned that the bureau may or may not market and sell him to clients; their first obligation is to the client, not the speaker. The bureau may offer several different speakers to each client and help the client narrow down the list. However, Scott may be the best choice for the client or prospective client, so a bureau will then sell Scott in an effort to close the sale. This bureau relationship isn't quite the boon that Scott was hoping it could be. Regardless of whether or not Scott works with the bureau (or they chose to work with him), he'll have to keep doing what he's been doing—recruiting new clients and serving his existing clients with care and excellence.

Arranging Travel and Accommodations

We'll move on now to Janice, who is headed to Dallas to address a convention of luxury auto salespeople sponsored by the manufacturer, Mercedes Benz.

Travel can be an exciting part of professional speaking as long as you know the ropes, so to speak. Unless you're speaking locally, you can expect your clients to reimburse you 100 percent of your travel expenses (including air travel, car rental, parking, meals, and so on).

Janice is running a little late this morning. In fact, she arrives at the airport just in time to watch her flight leave without her. Her ticket is nontransferable and nonrefundable. Now what is she supposed to do? Should she call the client and ask them to purchase another ticket for her? No way! This was purely Janice's fault and she's going to have to pick up the tab for the next flight to Texas.

 Words to the Wise

Some clients may choose to make all of your travel arrangements for you, both to ensure they're getting the best rate and to eliminate the hassle of expense reports. If this simply won't work for you, speak up before the client books your flight and hotel!

When to Arrive

In addition to being out several hundred dollars, Janice is in a real jam now. She had planned on preparing herself for her presentation on the flight and at the hotel; now she'll be arriving several hours later than she had expected. By the time she arrives at the hotel, in fact, it will be past midnight. Because her presentation is at 8 A.M. the next day, she has no other choice but to find an area in the airport and ready herself as much as possible there and during her late-night flight. Not only did Janice want to run through her speech several times in the comfort and privacy of her hotel room, she also wanted to get a good night's rest so that she would be at her sharpest during her presentation. The stress and anxiety of the situation is already starting to wear on her.

In addition, Janice shipped her props ahead of her and they're in her hotel room, unassembled and as unprepared for tomorrow's presentation as she feels right now. She also won't have much time to get a feel for the layout of the stage, to make sure that the audio-visual equipment is operating correctly, to test out the acoustics of the room, and so on.

Now, some people are last-minute workers and wouldn't let a situation like this get to them. These folks work best—indeed, often only work—under pressure, and might think to themselves, "Why arrive any earlier than a couple of hours before the presentation?" Clients often stipulate that the speaker arrive the day before so that any glitches in travel plans can be resolved. Also if the speaker is forced to cancel due to bad weather or some other sort of emergency, the client will have more than enough time to find a replacement speaker. If Janice acquired this booking through an agent or bureau, she would call them first, as the bureau or agent may be responsible for finding a suitable replacement.

If, for example, you are to give a speech or seminar after a noon luncheon—and there are dozens if not hundreds of variations to when and how programs are given—you would arrive at 11 A.M. (or earlier if you think the client would prefer it, or if you see benefit in sitting in on other programs before your message, or to have time to network).

Words to the Wise

With local presentations, arrive one hour before the program begins. Always check the audio-visual equipment, microphone, podium, or other aspects of the room where you will be speaking.

If Janice is wise, she has the cell-phone number of the meeting planner, and she'll be able to call him and let him know that she'll be taking a later flight. In the meantime, she'll have to make do with her surroundings and take this important lesson about punctuality to heart.

Typical Accommodations

When Janice at last touches down in Texas, she's looking forward to getting to sleep as soon as possible. Janice is a mid-range-priced speaker; she knows that her accommodations will be comfortable, but not luxurious. She has done presentations for a few clients who insisted on putting her up in the finest hotel in the city she was in, but that's a real rarity for a speaker of her caliber. Five-star speakers get the five-star hotel rooms. (After a client spends $20,000 or more for a speaker to give a presentation, what's a few hundred more?)

Although many clients make travel arrangements for their speakers, Janice opted to do this herself. She'll have to submit an expense report to the client, which, again, will not include the price of the replacement airline ticket, but will cover her rental car, all of her meals, and her trip home. Janice knows better than to rent a Hummer and order $400 worth of room service. Again, these amenities are reserved for celebrity-level speakers. Not only may her client (rightly) refuse to reimburse such extravagant expenses, but she will most definitely not be invited back!

Travel expenses can mount up fast, even when you're being reimbursed for the basics. Janice keeps track of every penny she spends out-of-pocket; she knows that travel expenses are tax-deductible!

Packing/Shipping Presentations Materials

Janice has several big visual props she uses in her presentation. Because they're quite large, she shipped them ahead of time and sent the shipping bill to her client. Now, this was a necessity, and Janice let her client know that without these materials her presentation wouldn't have the same "oomph." She also had an estimate for the shipping expenses, which allowed her to let the client know what kind of expense they were facing. Janice pre-planned so that her props, her handout materials, and books she'd be selling at the back of the room would arrive well in advance of her.

Speakers must realize that you must make one sale at a time. In other words, only after you close the sale and have a signed agreement for you to speak is it the right time to try to pre-sell books or other materials that might help enhance your presentation, especially so if there are additional prices involved. If materials are included in the fee, then of course you would bring that up in advance when negotiating the agreement with the booking client.

On occasion, Janice has custom-prepared her handout materials and an outline of her presentation and PowerPoint slides and e-mailed them to the client with an authorization for the client to duplicate these materials—that way, she didn't need to ship anything. Clients like to cut costs wherever they can, so Janice allows for this whenever possible.

Success Shortcuts

Create generic materials that can easily be customized for each client from your computer prior to your arrival. Sending materials via e-mail as an attachment is a wise use of time and saves money. And, since the materials may be originals or of a big dollar value, it may be wise to insure them or send them with a signature required upon receipt.

Preparing for Presentation

My research indicates that at least 60 percent of a successful presentation is due to preparation. What kind of preparation is standard? What does "going the extra mile" entail? Briefly, clients expect you to ask questions about their organization, the audience, the theme of the meeting or conference, what happens just before and just after you speak, and about the client's expected outcomes. These are minimums and, of course, you adjust and comply accordingly.

Going the extra mile in your preparation can create a greater bond with your client, increase audience approval, and create a greater likelihood of repeat business.

How Early to Prepare?

Some speakers like to begin preparing for a client presentation immediately after securing the booking, even if the booking is months away. The speaker we'll follow now, Alex, finds that it works best for her to do 80 percent of the preparation in the two weeks before a program, even if booked months in advance. Alex has one booking that's six months away. She sends an e-mail to the meeting planner once a month with a simple, "I look forward to being with you and I continue to look for ways to thoroughly understand your audience and your needs. Please remember to send me anything about your organization that might help me prepare. Thank you." She spends part of the last two weeks (unless it is a totally new presentation that requires much more time) gathering information and fitting it into her standard presentation;

it really is not like cramming for a final exam for the seasoned speaker, although a new speaker or a speaker working with a new presentation might be spending many hours to be properly prepared. But after you have done the same presentation over and over again, it takes less and less time to prepare each new time it is given.

Some clients do not plan very far ahead and hire speakers only a few weeks before an engagement. They have no idea how busy the speaker is in the weeks leading up to the engagement, and the speaker does not want to tell the client that very little time is available to prepare. Alex has her own personal rule about this: she does not accept any booking if she feels she won't have time to adequately prepare for it. The extra money just isn't worth the damage that could be done to her reputation if she presents a substandard speech or seminar.

Alex has a speaking engagement next weekend, which was booked just this week. She'll fly to Chicago Friday afternoon and give a keynote closing speech after the luncheon on Saturday. Her client has e-mailed her an itinerary listing the events: there's a dinner planned for the evening she arrives, a couple of breakout sessions, and a morning meeting on Saturday. The client writes in his e-mail, "Attending these events is of utmost importance. I want you to have a true understanding of our organization before your presentation."

Alex, who knows her own work ethic and needs for preparation, has written back, "The night before and the morning of the keynote speech, I can only attend very few minutes of these events. I will otherwise be sequestered in my hotel room preparing my material and reviewing information about your organization." This is not meant as a rude reply; Alex wants this presentation to be excellent, and she knows that bouncing from event to event will steal her focus and leave her feeling drained. She owes it to her client, she figures, to be at her best during her presentation—*not* at dinner or in the morning sessions.

Being Realistic

Alex's example is chock-full of tips. First of all, make sure you have time to prepare for a presentation. I know that speakers who are just starting out hate to turn down any offers, but if you just can't pull a presentation together with only two weeks' notice, then turn it down. It can't help your career to show up and give a crummy performance. Your client won't say, "What a trouper! Thanks for trying!" She'll say, "I thought you said you could do this!" Your reputation may be sullied, and you definitely won't get any repeat business from this client.

Another great thing to learn from Alex: stand your ground. Know your limitations, mentally and physically. Don't pretend to be Superman or Superwoman. If you can't do something, then say so up front. Maybe the client will appreciate your candor; maybe she'll be disappointed; but in any event, you won't wind up leaving her wondering why the heck she hired you. Be true to yourself, and you'll find the right clients and the right path to follow.

Procedures for Making Presentations

Daniel is a speaker preparing to address an audience of business leaders on the topic of safety in the workplace. He's done some research and has found safety tips from many sources. He's slowly working on his presentation, and has chosen to work the following seven-step formula. In 1975, I first learned from a great mentor, Carl Stevens, the procedure for making presentations that I now customize for any speaker to use in making a group presentation.

◆ Preparation: Research your topic, your client, and your audience thoroughly.

◆ Attention: Throughout the presentation, always look for ways to get and maintain attention.

◆ Examination: A professional speaker, just like other professionals, is a problem-solver and never offers a diagnosis without first examining the problem.

◆ Prescription: Demonstrate that you understand and have listened, and that your solutions are designed to solve problems.

◆ Conviction: In a great speech or seminar, you present facts, a few core points that can be easily remembered, and evidence as to why your solutions will benefit the audience.

◆ Motivation: Solutions must be presented in a way that motivates people, first to acceptance, and then to action. Use the right words in the best way to paint word pictures appealing to your client's desired results.

◆ Completion: A strong closing and a strong opening are vital, like the best of bread on the best of irresistible sandwiches. The content has points that are supported by colorful stories benefiting the audience.

Daniel will begin by researching his topic thoroughly (preparation). Daniel plans on using the space he's in to grab the audiences' attention, incorporating dramatic arm movements and using voice inflection at key points in his speech (attention).

He'll address—in depth—the specific problems (examination) he's there to address. Once he's covered that territory, he'll use transitional words like, "Because these problems occur too frequently, we have to find better ways to prevent them …" and "… Based on my careful research may I now present to you what is working for others in similar situations, step by step?" (prescriptive words of transition).

Then he'll mention that he's spoken with several other "safety in the workplace" experts who've offered up their suggestions (conviction). This step is important, and here is where he must make three major points, each supported with evidence—preferably visual—with questions for agreement from the audience. This is the "meat" of the speech.

He'll appeal to the audiences' sense of accomplishment by letting them know that they could be the first generation of business leaders who lower workplace accidents (motivation), and he will tell them what is in it for them as individuals if they each do so. Paint a positive picture!

Before closing, he'll describe how businesses of all types and "people just like you" across the country are benefiting from in-house safety programs like the one he is recommending: "Today (completion) is the day to make a commitment to improved safety, okay? Yes, great! Now, follow through when you are back at your workplace!"

Answering Questions

Daniel delivers a slam-dunk performance and then opens the floor for questions. For him, it will work. It will be important for him to repeat each question after it's asked so that every member of the audience has heard it.

Most speakers, however, approach Q&A sessions a little differently. By allowing for questions, the speaker risks losing the high energy she would otherwise leave the room with. All it takes is one bad apple, or someone with a confusing question, to undo all the work the speaker has put into this presentation.

So how *could* a speaker address questions without leaving herself wide open for criticism, or worse? One of the best techniques is to ask your audience rhetorical questions and then provide the answers. Daniel might interject the following questions and answers into his presentation:

- ◆ "How do business safety concerns take root? Mostly by management not caring and not paying attention to safety."

- ◆ "Who are the most unsafe people in your workplace? Identify them and get them thinking SAFETY FIRST always!"

- ◆ "How can we prevent injuries on the job? By slowing down, paying attention to what we're doing, and acting with caution, you can train people to do these things."

You see, by including rhetorical questions, the audience doesn't feel as though they've spent the time being lectured to on some dry material. They respond to the questions that they or their friends might have asked … and so they tune in a little bit more or often a lot more.

Add-On Materials

Add-on materials are things like books the speaker has written, DVDs showing the speaker in action, and other things of that nature. These can be offered for sale either at the back of the room, from a speaker's website, at bookstores, and so on. In the typical day of a great speaker, she is always thinking about how to sell her products—and if she doesn't yet produces add-on materials, she's thinking of ways to expand her marketplace, so to speak. Successful add-on offerings can have an astounding effect on your career! Not only are you putting your message out there so it can be shared with a larger audience (perhaps those who can't see you speak in person), you can potentially double your income by selling your books, CDs, DVDs, and so on.

The Least You Need to Know

- ◆ Even if you work with an agency or bureau, you'll have to continue looking for new clients on your own.

- ◆ Punctuality is not only a client expectation, it can also affect how well your presentation goes.

- ◆ Clients expect speakers to keep travel expenses under control.

- ◆ Delivering an effective presentation often depends on structuring your speech on a tried-and-true format.

Chapter 4

Speaker Career Paths

In This Chapter

- Learning about different career paths for speakers
- Sample contracts or agreements for engagements
- Working with bureaus can expand your speaking career
- Coaching or consulting can supplement speaker income
- Using your time wisely at all times

Recently, I contacted 17 speakers by phone to get a good idea of who's doing what these days. I found diverse offerings, to say the least!

One speaker, for example, is a vibrant and energetic caregiver. She addresses senior citizen topics. Another is a communication expert who inspires and challenges clients to put attitude and goals into action. I found an inspiring and motivating speaker/singer, focusing on communications and conflict resolution, health and wellness, and vocal dynamics. I also spoke with a former Top Gun instructor and a CEO who are now motivational speakers.

Needless to say, the path of a professional speaker doesn't follow any sort of map. Speakers come from diverse backgrounds and share their knowledge on varied topics. In this chapter, we'll take a look at the opportunities that might await you.

Speakers on Retainer

Some speakers book their presentations with individual clients. Other speakers are "on retainer" with corporations, which means they deliver a set number of presentations for a predetermined amount of money during a period of time. In either situation, you, the speaker, will most likely create your own contract, or as we call it in this industry, an *agreement*, which is a little like a contract minus the legal lingo (and the legal fees).

def•i•ni•tion

An **agreement** between a speaker and a client is a little like a contract. It spells out the date of the event, your payment, cancellation fees, and the like.

An agreement is really meant to protect both parties from the other party defaulting on the terms you've worked out. You don't need to hire an expensive lawyer to draw up a contract for you, but because you're acting as your own representative here, you really need to be on the ball. Ask all the questions you need to get all the necessary details before you agree to the speaking engagement. Often speakers arrange all the details by phone or by e-mail and then either fax or e-mail the agreement for a signature.

I recommend speaking at least by phone, if not face to face, with a client before a contract is hammered out and signed. This is a business where your voice is part of the product. Let them hear what they're paying for!

Contract A

The following agreement is a *boiler plate*, or standard-type agreement that was used by a speaker who has since left the business. You don't need to customize your agreement with your logo and name on it, as some speakers do, but of course you can if you want to. The speaker simply asks these questions of the client and fills in the blanks.

def•i•ni•tion

A **boiler plate** agreement indicates that the terms are fairly simple and standard. Neither party is asking for anything extraordinary (like providing room-temperature cola for the speaker precisely 38 minutes before his presentation); addendums could be added, however.

IMPORTANT

PLEASE READ ALL DETAILS CAREFULLY
(sample agreement to schedule speaker)

8-August-2008

RE: SPECIALIST ENGAGEMENT

Further to our recent conversation, I would like to confirm arrangement for your upcoming engagement between City of Kingston and Speaker Ltd.

Contract No: XXXX XX

Name:

Presentation: <u>**How to Create Time**</u> by **Mark McKeon**

Date: 24th April 2009

Timings: Keynote (approx. 75 mins) timing TBD

Venue:

Audience: 30–60 pax

Fee: **$8k + GST**

Retainer Required: 50% of fee upon signing of contract. Retainer required with this signed agreement to confirm booking. In the event of a cancellation, the 50% retainer is not refundable.

In the event of cancellation seven days or less before the engagement date, the full fee is payable.

Contract A is a standard boiler plate agreement where the terms are fairly straight-forward.

Payment:	By check to: Speaker Ltd. Electronic transfer to: Speaker Ltd. 123 State Street Anywhere, World 55555 Account No: XXXXXXXXX
Production Requirements:	Data projector for Intro
Dress:	Business
Travel:	N/A
Accommodation:	N/A

Should you have any queries or require any further information, please do not hesitate to contact this office.

Please sign your acceptance and fax to XXXXXXXXX or post to Speaker Ltd., 123 State Street, Anywhere, World, 55555.

Thank you. Signed on behalf of client:

_____

_____ (Name)

_____ (Company)

_____ (Position)

_____ (Date)

Signed on behalf of Speaker Ltd.:

_____

_____ (Name)

_____ (Position)

_____ (Date)

Although there is an area for expenses in the agreement, it is a good idea to be open to negotiating an all-inclusive fee for yourself. Keep this in mind for local presentations, too. Sometimes your only expense is the gas it takes to travel a few miles; many times, the speaker will waive this minor expense. This is especially important if you have a client who is "fee-sensitive" (i.e., very careful with their money). They may be reluctant to pay you $20 for gas. If you know this is the case, let it go. You don't want to lose a referral or another paid speaking agreement over such a small amount of money.

At the top or bottom of your agreement, place your contact information including phone number, fax number, e-mail address, and the address where your check will be sent, if that's applicable in your case. (Many speakers require a 50 percent deposit sent immediately after the agreement is signed and the balance due on the day of the event.)

Contract B

Now, here is another example of a speaker's agreement. Remember, you can also simply create a letter of agreement on your stationary or via a series of e-mail exchanges; however, it is best for all concerned to obtain signatures. This protects you so that a client doesn't back out on the scheduled date. Also, when you stipulate a 50 percent deposit by a certain date, the client is (at least) 50 percent less likely to postpone or cancel dates once that deposit has been paid. All of this is simply good business.

You may want to include a penalty for cancellation in your contract, because once you sell a date on your calendar to a client, that date cannot be sold to another client, even if someone else offers you more money for the same day. Honor your agreements and hold your clients to the same high standard!

What do you see that is added or different about contract B? Do you need these elements in your agreement? Before creating your own agreement, take a look at some of the elements in the agreement that follows.

John Smith Speaks
(sample booking agreement)

123 State Street, Anywhere, USA 55555

S P E A K I N G   C O N T R A C T

The Presenter: John Smith

Event: _____

ATTN: _____

Phone: _____

E-mail: _____

Presentation Dates: _____

Presentation Type: <u>Opening Keynote Presentation and Q&A</u>

Estimated Number of Attendees: _____

Session Time(s): _____

Specific Location of Presentation: _____

Address: _____

_____

Phone: _____

Note that contract B contains more clauses to protect the speaker's interests, such as penalties for the client's cancellation of the event.

Technical and Setup Requirements

These describe the ideal setting for the presenter to speak at his very best. If there are any details in here that are a concern, please communicate these concerns as soon as possible to the presenter. Please review these carefully and relay them to whoever will be responsible for the setup of the room.

Speaker Area

What matters most is that everyone in the room be able to see the presenter, and vice versa. Since Mr. Smith uses a wheelchair, eye contact is not possible with the whole room without some degree of elevation in relation to the audience—and they can't see the juggling!

If a separate platform is to be used, provide a ramp so that the presenter need not be lifted by helpers in front of the group. The platform should be, at minimum, 16 feet wide by 8 feet deep. In general, Mr. Smith's highest priority to is make as intimate and personal a connection as possible with all in attendance.

Provide a table for the stage big enough for a laptop computer, water, a couple of books, and the juggling balls. Leave an open area at the front of the speaker platform so the presenter is fully visible.

Microphone

Provide a hands-free, remote, lavaliere microphone. A remote microphone is important since a cord gets tangled in Mr. Smith's wheels and brakes as he moves around during the talk. And of course, Mr. Smith's hands have to be free for the juggling!

Video Projection

Unless you are informed otherwise, Mr. Smith will use video projection during his talk. He will bring his own laptop computer. Generally, advance copies of PowerPoint files are NOT provided.

Please ensure that there is a cable that is long enough to reach the speaker's platform from the video projector, since the presenter needs to be able to interact with the computer.

Book Signing

Following the talk and workshop, the presenter will remain on hand to sign books for those who care to purchase them. The table is best located near the exit from the room, and in an area where people can inspect and purchase books, and interact with Mr. Smith as he signs them. A single, 6-foot-long table will be sufficient as a minimum. Cash, checks, and major credit cards are accepted.

Intro/Outro

The presenter will provide text for the introduction. The introducer should plan to come back at the end with a final thank you, and to remind attendees of the book signing and where it is located.

Timing

The presenter arrives approximately one hour prior to the presentation to ensure that technical stuff is working, to set up the book tables, and to have a few minutes of quiet time (and juggling warm-up!) prior to the talk. Please ensure that the room will be accessible at that time, and that any AV and setup staff will be on hand to make any necessary adjustments.

Follow-Up

Following the presentation, at the soonest possible time, Mr. Smith and the primary client contact in attendance at the presentation will have a debriefing conversation to ascertain the success of Mr. Smith's work, and to discuss any ways it could have been even better!

Speaking Fee

US (fill in the blank)_____

Travel

Unless otherwise provided, Mr. Smith's office will make travel arrangements, seeking the most reasonable rates. Receipts will be submitted, using any forms and/or authorization information required by _____, as efficiently as possible following the event.

Payment

Payment of all fees and expenses will be paid in a timely manner, in no less a period than 30 days from presenter's submission of an invoice for fees and expenses.

Cancellation

If the presenter cancels the engagement, or fails to appear as agreed, all fees paid in advance shall be returnable to _____ and unpaid fees are voided. If _____ cancels this agreement, and the date is not resold, the following scheduled percentage of the fee will be in effect at the time of written notification:

0–14 working days or less prior to the scheduled engagement = 100%

15–30 working days prior to the scheduled engagement = 75%

31–60 working days prior to the scheduled engagement = 50%

120 working days prior to the scheduled engagement = 25%

Please complete and sign this contract and return to John Smith. Please retain a copy for your files.

Presenter Name: JOHN SMITH

Signature: _____ Date: _____

Client Authorizing Signature: _____

Name (PRINT): _____

Signature: _____ Date: _____

Contract C

Many speakers advance to the point where they are (or they would like to be) by working with *speakers' bureaus* or *agents*. Although I won't get into an in-depth explanation about bureaus or agents at this point, I want you to understand those relationships right now, because bureaus are increasingly controlling a growing percentage of the business for speakers.

def•i•ni•tion

> A **speakers' bureau** represents the interests of the client. Clients use the bureau to find an appropriate speaker for their event. The client pays the bureau, and the bureau pays the speaker. A **speakers' agent** represents the interests of the speaker, books him for speaking engagements, and takes a 15 percent cut of the speaker's earnings.

When you accept a booking through a booking company like a speakers' bureau, you may be asked to sign an agreement that looks something like the one my company uses. Do not let this intimidate you! No one is imprisoning you or locking you into a lifelong agreement. Speakers usually want to continue to create business on their own even if they have bureaus offering them.

In fact, I'll go so far as to say that you don't want to work with bureaus on an exclusive basis, because they represent the client. Because the client is considered the "property" of the bureau, this agreement obligates you to give the client the same stellar service you'd give the bureau. And if you don't, you'll have hard feelings between you and the bureau, which can significantly impact your career in a negative way, as bureaus work with many, many clients.

The agreement displayed on the next page has some clauses that are not in the other two agreements shown in this chapter. You can borrow some of these clauses for your own booking agreements; however, remember that with this three-way agreement, the client pays the speakers' bureau and then the bureau pays you. Therefore, it's a good idea to have a separate letter of understanding with the bureau indicating when you expect to be paid.

Agreement to Schedule Speaker   page 1 of 2
© from Speaker's Bureau

We (the client)_____ agree to hire
_____ (speaker) for an event on_____ (date(s)).
    This speaker, trainer, and/or entertainer agrees to do his/her very best!

This program will be a: _____ (speech, seminar, workshop, etc.)
And the starting and ending times are:_____

The location of the event is (address): _____
_____

There will be a meal at:_____; breaks in the program at:_____

Other pertinent information includes:_____
The title of the speaker's program(s) will be:_____
We need a photo:_____This program must include:_____

_____

We agree to the following fees and expense reimbursement schedule:

The speaker's regular fee is $ _____. This program will be $ _____
plus travel expenses _____ yes/no. Speakers/we require a 50% deposit to hold
the date/start preparation. All fees are paid to this bureau and we pay the
speaker. (Speaker fees are the same as if booking direct when booking through
us. We can save clients time and money or give you value added services).
The speaker is asked to minimize expenses. The client agrees to prompt
reimbursement upon receipt of an itemized statement by the speaker. In this
case, expenses could include: _____
(Speaker must send a copy of expense reimbursement request to the bureau.)

The balance of the fee (50%) is due the day of the event payable to: Professional
Speakers Bureau Int'l or within five working days after the event. A billing
statement can be provided, or you can pay from this agreement. The deposit now
due is: _____ Balance due: _____ (date)_____.
        (Mail checks to: PSBI, address at end of page 2)

This speakers' bureau guarantees a back-up speaker for this event. The clients
will provide us with their phone numbers. The speaker must call the bureau
before the event if an emergency takes place. The speaker will provide a full
refund of deposits to the bureau if he/she must cancel for any reason. We put the
client in direct contact with the speaker. The speaker agrees to learn what is
needed about each client to prepare properly. The client is that of PSBI only.

All billing must go through bureau as well as future bookings of this speaker.
Speakers' books or tapes, if approved by the client, can be offered for sale to the
audience _____. Speaker will notify the bureau-TTLG-PSBI of any sale of
products or other services. Client agrees to respond to the speaker's needs for
audio/visual equipment, meeting rooms aids, etc., if possible, and the speaker
will notify the client of all such needs in advance, if possible.

The bureau will provide an evaluation form to the client about the speaker's
performance. Please return it. The speaker agrees that if other business results
from this event, it is booked through this bureau. PSBI also is referred to as
PROFESSIONAL SPEAKERS BUREAU INTERNATIONAL (PSBI).

*Contract C is the stan-
dard contract my speakers'
bureau issues to speakers.*

Hotel reservation (if needed) will be made by_____. The speaker will stay at:_____ (if needed) the night of _____.   The phone # is: _____. The speaker's phone will be provided when the speaker signs below, or earlier: #_____

Speaker's email: _____

The client contact name, if different than the person below, for the speaker is: _____. This responsible person's phone is: _____

Upon arrival at the location of the event, the speaker must notify _____ _____ AND the bureau at 614-841-1776, leaving a message on voicemail if no live answer. Due to scheduling, various demands, and expenses, it is necessary to have a rather standard industry cancellation clause. This applies unless an "act of God" prevents the event from taking place. This protects everyone.

The speaker will sign this form, AFTER the meeting planner signs. A signed copy will be returned to the client. When this happens, and the 50% deposit is paid, **the client is guaranteed this speaker AND a back-up speaker.**

> 100% returned if the client cancels less than 360 days before the event
> 75% returned if the client cancels less than 180 days before the event
> 50% returned if the client cancels less than 120 days before the event
> 25% returned if the client cancels less than 90 days before the event

If the client does not sign this agreement within 30 days of receipt, this offer for this speaker at the stated fee is cancelled. Until then the speaker is asked to place a pencil **"hold"** on the calendar. Cancellation by the speaker after signature must include a 100% return of deposit money to the bureau, as this money then is paid to the back-up speaker, once the client approves the back-up.

No recording devices are allowed without the speaker's and bureau's approval. The speaker and bureau agree to abide by a code of ethics fitting to the profession of professional speaking and meeting industry standards.

X_____   X_____
      Client signature   Speaker signature

_____   _____
   Client name printed or typed   Speaker name printed or typed

Date: _____   Date:_____

X_____   Date:_____
Bureau signature valid if from President/CEO: Dr. Thomas (Thom) A. Lisk
Professional Speakers Bureau Int'l
Please sign and send original copy back to the bureau. Retain copy for your files. If you fax a copy with your signature, please send the original by mail as we may fax a copy to the speaker. Copies of faxes can be hard to read. Once the speaker's signed copy is received, the meeting planner will be notified and sent a copy. A 50% deposit is expected after you sign.
Please mail deposit check to PSBI: (**see/save: www.TerrificSpeakers.com**)
    ©Professional Speakers Bureau International
    1112 Firth Avenue, Suite 101
    Worthington, OH 43085-2914   **Questions:**
Please fax this after signing to ... F: 614-846-1377   **614-841-1776**

Professional Speakers, Professional Services

Have you heard the term *keynote speaker?* This term gets tossed around frequently when the subject of professional speaking comes up, so I'd like to address it here. A keynote speaker is an expert and the speaker at an event. She will speak on the topic that has everyone gathered together, whether it's industry, a hobby, religion, and so on. Her main goal is to present the issues related to the topic and garner a sense of unity. She's paid well for her appearance not because she's necessarily more skilled than other speakers, but often because the budget is larger for conferences where keynote speakers are used.

def•i•ni•tion

A **keynote speaker** is an expert who addresses an audience and covers the issues of the topic. Her goal is to inform and to create a sense of unity.

Now, as I said, the term "keynote speaker" is what many people think of when they hear "professional speaker"; however, as I also said in the opening of this chapter, there is no mold for the professional speaker. Speakers come from very different backgrounds, both professionally and personally; they each have unique skills and methods of reaching their audiences; and every speaker has his or her own take on the topic they share with audiences.

It should come as no surprise, then, to learn that professional speakers can offer a wide range of services. I'll touch on a few of them in this section.

Trainers, Workshops, Facilitators

Trainers often come from a strong background in corporate America and often belong to the American Society of Training and Development (ASTD). A trainer can be many different things to many different people, but for the sake of this book, please think of a trainer as an independent business person who gives training programs (on many different topics for all kinds of organizations) for a fee. Trainers are speakers, but they focus on giving longer, interactive programs, commonly called workshops or seminars. Many professional speakers first discover a love for speaking while working as a trainer inside of some organization. They enjoy the interaction with people and helping people grow. Seeing the light go on inside another human being is very rewarding for them.

A *workshop* has a misleading name. It isn't necessarily work; it can be a lot of fun. These sessions are usually about three hours (sometimes longer) and are meant to help people work through problems, come to some decisions, and work more effi-ciently. A *seminar* is also presented in an interactive format, complete with a learning objective. It's often longer than a workshop, either presented as a day-long event or presented in modules (maybe two hours at a time, once a week for several weeks). Handout materials are often provided to help you stay on track and remember all of the information being given to you.

def•i•ni•tion

A **trainer** is a speaker who specializes in interactive programs. A **workshop** is a trainer-led session meant to help a group of people work through problems and issues and develop workable solutions. A **seminar** is an interactive session led by a trainer, and is longer in duration than a workshop. Handouts are often provided to help the audience keep up with the information.

Independent trainers sometimes think of themselves as "only trainers," but most often, if they persevere, they begin to think of themselves as someone capable of giving speeches, offering coaching services, and maybe much more. Trainers are typically not paid as well as keynote speakers, so this is why some gravitate toward other areas of professional speaking. A speech is only a 30- to 90-minute event, and although it can take as much energy and preparation as a training seminar, it does not take nearly as much time to deliver. (Which means the professional speaker has more time to devote to building his business.)

Success Shortcuts

You'll see trainers and work-shop and seminar leaders when you go to public or open-enrollment seminars. Speakers will use this public strat-egy not simply for profit, but also as a way of finding new clients for ongoing or in-house training or speaking engagements.

Workshop or seminar leaders work in-house for organizations, although they may be independent contractors, not employees. Many large companies employ trainers who give all kinds of workshops and seminars for small and large groups of com-pany employees. There is a great need in corporate America for outside trainers to deliver seminars and workshops, so you could be a contracted seminar leader for numerous companies.

If you think you'd prefer to be a workshop or seminar leader, then you should know that the market for trainers and workshop leaders is bigger than the market for "regu-lar" speakers!

Facilitators are often highly skilled trainers or workshop and seminar leaders. Some clients prefer a facilitator who simply helps a team of people think through some complex issues or solve challenging problems by, yes, facilitating a discussion and asking well-crafted questions. The facilitator may post responses from audience members to a white board or a flip chart for later reference and decision-making.

def•i•ni•tion

A **facilitator** may give either seminars or workshops; this person is a speaker who does as much listening (or more) during the group event as speaking, and helps a team of people work toward a desired goal.

A speaker may ask a lot of rhetorical questions and allow little time for each audience member to respond, but the facilitator goes slowly, allows for questions, and lets everyone hear each response, maybe repeating the response so everyone is sure to hear.

Continuing Education Programs

Most medical professionals, lawyers/attorneys, accountants, university faculty members, early childhood professionals, financial services, realtors, and human resource managers (to name just a few) are required to keep up to date with the latest information and research in their career fields. They must earn a number of continuing education (CE) credits before they can become relicensed. And guess who sometimes delivers the information on those CE credits? That's right—the professional speaker!

There's one caveat: in most cases, CE classes or seminars must be delivered by speakers who are in the given profession. For example, the speaker providing information about Certified Public Accounting CE credits must be a CPA herself. What do you think? Could you help out someone in your own career field (or other career fields) and speak about the latest advances in the industry?

Entertainers or Entertaining Speakers

Entertaining speakers are some of the most in-demand speakers and trainers. In truth, to be great, every speaker needs to offer some kind of entertainment value to some part of the program, even if it's only some cartoons projected on a screen with a punch line.

The most entertaining speakers are often very interactive. I think of Dick Stoner who owns a comedy store in Ft. Wayne, Indiana. He is a legendary comedy magician who

Success Shortcuts

Consider people like Jay Leno and David Letterman, who earn at least 10 times more than the president of the largest university in your state. What does that tell you about entertainment versus education? (Hint: put some humor into your presentation!)

appeared on *The Late Show with Johnny Carson* years ago. He has many bookings that could have gone to other speakers, but when clients see his demo tape, they forget about wanting educational value from a speaker; they would prefer to be entertained by Dick.

You may find more buyers if you find a way to make your presentation entertaining. Just keep your audience in mind and make sure your "entertainment" will appeal to them based on their age, profession, gender, and so on.

Coaching and Consulting

More than any other type of services, speakers create a base of income from *coaching* or *consulting* with clients.

In using the word "coach," we often think of the world of sports. Just as in baseball, football, hockey, or any sport, a great speaking coach brings out the best in each individual and the entire team and inspires his "players" to be their very best.

def•i•ni•tion

A **coach** in the world of speaking holds a team of people accountable to their goals while helping them to come up with solutions. A **consultant** is an expert with very specialized knowledge who works with larger groups or corporations. He is a professional problem solver.

Continuous Revenue

Coaching is usually done one-on-one or in a small group setting, whereas consulting may be working with a group or people or on a contract to serve a company. Both coaches and consultants are professional problem-solvers, but they approach it in different ways. Coaches and consultants usually serve more than one client at a time and have long-term contracts or agreements with clients; these relationships generate ongoing revenue, which in turn enables the coach or consultant to continue to serve as a professional speaker, if she so desires.

Believe it or not, some speakers make over a million dollars a year as consultants and/or coaches. How do you become a high-paid coach? That's a subject for another book. For now, consider that to become a coach, you must have many of the skills of a facilitator or workshop leader—e.g., you must work well with people, offer solutions to problems, and be wise enough to have some kind of written contract or agreement that calls for these ongoing services.

Certainly some coaches and consultants have niches within their expertise; so, for example, an executive coach would work with executives one on one, and an executive consultant may use a group approach within a corporation and do some group facilitation each week or month. Both a coach and a consultant may bill by the hour; however, many prefer to work on retainer, requiring a fee each month for six months to a year.

Time-Consuming but Well Worth It

Coaches or consultants are into reliance-building and making lasting commitments with clients. One-on-one coaching can be very time-consuming, but because you can earn $500 or more an hour as a great coach or consultant, you can get a great return on your time investment! All things considered, a $10,000 speaker may still have to invest 40 hours to secure one engagement, prepare for it, and deliver it. A consultant who works 40 hours at $500 each hour ends up with the same amount of money. The trick (don't be crafty, just set your contract up properly) is not to have to be on premises with your client or on the phone every one of those 40 hours; otherwise, you won't have time to prepare properly to serve.

Years ago, I was a member of the Independent Professional Consultants Association in my home state. I was honored when this association asked me to serve for a year as their president, a volunteer position. During that time, I learned a great deal about consultants' time and earnings. Consultants and coaches have to be perceived as experts in their field, but they must also have time to continue their education so they can continue to serve. Consultants and coaches, therefore, keep this in mind when managing their time and structuring their fees.

Please place great value on your time. You must if you expect to be paid enough to survive, let alone succeed, in the world of professional speaking. You are worth more than you think. Your time is more valuable than money. You can always get more money, but you will never regain a moment of time.

The Least You Need to Know

◆ Speakers can follow a number of different career paths.

◆ Clients and speakers enter into an agreement, which spells out the terms of the speaker's fee and the client's expectations.

◆ Trainers and consultants often work for large corporations.

◆ Coaches often work one on one with individuals who need their help.

In Pursuit of the Profession

Professional speakers certainly need to be organized, motivated people. But it's just as important to have good marketing skills if you want to survive in this profession. In this part, I'll give you an overview of how to find an audience, how to keep it, and how to expand it.

Chapter 5

What Are You Talking About?

In This Chapter

- ◆ The process of choosing a topic
- ◆ Engage your brain!
- ◆ How to become an expert
- ◆ Reworking material to stay current

It's sad to say, but even the best of speakers are forgotten way too soon unless they make a lasting impact or difference. What determines longevity in this business? Well, there are several factors, but some of the biggest are your topic and how well you present it, your intelligence, and how well you adapt all of these things to suit your audiences' needs.

But your topic and intelligence can take you only so far as a speaker. Even the timeliest, most interesting topic in the world needs to be reevaluated and reworked from time to time. Keeping yourself open to new ideas, having confidence in your abilities, and addressing changes in a timely manner can keep you on top of this game for many years to come.

Determining Your Best Topics

When you enter the professional speaking world, you need to determine where your energy is best applied. Your potential energy is stored in the topics that you're so passionate about. When you speak to audiences, you want that passion to come through, no matter what subject you're speaking on!

One way to determine your best topics is to carefully assess your background and educational expertise. After doing so, which topics do you think suit you best? Write down the top three. Next, you can determine potential topics by asking yourself about your hobbies or special areas of interest. Which of these topics would you be able to speak about? Again, write them down. Last, ask yourself, "What topics would I enjoy presenting?"

Also, consider that your topic(s) are important to the people who are listening to you speak, especially when delivered on the wings of inspiration. Maybe you'll get rich as a speaker, but wealth shouldn't only be measured in terms of the money you've earned; richness can be measured in total numbers of lives benefited. If there's a subject that you can deliver in an inspiring manner (and change lives in the process), consider that to be one of your best topics.

Your Brain Is Your Best Asset

You must be enthused about topics to be an enthusiastic presenter. (There's nothing worse than a boring talk!) In an ideal world, that would mean every aspiring speaker who feels a genuine attachment to her topic would find her niche and go on to have great success. But in the business world, clients want that passion to be paired with smarts.

Does a so-so IQ preclude you from becoming a great speaker? Not at all! As you'll read in this section, your intelligence and determination to succeed are determined by nurture as much as nature … and that means you have a lot of control over how far you'll go in this business!

The brain is an amazing instrument. And if anyone understands the value of the brain and how it functions, it's the professional speaker. Great speakers aim for the audiences' mind—they understand that men and women learn and communicate differently and go to great pains to adjust their presentations accordingly. Great speakers also take the time to study the differences between the brain's hemispheres (the left side is more rational; the right side is more creative) in an effort to present information that appeals to the entire brain.

Terrific speakers have outstanding ideas because they know the importance of learning all sorts of information from all kinds of interesting people. Back in the day, there was a term for a person who had a great love of learning: a "Renaissance man (or woman)" was someone who knew a great deal about a great many things. He or she was a well-balanced and interesting person, the kind of person a professional speaker should strive to be.

Henry Ford, the great industrialist, was as close to being a Renaissance man as anyone I can think of. Known for his amazing innovations, his brain never seemed to run dry when ideas were needed. Ford admitted that he had a philosophy of surrounding himself with people who were, as he said, smarter than himself. Ford was once asked, "What would you have done had you not gone into the automotive industry?" He responded: "I would have merely found another great need, come up with other great ideas, and made my millions another way."

Ford—one of the greatest inventors of all time—obviously knew the power of engaging one's mind. Speakers (who are themselves inventors of a different sort) have to tap into this power to create unique ideas and present them with excellence. It's one thing to have an entertaining personality and the gift of gab; however, clients want to know that their speaker is imparting some kind of wisdom to the audience. And because those clients are paying your bills and handing out references (you hope), you need to be able to give them what they want and need—brainpower!

Everyone loves a good showman, but to be a successful speaker, you have to tap into your brainpower. In-demand speakers are highly determined and intelligent folks: above all else, they know their topic inside and out, and they aren't shy about sharing that knowledge with their audiences. (It's good to be entertaining, too, as I mention in Chapter 14, but if you don't have the brains to back up your presentation, it will be painfully obvious!)

We'll talk about "experts" in the following section. For now, I want to talk about how important it is to create an environment for yourself where you're always learning, questioning, and creating. Speakers are supposed to leave their audiences feeling uplifted and inspired, no matter what the topic!

There's an old saying, "Garbage in, garbage out" (or "GIGO," as I like to say). There's another saying, "Guilt by association." What do these philosophies have in common? What you choose to read, what you choose to watch on TV, the people you surround yourself with, the entire environment you create for yourself impacts your mind, your spirit, your life … and by extension, your profession. Believe me, successful speakers don't make it to the top by wasting time, reading and watching junk, and hanging around with questionable characters.

Dedicate yourself to shaping the best thoughts possible and expressing them in the most positive ways you can. As professional speaker Ed Foreman advises, "Upgrade your thinking: feed your mind properly."

Intellectual Property

Truly wise speakers understand the value of intelligence. They know they have a unique gift to offer and most want to offer it as often as possible. Once you determine your best topics and develop your presentation, everything that's contained in your presentation is *intellectual property*, which can be loosely defined as your unique ideas and the manner in which you present them. For something to be proprietary material, it has to be original.

def•i•ni•tion

Intellectual property includes your original ideas and opinions and the way in which you present them.

Okay, so what is the value of your intellectual property? First, like most things in life, it depends on what someone might pay for it. After you assess yourself in Chapter 7, you will have a better handle on your intellectual net worth. And remember: you are not to overvalue yourself simply because you have an MBA, MS, or Ph.D., or maybe even an MOT after your name. (What is an MOT? One speaker sent her credentials out as "Mother of Triplets.")

Now allow me to introduce you to the wisdom of Alan K. Mooney, a great speaker, full-time business owner, and financial guru investment counselor and supervisor. This humble man claimed in public to have created 600 percent more income in 2006 than in the prior year (when he had probably grossed seven figures). Even he was amazed by this. Mr. Mooney had been concentrating on building a "business infrastructure to make growth more possible and manageable."

Consider Mooney's calculations:

◆ Fifty work weeks a year × 40 billable hours = 2,000 possible work hours. (Note: no one, not even a top-notch attorney, can ethically bill for 2,000 hours a year.)

◆ Subtract holidays: 10 per year × 8 hours = 80 hours, giving you a new total of 1,920 working hours per year.

◆ Subtract 10 more days off, for sick days, emergencies, and so on. Now you're minus another 80 hours, so you have 1,840 working hours maximum in one year.

Consider this: if you were to project $100 earnings for each possible hour of each year, you'd make $184,000 each year. That's not bad, but you can think bigger and do better—much better—than that if you add the worth of your intellectual property to the mix. This formula only begins to illustrate that you cannot exchange time for money if you intend to get rich as a speaker; rather, you must put a price on your intellectual property!

Now, because intellectual property comes from your best asset—your brain—how on Earth can you protect it? Can you really horde an idea and safeguard it from other speakers? Well … not if you want to share it with audiences! The first thing I advise speakers to do is to Google their ideas. You might be surprised to learn that your material isn't original at all, and that you are (inadvertently) ripping off someone else's presentation! Second, I advise that speakers copyright their material in a very simple way—by placing either a © or a ® next to their name and material. For more information on registering your copyright, visit www.copyright.gov/faq. Visit www.uspto.gov for more information on registering your trademarked material.

I don't advise spending a lot of time and money with an attorney right off the bat, but you should note the dates that you first present or publish your material. From that date forward, it's your intellectual property. Like a classic car or fine wine, it may improve with age. Expect that and protect it accordingly.

You're the Expert!

People like to do business with experts. If you hang around a so-called expert, then that makes you very smart, right? Needless to say, clients want to book *expert speakers*, no matter what the topic is. (No one wants to listen to a speaker hem and haw on an issue—they want to hear a confident message of, "This is the way it is, and I know because I'm the expert!")

How does someone become an "expert" in a given field? Is there an expert-certification course that one must pass with flying colors? And if there isn't any official licensing of experts, then is it reasonable to assume that anyone can pass himself or herself off as an expert? Doesn't that harm the credibility of the title?

def•i•ni•tion

An **expert speaker** is someone who has greater expertise in specific topic areas than nearly all other people. He has the credentials and documentation to prove it.

Generally speaking, an expert speaker is someone who has more experience, has done more research, or has been otherwise involved in a given profession or interest than almost anyone else. This person has been in the trenches, so to speak; he has seen all sides of the issue; he's formed well-thought-out opinions and has no qualms about sharing them.

What are the benefits of being an expert, at least as far as the professional speaker circuit goes? First, there isn't really a "circuit" as such, so don't worry if you are not a part of it. One of the big benefits of being an "expert" is the recognition factor, which in time can help you justify raising your fees. Often an expert is in demand by the media for comments on issues of concern; however, don't wait for the media or others to discover you. Seek them out and let them know who you are and what you have to offer them!

Sometimes being an expert can actually be rather burdensome. You have to be on the cutting edge, up to date in your topic area. This is why having a passion for your topic is important: you need to stay motivated to develop, add to, and share your expertise. Also there's little room for modesty when you're an expert: you have to be willing and able to present yourself as the person with the solutions.

Selling Yourself as an Expert

Let the truth be known: many people do not believe in themselves or their topic or their ability enough to sell themselves as a top-paid speaker. You don't like the word "selling"? You don't see yourself as a salesperson? Tough! You had better learn how to sell yourself and your programs if you intend to do more than stumble into one or a few paid speeches or "gigs."

 Success Shortcuts

Selling your expertise is first and foremost transference of belief. If you do not believe in yourself or your topics and your ability to solve problems through your messages, you cannot expect others to believe in you and buy from you.

Because selling mostly begins with believing in yourself (and you must sell yourself to speak a lot; and you must sell your ideas, material, solutions, and so on), take a check-up from the neck up, as well as a check of your heart, self-esteem, and self-image to see if you believe in yourself enough to become a great speaker. (Read and review what you just read as often as you need to. Repetition is called the Mother of Learning.)

You don't think you're an expert in anything? What is it that you're passionate about? What kind of information do you soak up when you hear it and share with others as soon as you see them? Are you an artist, a business person, a marathon runner? Find a group that shares and discusses your main interests and join! Look in any Yellow Pages (the old-fashioned paper version or the online version) or your local newspaper, or check fliers in the grocery store and library—you may be amazed at how many clubs and associations you can locate. Many of these associations have common needs: a well-crafted and custom message from a terrific speaker is welcome, and actually needed. Some have weekly, some monthly, some quarterly, and some have annual meetings.

How many Fortune 500 companies purchase speakers? All of them! Corporations need speakers and sometimes hire outside trainers or other kinds of folks to meet internal needs. Again, look through the Yellow Pages, read business journals, and ask around to find organizations that may need speakers in your specific area of expertise. Find out who the decision-makers are (as far as hiring speakers goes) and start selling yourself! (More on this in Chapter 7.)

Examples of Expert Topic Speakers

Ideally, experts are pulled into organizations that benefit from hearing the topic at hand explained. Topic experts are all around—in every industry—and you need only contact almost any state or national association for a list of topic experts relevant to their industry or niche. Almost every day in the mail, you can find some sort of invitation to hear an industry speaker. A recent mailing invitation said: "Everything you wanted to know about precast concrete."

As you can imagine, the audiences are fairly limited for many industry topics, and industry speakers typically aren't paid much to speak, other than a free lunch or dinner. However, don't let the typical low pay scare you away from industry speaking! Some topic experts offer presentations for CE (continuing education) credits in their niches and are content with making a minimal commitment to public speaking. The minimal pay augments their full-time job income.

And anyhow, speaking directly to your colleagues can become part of your game plan. These presentations may lead to more credentials for you that result in a pay raise, promotion, or maybe a new or better position elsewhere. Some industry speakers make over a million dollars each year.

If you want to become an industry speaker, look in the Yellow Pages for clubs, associations, or niches in your topic. (For example, a musician might speak to a gathering of therapists, addressing the soothing effects of certain types of music.)

Timing Is Everything

Earlier in this chapter, I talked about selling yourself and your intelligence to clients and developing your very best topics. However, even if that topic is in high demand and serves you well, today's high-demand topic can become tomorrow's old news, so it's important for you to keep an ear to the ground, so to speak, in order to accomplish the following:

 ◆ Determine which topics are on their way in and which are on the way out.

 ◆ Adapt your message so that it fits with the "in" topics.

 ◆ Do it faster and better than your competition.

Audiences want timely topics! Most topics change for various reasons, often because of shifts in societal or technological thinking. Keep up with these trends and work them into your presentation!

Who Can Relate to Your Topic?

Everyone thinks, "My business is different and unique!" This is seldom true for a speaker whose message is malleable for different clients. But because your message must appeal to several different audiences (or markets, as we'll discuss in Chapter 7), you have to be able to mold it, shape it, and present it in a unique fashion, no matter whom you're speaking to.

Some speakers are coming close to their full potential because they have found gold mines within their own topics—in other words, they've found a way to make their message appeal to audiences they never would have dreamed would be interested! These speakers know how to tweak their presentations so that many, many people (often from diverse backgrounds) can relate to what they're hearing.

As a professional speaker, you need to know what people want and how to give it to them. You may end up speaking to some groups that need complex technical material explained and presented. By their very nature, presentations of this sort provide lots of content and "meat on the bone" for the audience members to chew on. But some people are vegetarians, if you get my drift. They don't need as much information; you can pare it down for them. I'm not encouraging you to be simplistic in your presentations—I'm suggesting that you size up your audience before you speak to them and personalize your message for them. It could be the same information presented in a different manner, or it might be an overview of the topic minus a few points that are of no use to this particular audience.

Learning to relate to audiences is as vital to your long-term success as your topic, and it takes intuition and intelligence to be able to stop and say to yourself, "Hmm ... I gave this speech to a group of engineers last weekend. This weekend, I'm presenting it to the road crew. What can I do to make it appeal to their line of work?"

Can You Adapt Your Message to Be More Timely?

Most important, you the speaker must communicate to potential clients that you care about their needs and are willing to go the extra mile, if needed, to customize or tailor your message just for them. This helps you reach your potential.

Sure, you may be considered an expert on certain topics, but you don't have to fence yourself in. Start thinking outside the normal parameters of your expertise and you'll find fresh, new material just waiting to be exposed (those gold mines I was just talking about)! There are plenty of angles to work on any given topic (what we might call subtopics, although almost any subtopic in and of itself can be expanded into its own topic).

Use what you already know to help you think about seemingly unrelated topics in a whole new way. A cardiologist, for example, might seem like a natural to present complicated surgical and medical matters. But what if he chooses instead to speak on the emotional impact that organ donations have on families (of the donor and the recipient)? Well, the latter is certainly a timely topic, and the former is a timeless presentation .... He could reasonably do both, expanding his audience base, his bookings, and his earnings.

It's also important to keep your message relevant so that your audience feels as though they're getting real value out of your presentation. For example, let's say I've been presenting information on how to win big in the stock market for the past 30 years. If my presentation isn't updated to include the very latest trends and technological advances in the financial world, then I'm not going to attract a large audience. People want to know what's happening right now in the field—they come to hear you because you have expert information! Use your brain! Tie all of this together to give a presentation that's chock-full of relevant tips, knowledge, and even a little entertainment!

Speakers must be willing to change, and change quickly. Part of keeping a topic timely is reevaluating your audience from time to time. Do they still want and need to hear your message? How does it relate to modern-day life? What kind of practical advice are you ready to share?

"Wait a minute," you might be thinking, "there are some topics that really don't change very much. Do these 'timeless' pieces really need a modern-day overhaul?" Any topic can—and should—be made to sound 100 percent up-to-date, and sometimes it only takes minimal effort. A topic like "Body Language in the Workplace" can be transformed into "Body Language and the Twenty-First Century Business World." That makes the topic sound of-the-moment, even if some of the information is, indeed, based on Charles Darwin's studies of animal behavior in the 1800s.

An important part of professional speaking is listening to feedback and—dare I say it?—criticism, which is never pleasant, but can be a great impetus for positive redirection of your message. Professional speakers need to have a thick skin, so if you don't have one … develop one! Allow people to help you restructure your presentation. Pride is not a virtue; it is a vice. You can program your brain to welcome change, and as a result you become a great element of change for good in this needy world.

You have heard of (and I hope you operate by) the Golden Rule, "Do unto others as you would have them do unto you." Follow this advice when reconfiguring your materials to help your clients, but please also remember that usually, "Those who have the gold make the rules." Find those speakers who have found the gold, and play by their rules!

The Least You Need to Know

- Your education, work background, and interests all combine to determine your best topics.

- Your ideas and the way you present them are your intellectual property and can be trademarked and/or copyrighted.

- Speakers charge clients according to the worth of their intellectual property, not by the hour.

- Be willing to adapt your message so that it can reach as many audiences as possible.

Chapter 6

Refining Your Speaking Skills

In This Chapter

- ◆ Groups to help you sharpen your skills
- ◆ Becoming a certified expert
- ◆ Improving with age
- ◆ Simple speech structure

As I've mentioned throughout this book, professional speakers strive to continue learning, both in their personal lives and careers. No matter how successful you become, you will always have competition. If you aren't willing to put the time into improving or maintaining your standards of excellence, you can bet that the speaking engagements you want will go to a speaker who's devoted to being the best that she can be.

Now, if you're just starting out, it's obviously vital to develop rock-solid speaking skills. Even if you believe you're a natural in this area, you simply can never be *too* good, so be prepared to put lots of effort into planning your presentation! In this chapter, I'll cover the ins and outs of polishing and refining your speaking skills.

Toastmasters and College Classes Can Help

Recently I received a phone call from an aspiring speaker based in South Carolina. John is a high school teacher with 29 years' experience, and for the past two years he has led a class on Presentation Skills for his students. John is a skilled presenter himself, having been a member of his local *Toastmasters International* club. (In fact, he made it all the way to the state finals of their annual competition!) He is laying the groundwork to retire after 30 years as a teacher and to become a paid professional speaker (full time), and his experience with Toastmasters may serve him well in this venture.

def•i•ni•tion

Toastmasters International is a collection of small, local groups who are interested in refining their speaking skills.

Toastmasters is an international organization made up of thousands of local clubs where one can practice speaking and receive some peer review. Not everyone who joins is an aspiring professional speaker—some folks want to feel at ease when speaking in front of a group at work; others are shy people who want to increase their self-confidence. These are intimate groups (about 20 members each) that usually meet once a week to practice all sorts of speaking skills. Members might be asked to deliver a prepared presentation or a spur-of-the-moment speech. You may be timed, your word choice will be critiqued, and you must be prepared to offer up your honest opinion of others' work.

Because these groups are small, they enable members to get comfortable speaking in front of a nonthreatening audience. Once those skills are perfected, it's somewhat easier to move onto giving a presentation to a much larger group of people. Regardless of your skill level, you can benefit from Toastmasters in a variety of ways. (Anytime you get together with a group that shares a common goal, you're bound to pick up some great ideas—and you'll also learn what *not* to do!) There is a nominal fee to join. Go to www.toastmasters.org to check out this nonprofit association.

College Courses

When I was considering entering the world of professional speaking, I went back to college at Ohio State University and took an evening class for credit in speech communications. In this class, I learned about presentation skills and had to give two or three mini-speeches in front of my classmates and teacher to earn my A. This three-month learning experience convinced me to say, "Yes, I can do it! I can become a paid professional speaker."

Drama classes and theatrical education are also helpful for aspiring speakers. Actors are taught to project their voices and create a dynamic stage presence. Because they perform in front of groups of all sizes, they learn early on to be comfortable in the spotlight. Most also develop an appreciation for constructive criticism (because they're exposed to it nonstop in their classes). All of these skills are part and parcel of the professional speaker's career!

College is not a prerequisite for success as a professional speaker. Speakers come from all kinds of backgrounds in both education and work experiences. The only common thread that seems to run through the life experiences of great speakers is a love and passion for speaking and a desire to get their message out and thereby make a difference. Tony Robbins, for example, who has written several great books and has been on national TV with *Larry King Live* (and others), and has made millions per year as a speaker, motivator, trainer, or extreme seminar leader, had little college before he began.

Here's my take on higher learning for the professional speaker: if you have a great mentor who has a Ph.D. in speech communications and this person works with you to impart his or her knowledge, then you can get the equivalent of a four-year degree in a year of working in an apprenticeship situation. This kind of education, in my opinion, is often better than a college education, in that you receive very specialized and proven knowledge (and practical experience) directly from someone who is where you want to be.

Certification Programs

So now you know that you do *not* need to acquire formal college education in order to demonstrate to others that you are an expert in a given field. However, formal education can be a very good and sometimes necessary thing, especially if it helps you, the aspiring speaker, to refine or improve your knowledge base (which, in turn, will be converted into improved presentation skills). Instead of committing yourself to earning another college degree, however, you may be able to gain *certification* in your area of expertise, which is verification that you've expanded and/or maintained your expertise. Certifications are increasingly common in all professions; some are truly earned, some are awarded for more education, and some are a combination of both (and a few might be bogus).

def•i•ni•tion

Certifications provide verification that you have arrived at a certain level of competency. They are typically issued by professional boards or state-governing bodies.

Today it seems with every business card you collect, you will find names with initials after them. We all know that educational degrees like M.S. after a name means Masters in Science; an M.D. of course means Medical Doctor; my B.A. stands for Bachelor of Arts; and the treasured Ph.D. is a doctorate degree and could be from many different disciplines. (Some say a Ph.D. stands for "piled higher and deeper" ....) My L.H.D. stands for Doctor of Humane Letters. There are so many combinations of letters these days, you may not know what some of them stand for. Don't be afraid to ask someone, "What does this X.Y.Z. after your name stand for?"

As with nearly every profession, the association attempting to shape the industry—the one with the most powerful or largest membership base—usually attempts to promote their certification and make it seem nearly mandatory for those in the profession. The National Speakers Association, for example, has a certification program that results in participants earning a CSP (Certified Speaking Professional). Certification is seldom truly necessary (you do not have to have a CSP, for example, to succeed as a professional speaker); however, it certainly can be an asset to you as you develop your career.

Destined to Succeed

Realize that your thoughts determine your actions, and eventually your success or lack of success. Furthermore, as a speaker you must realize that your actions determine your habits, and like it or not, your habits determine the way you feel about yourself and can eventually affect your skills and results.

Words to the Wise

Over the years I have known dozens of speakers, maybe hundreds, who work for a while and then are never heard from again. Don't end up like this! Continue to refine your speaking skills! It's the only way you're going to improve them and become a more skilled presenter!

Work habits are especially important. Having the courage to believe in yourself and to persevere even when things aren't going your way is, perhaps more than anything else, the one thing that can make or break your career.

Recently I heard a retired priest give a sermon in a Catholic church. To look at this man of God, you would think he is all worn out with nothing to say, or if he did have something worthwhile to share, it would be delivered in a boring way. Just the opposite was true. This veteran speaker—a man who spoke to audiences every week, and probably every day at times during his 50-year career—still understood what brings success for speakers, even when others don't seem to care. He stood about 5'4" and had a booming voice. He used dramatic pauses, good nonverbal communication, and he chose words that stuck with his audience, and moved us to action. In other words, he had great skill and was a much better speaker than most people who are much more physically attractive and are one third his age. The seasoning of the years brought an interesting, comforting tone to his voice that left us wanting more. Perhaps he wasn't so skilled during the first 10 or 20 years of his career. But I am sure those who hear him now are very glad he stuck with it and continued working to refine his delivery!

Expect that kind of thing to be said about you many years from now. *That's* your destiny!

Determination Affects Success

We have to aim to be the best we can be today, but we must also keep in mind that we always need to learn more. And as we learn more, we can—and should—embrace the chance to do things better. In other words, your "best" today won't be as great as your "best" next year, and that's all right! Be determined to continue growing and improving, and don't ever stop!

I remember one of the first paid speeches I gave in the early fall of 1977. Am I a better speaker today? Of course! Should I be paid more today? Of course! Do I value my experience and additional education? Of course!

In addition to having the determination to continue to be better with every passing year, find some determination to convince any kind of buyer, regardless of age and experience in working with speakers, that you are a great speaker, the best and right choice, and worth every penny of your asking price! (It's tough to grow in a business if your pay is not commensurate with your experience, after all.)

Methods for Improving Your Speaking Skills

The best athletes know that as long as they want to compete, they must discipline themselves with exercise and work to perfect their skills. The baseball player who wants to be the best comes in early and takes extra batting practice. The great golfer works out at 6 A.M., five to six days a week. The tennis pro practices until his hands are raw.

Like world-class athletes, super-terrific speakers—truly the best ones—don't take *anything* for granted. They practice all the skills needed for excellence relentlessly. What kind of methods can you borrow from these pros?

◆ Exercise your voice. While you're driving (especially by yourself!), practice voice inflections, exercise raising and lowering your voice, work on improving the tone of your voice, practice your dramatic pauses, and strengthen your vocal chords by speaking very loudly (singing can help, too).

◆ Practice your delivery of humor and other material to perfect your sense of timing. Then ask your significant other or family member to be an audience of one and to applaud, respond appropriately, and give you written evaluations.

◆ Be your best! You can't be 50 pounds overweight, smoke cigarettes that produce a hacking cough, neglect exercise, stay up half the night, and so on, and expect to last for long as a speaker. This business takes stamina, both mental and physical! Take care of yourself!

Most speakers who sustain themselves and survive long term in this business are simply determined to succeed and will do whatever it takes to do so. These folks can't leave things undone. For example, I'm writing this chapter on a summer Sunday afternoon. I assure you, there are a couple of other things I would like to be doing at the moment (as I have a full speaking workweek ahead of me), but I have my laptop with me at my 88-year-old mother's home. My wife and I had lunch with her, some nice discussion and prayers, and now I am back to work. I know I will finish this on time, not only because it will help my career, but because I am determined to do so!

Image Factors Determine Success

Videotaping yourself may be one of the best ways for you to critique and improve your speaking skills *and* your image. I think it is a great idea to tape every message the first couple of years, and doing so with your own home video camera on a tripod from the back of the room is good enough.

When you are ready to hire professional videographers to make you look like a saint on camera (better than a devil, for sure) you will have already mastered some of the benefits of being taped, which include some simple, but important, things. Make sure you do the following:

◆ Understand which colors look best on you.

◆ Appear confident and poised before the camera.

◆ Look into the eyes of various audience members.

- Be microphoned properly with a back-up battery.

- Have extra lighting so that no shadows are showing.

- Have an interesting and attractive backdrop.

- Have your material memorized.

- Have the camera focused always on you, not on your slides.

- See to it that the audience response is recorded.

- Laugh at your own humor; it will prompt the audience.

> **Words to the Wise**
>
> One big reason that you may not be a better speaker 10 years from today is the development of bad habits. If you regularly watch your performances, you will see with your own eyes any issues that are dragging you down.

Keep a notebook marked VIDEO REVIEW, and every time you evaluate yourself on tape, make some notes as if you are journaling to yourself. Gee, I wish someone would have given me this great advice 30 years ago. I really believe I would have had twice the success I've had …. Maybe *you* can have that success now!

While we're still on the topic of image, let's talk about some master image-makers. Recently, I was inspired by the great image of our U.S. President when he gave a tele-vised speech from the Oval Office. I realized that no matter how intense this business is or how far I go in it, I will never be scrutinized like the President of the United States. Nor will you. But we can certainly learn many things from how politicians project their image. What are some of those factors you can observe and possibly emulate to become a much better speaker?

Speaker politicians …

- Know how and when to project a serious image and when to shift gears and present an upbeat, hopeful image.

- Know how to bring up a problem, explain it, and then present their analysis and solution in a persuasive way, steps that improve their image.

- Have advisors coaching and critiquing them—trusted advisors whom they con-tinually get feedback from.

- Learn how to turn a phrase to make their points and repeat their ideas or deci-sions in different ways for impact. Repetition can improve learning.

Words to the Wise

Professional speaking is one of the most, if not the most, competitive businesses in the world. Even if you become your area's number-one topic expert speaker, you might be competing for a limited number of openings for paid speakers with the likes of prominent retired politicians, big-name sports heroes, and celebrities.

◆ Have learned to never give up or give in just because people are critical of them; rather, they keep looking to improve.

◆ Must be willing to see themselves on videotape, laugh at their flaws and mistakes, and simply set goals to project a more believable ethical image.

You can—and should—be able to meet every suggestion on this list. There's a reason why politicians are so persuasive and why ex-politicians go on to have long, successful speaking careers: they stick with these actions, which have proven to be helpful in improving image!

Speech Preparation

At this point I want to talk to you about the *vignette* approach to creating a speech. This method of structuring your speech (or seminar, or workshops, or training programs) is the best I have ever discovered in 30-plus years of professional speaking. Although I will cover other aspects of speech preparation elsewhere in this book, I want to introduce the vignette approach here and now. *This is basic, and needs to be mastered.* It's really this simple: you can't succeed in this business unless you have sharp speaking skills; and you can't sharpen those skills if you present your speeches in a haphazard way.

The vignette method to creating a speech is basically stringing a series of short stories, one liners, quotes, short paragraphs, and so on together under a speech theme or title or topic. An average 45- to 60-minute speech would have three major points. Each of those points would be proven by vignettes supporting each point, and the better the variety of vignettes, often the tastier and more memorable the message.

So here is how you can outline your greatest speech:

I. Title of the message (usually ties into a topic area, and possibly the theme of the meeting if one exists). Sample title: *You Are Not an Idiot: You Can Succeed.*

II. Opening: Attention-getters can include three or four small vignettes:

A. My favorite first one after saying, "Thank you for that kind introduction!" Then, "How many of you have heard of Thom Lisk? How many of you don't care that you have never heard of Thom Lisk before?" (Laugh expected.)

B. "Well, that makes us even. I have never met most of you, either—I have never heard of you." (Another small laugh.) "Now that introduction reminds me ...." (Tell a quick humorous anecdote.)

C. "I would like to acknowledge your entire executive management team who are so dedicated to your success, and thanks especially to ... (mention names of significant people, and ask for applause for them, if not spontaneous)."

III. Tell the audience what you are going to tell them in overview before you explain it in three major points with vignettes to support each point. Note that at the end in your overview, you may be wise to remind them of what you told them. You might begin by using these kinds of words, "Today let's please consider ...."

You could call this the introduction to your speech. Make it memorable and attention-getting, and build some suspense and a desire in your audience to want to hear more. "Now, even though in your childhood some may have referred to you as an 'idiot,' you know better. You have had many successes, and this message will provide a great guide so that you can and will have more ... SUCCESS." The last dots represent a dramatic pause, and the capital letters on the last word imply that you raise your voice on that word and say it with added emphasis.

IV. Point 1: The theme of your first point is, "Let's first think about a definition for the word 'idiot' ...."

Give a definition, and then proceed to prove in this speech that no one in your audience is an idiot. This is vignette 1 of your first major point. (Remember, you'll make three major points and support each with vignettes.)

A. Point 1, Vignette 2: Give an inspirational story about some average-IQ person who became famous through intellectual curiosity. At the conclusion of a one- or two-paragraph example, you could say, "Now, if this person can succeed, so can you!"

B. Point 1, Vignette 3: You could do more of the same as 1 and 2, but this time with some great humor included. (You should shoot for humor every seven minutes.) Use a PowerPoint slide for laughs until you're comfortable delivering this important humor-point verbally.

By now you are about 10 minutes into your 45-minute speech. If your speech is shorter, you must shorten some of the vignettes, or use fewer. Likewise, if your speech is longer, let's say 90 minutes, you might attempt to bring out six major points instead of three.

V. Now on to Point 2, The Definition of Success.

Introduce Point 2 with a memorable attention-getting device, or in such a way that they will know you are transitioning to something new, but equally important.

A. Point 2, Introduction: "We looked at the definition of idiot and we all agreed, no one in this room today is an idiot … You are all capable of more success. Now, words mean different things to different people, so let's define the word SUCCESS. What is success to you? Let me see a show of hands, please: how many of you truly want more success?" (This is an involvement technique to keep people interested.)

B. Point 2, Vignette 1: "Great! Everyone is in agreement: you all want more success. Now, let's think about a classic definition of success from Napoleon Hill's famous book, *Think and Grow Rich.* How many of you would like more money, more wealth? (All hands usually would go up again.) Okay, then, the definition that successful people have agreed to for the past 70 or more years—since the Great Depression of the 1930s—is that 'Success is the progressive realization of a worthwhile and predestined personal goal.'"

Comment about the definition, and make sure everyone's with you while tying it back into the title of your message and *also* back to the theme of the meeting or the objectives of the meeting planner who hired you to speak.

C. Point 2, Vignette 2: Point 2 is that everyone wants more success. "You have agreed you want more success, and that none of you are idiots, so now (at the heart of the message) let's consider how you can overcome obstacles in your life, in your organizations, and make needed changes so you can all create more … SUCCESS. Okay?" Here, give a how-to story from an organization or person the audience can identify with.

D. Point 2, Vignette 3: For the analytical types in the audience you want to include some hard, cold facts, some research that proves your points. Remember that you have different types in your audience; not everyone likes the same kind of food to eat, or the same words in a speech. People have different learning styles (which we'll discuss in Chapter 14), so make sure to appeal to those who are left-brain dominant (those who want empirical facts) as well as the right-brained, creative (emotional) types.

E. Point 2, Vignette 4: It's time to bring in some levity again, of course ideally tied closely to your message, and delivered in such a way to support Point 2. This one might be brief and help transition you into the next and final major point of the speech.

VI. Point 3, "What is change?"

You're about 25 to 30 minutes into your 45-minute speech. By now, you have your audience's respect and attention, and they're thinking about the first two points you've made. You just used humor to close Point 2, so if you have to deliver a sobering message, now's a good time to do it.

A. Point 3, Vignette 1: "You may have heard it said that the only person who likes change is a wet baby. Well, change is a fact of life, and as we change we grow—the alternative to change is not good. Sometimes to learn what is good, we must compare and contrast with other possibilities. Let me tell you a sobering story about someone who refused to change." Here, you would tell the story, the point of which is that change is a good thing.

B. Point 3, Vignette 2: "Do we have any gardeners in the room?" (Lift your own hand as a nonverbal example of what you want others to do.) "My father loved to work in his garden; it was a wonderful stress relief for him. I hope you each have found such a stress releaser. Now, his favorite thing to grow was his big-boy tomatoes. He started them in a hotbed with a greenhouse type of effect before transferring them to the garden, and then later he staked the plants as they grew and matured. Dad pointed out to me one day when working the vegetable stand we had in front of our home at the end of each summer, 'Son, notice a tomato when it stops ripening on the vine, because it is ready to pick. If it's fully ripe and you don't pick it, the tomato may fall off the vine and begin to rot. Timing is everything.' See the points in this story? You must keep growing and improving, or what is the alternative? You must time your important changes."

C. Point 3, Vignette 3. What's needed at this point? Humor again? You may need to read the nonverbal cues from the audience before making your decision. But consider that because you are approaching the end of the speech, you want to make sure you are getting ready to close on a high note. You are not simply trying to cram as much information into a speech as possible. You want to reflect on the needs of the meeting planner who hired you and the objectives they want from your message. If that has not yet been accomplished, now is the time to go for the throat (but in a pleasant way), like so: "The facts are, ladies and gentlemen, we must change and improve the culture of our organization to stay competitive in the current economic conditions. We must all pull together, make sacrifices, change as needed, and stay focused on the new, improved mission and vision statement the company has published. Some job is better than no job, and your loyalty to your employer is needed now more than ever. A great deal is at stake. It is not a laughing matter: it is the future of your company."

VII. Now you are ready to close your speech.

A. Humor. Tie a funny story or one-liner back to the theme of title of the message.

B. Review. Tell them what you told them: "Thank you for considering my message, *You Are Not an Idiot: You Can Succeed.* It is true that if you think you can, you can! And, if you think you cannot, you will not. I hope I have given you some ideas and words (and images) to strengthen your willpower so you will have more success. In helping others on your team, you will have more success; never forget that. Excellence in both internal and external customer service demands that you—that we—place others' needs ahead of our own, and certainly you can see that now."

C. Final closing thought: "In final summary … may I respectfully challenge you to change your attitude toward change? I ask you to embrace change … and have fun doing so. You can if you think you can … after all, you are not an idiot; you are capable of much more success!"

D. Use a closing poem, if you have an appropriate one, or closing music that is upbeat. Many speakers use them these days.

E. THANK YOU. "You have been a terrific audience! You are terrific! May God bless you, God bless your organization. I applaud you for your success to date, and in advance for your future successes." (This may stimulate them to applaud you more as you actually applaud them!)

By providing one outline with samples and examples, I am in no way saying that this is the only way to structure a speech; however, this is one great way to refine your speaking skills and increase the likelihood of being invited back to serve your client again and again. Combine and apply all of the ideas provided in this book about improving your presentations and you will be on your way to great success!

The Least You Need to Know

- Clubs like Toastmasters are a great way to sharpen your speaking skills and make contacts.

- Gaining certification in your topic area is one way to prove your expert status as a speaker.

- Focusing on a positive destiny is a great way to ensure your success.

- Image is everything as a public speaker; sharpening your skills improves that image.

- The vignette approach to speech preparation is one of the best and most basic formulas you can use.

Chapter 7

Who Wants to Hear You Speak?

In This Chapter

◆ Who's your audience?

◆ Angling your message toward different groups

◆ Testing the marketplace

◆ Expanding your audiences

Imagine a college professor who has a true love of her topic and a gift for imparting her knowledge to others. Now imagine she wants to branch out and become a professional speaker … but her new career goes nowhere, fast. How could this happen, you wonder? She's highly intelligent and very personable. Why, you'd love to sit and listen to her speak for hours on end! So how and why did she crash and burn as a professional speaker? Chances are she wasn't addressing her best audiences, or as we call them in this business, her best markets.

A professional speaking career is essentially a small business. You have to know your markets, be aware of who needs your services, and find a way to reach your best potential clients.

Prioritizing Markets

Have you seen the movie *Iron Will?* The main character is a young boy who competes in a dogsled race, fighting against all odds to persevere and win. When I saw this film, I couldn't help but think that marketing yourself as a public speaker sometimes feels like you're running a circuitous race. It can take an indomitable will to say, "I won't give up!" and win at this game.

If you truly love your topic and your area of expertise, it will show in your presentation. People will take notice; ideally, the word-of-mouth praise and referrals from pleased clients would ensure that you'd never have to go looking for clients again! They'll run to you!

Unfortunately, this is rarely the case. Most clients won't come looking for you; you'll have to go out and find them, and not only find them, but convince them that they need a speaker just like you! This sometimes seems like an overwhelming task to speakers who are just starting out, so let's put it in terms of a more familiar situation: if you were job hunting and needed to sell yourself to a potential employer, what would you do? You'd probably start out with a well-crafted resumé and then brush up on your skills before walking into an interview.

The initial steps to marketing yourself as a speaker aren't much different. In both cases, you start by thinking about the kinds of organizations where you'd be most likely to land a job. Career counselors often tell their clients to find 100 (that's right, I said 100) prospective employers and go after them. As a professional speaker, you have to be prepared to do the same; in other words, you have to be geared up to be a real go-getter. I've said it before in this book: as a speaker, you can't be shy and you can't be modest (though you can—and should—be gracious and humble). You have to be willing to tell prospective clients in the right *markets* everything they need to know about you to sway them in your favor.

def•i•ni•tion

Markets are groups or organizations broken down by industry type or niche or kind. Markets essentially refer to your best prospective clients.

Narrowing Your Search

How do you choose your top markets for speaking? It isn't always easy. Some speakers search for industries similar to the business they're currently employed in (a nurse might contact a nursing union or a health-care organization, for example) and look for contacts there. This works pretty well for some folks; however, it never hurts to have a couple of other plans in the hopper, so to speak.

Here's a story to illustrate the importance of having several marketing plans: Steven Newman was the first person to walk all the way around the world. He wrote about his adventures in *The Worldwalker* and later parlayed his experiences into a successful speaking career.

You might think Newman spent his time addressing outdoor clubs or exploration groups. You'd be wrong. Newman became the top speaker in elementary schools in Ohio (and surrounding states, too) for about 10 years after his endurance walk. His tales of adventure wowed the kids, but he also imparted a larger truth: "People can be trusted worldwide; if you love and respect them, they will love you and show you hospitality in return." He hand-delivered a personal message of caring love, tolerance, and positive expectations to countless children, which couldn't be a more timely issue in this day and age.

Creative Plans Go a Long Way

Newman could have talked about the gear he used, his nutrition, how he managed dangerous terrain—all topics that outdoorsmen and women would gobble up. However, Newman realized that in order to appeal a larger audience (nothing against sportspeople or their organizations—there just isn't a huge market for those types of speakers), he would have to find some other angle. He must have asked himself, "What else could I talk about? Would people listen to stories about cultures around the world? Who would most appreciate my stories and the lessons I've learned?" As you can see, his creative mind-set worked out pretty well for him!

To find your best markets, you need to ask yourself the same kinds of questions about your topic. Newman had a Plan B centering on delivering his message to middle schools and high schools; he also planned to transition his message for adults (we'll call that his Plan C). So you see, he had a solid plan to continue his work for years to come. In real life, he skipped over plans B and C and went on to speak for a Fortune 500 company, earning four to five times what he was making speaking to grade-schoolers.

Success Shortcuts

If you only offer one primary topic, be prepared to offer at least nine subtopics from that one "umbrella" topic. From this one large topic, then, you may be able to work in several different markets.

The lesson to be learned here? Don't put all your eggs in one marketing basket. Develop several different options for presenting your topic. If Newman had relied on his Plan A, he wouldn't have been able to branch out and reach other audiences. Your Plan C could turn out to be your best market of all … but not if you don't dream it and develop it.

How to Test a Market

You might be so excited about your topic that you're ready to jump right into the marketplace, but be forewarned: it's essential to test the waters before committing all of your time, money, and energy to any particular group. Marketing 101 classes always include an overview of the subject of *test-marketing;* unfortunately, those who go on to become public speakers often have not had any marketing courses (and if they have, they've often long forgotten those courses). Now don't worry about what you might have missed or forgotten. You don't have to go back to school to cover the basics of business. I'll tell you everything you need to know here.

def•i•ni•tion

A **test market** is a relatively small region where a product (in this case, a presentation) makes its debut. Test markets help to determine whether the product will sell and whether it needs a little tweaking to appeal to more people.

Here's something to keep in mind when you're testing out your new material: you haven't sold it to a client yet. If you think you're such hot stuff that your credentials and good looks alone are going to pull clients toward you, you're probably in for a rude awakening. Professional speaking success relies on a combination of intelligence, skill, and an interesting topic. Test-marketing gives you a chance to see what's working in your presentation and what isn't; it's a time to be open-minded and listen to criticism. This is an opportunity to correct any mistakes or things that simply aren't going over well with the audience. So keep in mind during this time that even though confidence and self-belief are essential building blocks of a professional speaker's success, egotism and stubbornness (an unwillingness to acknowledge which areas of your presentation need improvement) are not.

The beauty of test-marketing is that it allows you to start out slowly and evaluate your audiences' reaction to your message. It's not quite as exciting as making a big entrance on the professional speaker scene, but as the old saying goes, slow and steady wins the race.

Wal-Mart Exec Spreads the News

Michael Bergdahl is a former Wal-Mart executive whose major life lessons came directly from the top—that's right, from Sam Walton himself. I'm sure you know that Walton built an empire based on giving the customer the lowest possible prices. At the time of his death, Walton was one of the wealthiest men in America. Not bad for a poor country boy from Arkansas.

After leaving his position with Wal-Mart, Berghdahl began to test-market the idea of sharing Walton's success secrets with others. Once he had nailed the message and the method for delivering it, he took his presentation nationwide. *How to Compete and Thrive in a Wal-Mart World* is now heard in countries around the globe, but specifically in market areas where Wal-Mart is expanding.

Granted, Bergdahl had a couple of big advantages that you and I may not have: he was already well-off, and as huge (and controversial) as Wal-Mart is these days, his topic was situated to sell itself. However, if he had given a bland presentation to a disinterested audience, his speaking career would have fallen flat. So despite those advantages, Bergdahl still took the time to test-market his presentation. That's a pretty good example of how important test-marketing is in this industry.

Where to Test Your Message

Fast food restaurants choose certain test markets to see how the public responds to a new product. If the new Double-Whammy Triple-Bacon Upside-Down Burger doesn't sell well in the test market(s), it probably won't sell well in other locations. The companies know that it's better to lose a little bit of money by testing the product in a small region than to overextend themselves and lose a bundle. The companies also know that a losing product can be turned into a winner with some fine-tuning and changes—and that's a lesson you can learn from, too.

Start your test-marketing by giving free speeches for local audiences. This is a perfect opportunity to hone your speaking skills and learn which elements of your presentation work well with which groups. From there, you'll learn how to work the different angles of your presentation so that you appeal to different audiences. (Here's where Plans A, B, and C are developed.)

So how will you find appropriate test markets within your area of expertise? Join a trade or professional association and volunteer your skills. Sound too easy? There are associations for almost every profession and any niche market in America, and this kind of association test-marketing, possibly more than any other method, is how some

Words to the Wise

Some speakers make the mistake of thinking that marketing themselves is a luxury rather than a necessity. Selling yourself to clients is part and parcel of a successful speaking career—you simply can't have one without the other.

of America's best-known speakers have fine-tuned their messages and their public speaking personas.

Join. Volunteer. Serve. Speak. Become an officer and leader, and you'll have a platform; in the process, you'll also meet some people who can hire you to speak. Plus you'll learn more, so you can be more and do more and do better.

You'll find contact information for these groups in Appendix B.

Committing to a Market

Earlier in this book, you were asked to make some commitments to the profession of speaking—specifically, to be your best and make a difference in your audiences' lives. Now you have to make a commitment to market yourself and your programs, even if they aren't yet fully developed. There's just no point to putting your time and effort into your presentation if you aren't going to actively sell it. Speaking deals aren't going to fall into your lap—you have to seek them out. Keep in mind that your best opportunities may come from the least expected markets, so you must keep an open mind.

The questions in this section will help you focus on your message, your potential clients, and how ready and able you are to sell yourself. Once you have these answers, you'll know where and how to expend your time, money, and energy.

Score Yourself

You can't start a speaking career if you don't know who to speak to. Theoretically, you could book a hall and speak to just about anyone, but the strength of your message has to be coupled with an audience who's eager to hear it. To narrow down those options, mull over these questions:

◆ Based on your professional background, what is your number-one market? What's your number-one market based on your educational background?

◆ Who or what kind of person has responded best to you? (Age, gender, personality type, profession, and so on?)

◆ What do these people like best about you? (Your sense of humor, your intelligence, and so on?)

- Where and how can you find more people like these? (At work, in schools, in trade organizations, in a particular community?)

- Can you become more likeable or personable and, therefore, easier for a client to hire on a retainer basis?

- What do you most need to learn about offering yourself as a speaker? (Do you need to be more outgoing, friendlier, better organized, and so on?)

- Have you completed a thorough Internet search of your topic area, competition, and your primary market(s) so that you know who and what you're going up against? (Keep this info for ongoing review.)

Think about your answers to these questions. Write them down in a journal. Can you summarize your responses into a statement or a paragraph that helps you narrow down your best markets? For example, say you're a high school baseball coach and your team responds well to your methods. You have some choices to make right off the bat (no pun intended): Do you want to speak to high school athletes or to other coaches? What aspects of your personality would appeal to each group? Where will you find these groups?

In asking the questions, the answers will lead you to more answers. The goal is to come up with at least a couple of different angles for your message. In the case of the coach, you might gear your presentation first toward other coaches, second toward high school athletes, and third toward younger athletes.

Creating a Potential Client Base

Finding success as a professional speaker depends on selling yourself and your best topics to the right clients in the right markets. Sounds like common sense, right? Well, I can assure you that some partnerships look great on paper but fall apart in practice. So how do you go about finding the perfect match?

I've listed some of the most important issues in considering your best markets:

- How does your expertise transfer into speaker topics?

- What kinds of organizations would be most likely to hire you because they need your topic expertise?

- Are you aware of all the organizations that can hire (or have hired) speakers in your best topic areas?

◆ Does your topic need customization so clients can better understand how your message fits their needs?

Let's go back to the example of you as a high school baseball coach. First, you would list the areas of your expertise that you believe others will be interested in. Next, you take a look at those topics and decide if high schools are your prime markets, or if you'd be better off looking for coaching organizations to speak to. Not content to stop there, you research more organizations—perhaps you find that your local YMCA is looking for a speaker to address their young athletes. Because the Y doesn't have a baseball team, you customize your message to apply to other sports as well.

Success Shortcuts _____

Evaluating your strengths and weaknesses before contacting potential clients can save you a lot of time and energy. Appeal to the people who need to hear your message (but be prepared to convince them of that need).

You may not have responses to all of these questions now, but as you proceed through this book, you'll find your answers. So mark this page for easy reference and flip back to it as necessary during your reading.

Sell Yourself!

Now put together a series of questions that will lead high-priority clients to realize that they not only need a speaker, but they can afford a great speaker (namely you).

The best way to interview potential clients is by phone or in person; e-mail also works, but you run the risk of being flat-out ignored or having less of a personal connection to the person you're dealing with. Remember: a speaker's best tool is his voice—let those clients hear you loud and clear!

Before you start in with your list of questions, make sure you're speaking with the decision-maker. This may be the head of a particular department, the head of human resources, or the president of a particular organization. If you aren't sure, ask who hires speakers. No sense wasting your time with the wrong people. Being respectful, polite, and just pushy enough (as opposed to far too aggressive) will help you get all the answers to your questions.

Here are questions for potential clients:

◆ Has your company ever used outside speakers?

◆ How much did you budget or pay for your last speaker?

◆ What did you like most about that speaker?

◆ What did you like least about the speaker?

Once you have those answers, you can let the client know why you're the better (or best) option the next time she needs to hire a speaker. (For example, you might be more knowledgeable in a certain area of expertise than another speaker, or you may be able to offer the company a better rate for a presentation.)

Updating Your Offerings

Once you become a veteran speaker, you may need to retool your offerings every so often, depending on the timeliness of your topic and the saturation in the marketplace. So do your research and visit speaker websites to stay current.

Be aware that small changes in how you market your message can have big results. Your speech titles, for example, can be updated to reflect current events. For example, a speech titled *Change Management* is timeless, but it's also kind of flat and dull. Updating the title to *Dealing with Change in Our Changing World*, however, really catches a client's attention and their imagination. Both speeches may include the same exact content, but revising the title makes the presentation seem fresh and current.

Success Shortcuts

Take note of the top speakers in your area of expertise and Google them. Which marketing materials seem to work best for them? Can you learn anything from their marketing strategies? You can always borrow ideas from leaders in the field—just be sure you don't plagiarize their work.

For more information on marketing materials (books, pamphlets, videos, and so on), see Chapter 12.

Preparing to Expand

When you ask an aspiring speaker, "When might you think about expanding your market?" many will say, "Oh, I haven't really thought about it. Later, I guess."

So … when is later? If you are truly committed to success as a professional speaker, it's best to start thinking about other, bigger markets sooner rather than later. This is business, after all, and if you aren't providing clients with needed services or looking for new clients, someone else is going to slip into your spot. Once you've put the time and effort into selling yourself to several clients, keep that momentum going and look for new ways to market yourself, even if that means making yourself available to a market far, far away ….

Time Is *Not* on Your Side

There is a speaker whom we'll call Bill (not his real name—he's a very humble soul) who was shocked by the speed of his own success. Within five years of entering the business of full-time speaking, Bill had spoken to countless audiences, co-authored a book, and flew to Chicago to speak to an audience of international managers employed by a major beauty chain.

At that speech, the CEO was so impressed with Bill as the keynote speaker, he said, "I want to purchase 100 copies of your book, but I need them autographed and on my desk by 3 P.M. tomorrow." Well, Bill knew it would take some extraordinary effort to get those books signed and shipped to Chicago, but he also recognized several important facts:

- His earnings for this speaking gig were about to increase significantly.

- The exposure he would receive by putting his book into the hands of 100 readers furthered his career.

- The word-of-mouth praise he would receive by meeting the client's request could mean more speaking engagements.

Needless to say, the books arrived on time and contributed to Bill's continued success as a speaker.

Now here comes the point: when you're just starting out in any business, five years can seem like an awfully long way off. This speaker didn't just sit on his behind waiting for opportunities. In addition to booking numerous speaking engagements over that five-year period, he also took the time to co-write a book, which not only expanded his audience, but added to his success. He committed to branching to all of his potential audiences; he gave it everything he had … and it paid off, big time.

Moving It Along

Experts sometimes find that in order to tap into their best audiences, they have to change the horizon they're looking at. Lawrence Willis, a successful speaker from Ohio, has moved several times in the past 10 years, each time to plug in to his best client base (something that can shift around with time). He currently resides in Atlanta, but he's ready to follow the market to another location if and when the time comes.

Of course, you may feel that with modern technology, there's no reason to uproot your entire life to find success in the professional speaking world. You figure you could hop on a plane and be anywhere within 24 hours, so why relocate? Well, even with modern advances, it can be hard to network and make strong interpersonal connections if you aren't physically present in the marketplace. It's the difference between a total commitment and a so-so dedication to the profession. Of course, that difference can translate into great success or disappointing results.

To succeed in this profession, you have to create a vision of what you want to achieve—that's basically what a marketing plan is all about. Think of a good, solid marketing plan as a one-way escalator going up. The steps on the escalator are your sub-plans, your test markets, and your overall effort. How far you go depends on you—will you make it to the top or get stuck on the bottom step?

 Words to the Wise

Even though it's important to be flexible as a professional speaker, I wouldn't recommend jumping the gun. Many speakers hang on to their day jobs for several years after entering this profession … just in case things don't pan out as planned.

The Least You Need to Know

- Have three or four marketing plans in place for each topic you offer.

- Prioritizing your markets includes performing effective test-marketing to save yourself time and money.

- Test-marketing is also a great way to hone your presentation skills.

- Don't waste time waiting for opportunities to present themselves! Throw yourself into this profession with everything you have!

Chapter 8

Speaking to Promote, Market, and Sell Anything Better

In This Chapter

- ◆ Bigger benefits than money
- ◆ Tips for successfully selling yourself
- ◆ Always behave as though you're being paid to speak
- ◆ People want to be sold on something!
- ◆ Ethical behavior leads to long-term success

You have undoubtedly come into contact with speakers who may not have really been professional speakers at all, but rather people promoting some product, service, idea, or image—their company or themselves. Some speakers are promoters, marketers, or salespersons—or all three! These folks are offering not a message, but *something* to the sometimes unsuspecting public or attendees at all kinds of meetings.

Don't get me wrong; I am not against this. I am actually for it, and I want to help *you* if you are one of these people who only wants to use speaking to accomplish some other objective. I do *not* advocate calling yourself a professional speaker if you are not paid to speak but rather are promoting something; however, I am for you promoting, marketing, and selling your way to great success as a speaker in a professional way.

Words to the Wise

> Although I am not against speaking to sell something, I *am* against people calling themselves professional speakers if they may have some ulterior unknown motive when they speak to audiences. I am against *any* kind of coercion or unethical behavior when it comes to serving audiences with any speech or message at any time and in any place. You can wisely use speaking to sell just about anything. Do so ethically by letting your meeting planner know up front what you are attempting to do, and everything will turn out great.

Speaking to Groups to Save Time/Money in Promotion

Carl Stevens—my first great speaker mentor 30+ years ago to whom I will always be grateful—taught me a great deal about how speaking can save one's time and money promoting. In this chapter, I will share with you current and refined methods; however, let us first consider this example.

Like some of our readers, Carl had a product to sell—his seminars, for one thing. When I first joined him, we were offering a $2\frac{1}{2}$-day seminar every month on an open-enrollment basis at our headquarters building conference room in the Management Horizons International office in Ohio. My first assignment was to promote these events, create effective marketing materials, and then use anything I could to sell seats to the open-enrollment seminars at $295 per person.

I was told in so many words that the very best way to give a sales presentation that gets "bigger results" is not to bring in one person at a time (that is too slow!), but rather to look for appropriate groups I could speak to for *free* (promoters' favorite word!) where I would have a captive audience to promote, market, and sell to in an ethical way. Now where does one find these group audiences? They are everywhere, I soon learned … and you will soon discover this, too.

At the beginning, I was a very green 27-year-old speaker; however, I was already a very proven and successful salesperson and manager. My classes at Ohio State University in speech communications, and other in-house group presentations to small groups of client employees at my prior employers, helped me to understand the wisdom in group promotion and selling, and as a result I had a springboard to more success.

You can find that speaking to a group in the best targeted niches for free can save you heaps of time and money. In my case (learn from this please), I came to quickly realize that any company with salespeople, especially a great many salespeople, were *hot* prospects for my presentations. Nearly any kind of company with six or more local salespeople has a weekly or monthly sales meeting where a guest speaker, especially one who has a valuable and motivating educational message (and especially one that is free), is very welcome.

Examples of Speakers Who Promote from the Podium

So I am the first example of a speaker who promoted, marketed, and sold from the platform that I will give you. I am an expert in this area through the fire of some trial and error, but I was lucky: I had a great mentor to critique me. When I first started, I would sometimes speak to community service groups and local associations who had absolutely zero budgets for speakers, but I went away from those speeches with hundreds (later thousands) of dollars in sales and income. Is that what you want? Keep reading!

Free ... for Now ...

If you live in or near a big city, you may have seen the Peter Lowe "GET MOTIVATED" seminars. These are an inspirational recreation of the group sales effort approach. They sometimes get 20,000 or more people into an arena for a free (or nearly free) business seminar with some of the world's top-name speakers. Where they make their money is on the sale of products or other services at the seminars.

In the past year my company, Professional Speakers Bureau Int'l (as seen at TerrificSpeakers.com), purchased 25+ tickets for one of these events. I gave them to business associates, staff members, family members, and so on. One of my family members went to this "free" event and then gave her charge card and invested $1,000 for another seminar promoted at the event. See what I mean?

Maybe a better example would be the expert speaker who is always speaking at your industry annual convention. This guru, in my experience, often is a business owner or top manager or technical "geek" (I use the word with the utmost respect for these intelligent folks) who sometimes has a kind of hidden objective. Have you seen the type?

Maybe the person is trying to connect with suppliers or customers and uses the vehicle of speaking to enhance credibility in an already very competitive marketplace. To me, this has its good points and bad points. I will not belabor them other than to say it sure can help the speaker. It can help the meeting planner (maybe because her pay or company budget is affected if she pays a speaker) who gets a free speaker over a truly professional speaker.

Words to the Wise

For those of you who are interested strictly in professional paid speaking, be aware that you may be going up against free promotional speakers when you are trying to get meeting planners to pay for your program!

In my long and varied history in speaking, I have often been the first speaker an organization has ever *paid* to have come speak! Remember, as I candidly admitted, that I started out giving free speeches to promote, market, and sell seminars (and related services and products). However, my goal from day one was always to become a paid professional speaker, not simply a speaker who spoke to promote, market, and sell. Later my goal included developing a bureau to book other speakers.

Promotion Shortcuts for a Speaker

I have already shared some ideas with you that are shortcuts for a speaker wanting to promote, market, and sell. Here are more ideas that work, if *you* work *them:*

- Get a good marketing brochure together that you can give to each person in the audience where you speak. This brochure is not to sell you as a speaker; it is to sell your products, services, ideas, or company (or it could at least be your image piece).

- Create a good image in all ways possible, but don't personally go into debt for it. Stay out of debt unless you can pay off your self-promotional "tools" (whether these are actual promotional materials or a professional wardrobe, or both) in 30 days, even if your speaking career flops.

- You might be surprised who you can get to fund your promotional materials. Ask for help and expect it.

- Press releases sent to your target markets can get your name in the paper or trade publications, help brand you, and create invitations to speak! You can write articles that create speaking invitations, too.

- You can create e-mail lists and send out your newsletter periodically with an offer to speak for free to any group over six people.

◆ Promote with your own voice—first in person, and if that's not possible, then by phone.

Color glossy marketing materials may not always be necessary, but consider that for the price of a few pennies more, you leave behind a lasting impression. But if in 90 percent of the cases, you're certain that your marketing materials just get thrown away (or at best put in a file never to be seen again), then by all means be frugal.

Professional, Not Huckster Please

Not long ago I received a phone call from the Bush Chamber of Commerce in Bush, Colorado. They needed a speaker: "We have a farm community and we want a humorous speaker who can relate to our unique audience for our annual banquet on a Saturday night in March. Now we don't want some huckster. We want a great speaker within our budget, someone who has great, clean humor for both men and women, as the farmers bring their spouses."

Huckster? I had not heard that word in quite some time, but I knew exactly what the chamber leader meant: they didn't want someone who appeared to be "cheap" in any sense of the word—in his dress, his language, his intent, and his message. Speakers who have something to sell can be perceived as hucksters, but this isn't always the case.

The four things mentioned that you have to sell are (generically speaking): products, services, ideas, and image.

Think about how you have sold these things, or how you would like to come across as you make a group presentation with at least one motive to sell something at the end (and/or later) as a result of your message. For the sake of this chapter, I am not presenting skills for presentations, but rather ideas and principles for your success. Follow this, please …

Product: You really don't market or sell products; you sell the product of the product. In other words, sell the *benefits* in; sell the answer to the question that audience members have in mind: "What's in it for me?"

Service: People can discern if a speaker is concerned about them, if you are present to serve or sell. Always be present to serve *first*, then selling will be easier.

Ideas: People are always interested in ideas, especially better ideas that can benefit the listener. More money is made with better ideas—get them and present them better than anyone else and you will succeed.

Image: An image can be rather elusive for the speaker who wants to sell something with his message. You must present an appropriate image, but also the *professional* image of the organization you represent. People will pay more for and respond more positively to image and quality.

Success Shortcuts

When I was chairman of speakers and programs for my local Rotary, I arranged for a high-ranking politician to speak. This man sat and spoke at length with me as if we were long-time friends. He didn't even know (or ask) my political party! I really think he treated me with dignity, respect, and care. How can you not like someone who treats you like that? Are you like that when *you* speak, in all regards?

Look in Your Local Area for Examples

You can easily plug your promotional message into your local speaking network. In most counties and cities with over 50,000 people, you can find numerous examples of people who are in need of speakers. You can look in something as readily available as your Yellow Pages under "clubs" or "associations," and you may find dozens of them. Based on your objectives and plans, which ones are good targets for your message?

You could also go to your local Chamber of Commerce and (whether you join or not) acquire lists of all kinds of organizations that may be open to have you speak—especially for free—to their people. Give it a try and see what happens!

Also, in any county or city of 50,000 people or more, you can find people who want to become professional paid speakers (some think of themselves more as trainers or educators) and other people who would like to speak to sell something. Who are these people? Why not find them and network with them?! Learn from them or offer them your services. Network!

Follow Leaders Who Create Business from the Platform

Politicians are not necessarily the best examples to follow for most speakers; however, they sure are selling ideas and an image, if not a product or service, wouldn't you agree? In the political campaign of 2008, we learned a great deal from both the Republican and Democrat candidates leading up to their party's nomination before the general election. Maybe all you learned was their positions on issues important to you, you might claim. But I think you learned more—maybe much more. What kind of information did we glean from this process?

◆ Did you learn how the wrong use of one word can backfire on you and hurt rather than help?

◆ Did you learn how fund raising is handled and that the person who sells himself or herself best (thus raising the most money) has a greater likelihood of getting elected?

◆ Did you learn how to ask for action at the end of a speech, as in, "Please, I ask for your vote on election day"?

◆ Did you learn how image affects your choices?

◆ Did you learn that you prefer people just like yourself ... or did you learn that you are open-minded?

◆ Did you learn that it is nearly impossible to please all people all the time ... so why would you expect to with one of your presentations?

◆ Did you learn about speakers who have more substance versus someone that is more inspirational, and which you (and others) preferred?

You could make a short list here and now in this book or in your planning journal of speakers you have seen in action, whether it was first-hand or via television. What did you like most about their presentations and what did you like least? Adapt and use the good, and discard the bad.

Everyone Is Promoting Something—Why Not You?

Hey, look around. Think about it; everyone is trying to promote or sell something. It's true—not just the United States, but much of the world is consumer driven. We are all so oriented to look for something to buy, something that meets our needs, something that solves our problems and makes our life a little easier.

I have heard the pastor of my home church, Father Richard Pendolphi, say from the pulpit on more than one occasion, "I am in sales, not in management." And you'd better believe he is proud of the product he sells! He serves with excellence, as does his friend and associate pastor, Father James Coleman. The point? The best of salespeople (and speakers, too!) *must* believe in what they are selling!

 Words to the Wise

You must personally be sold on what you are offering to have maximum success in your promotional efforts from the platform as any kind of speaker.

If you are going to be successful in any and all of your promotional efforts, you *must* believe in the proposition (the offer you are providing). Selling is always first and foremost the transference of belief. Enthusiasm sells if it is genuine.

Lessons Gleaned from Master Promoters

Now, again and maybe in more depth, look at all the lessons you have gleaned from master promoters you have encountered. As for me, I think of people I have met like Bob Evans, founder of Bob Evans Restaurants. He was recognizable in one of my audiences several years ago due to his string tie, one of his trademarks that helped make him memorable.

I think of those on TV like Ed McMahon—remember him from the Johnny Carson show? (Are you old enough to remember?) Maybe you prefer Glenn Beck or Lou Dobbs on CNN, who are always seemingly championing some cause—this is why we listen even if we do not agree. They are masters at promoting their ideas. Can you see that? You can learn from lots of personalities on TV. Are *you* doing that?

Speech and Accountability

Sometimes (if not most of time for most of my readers), in order to use our gifts better on a consistent basis, we must make ourselves accountable to others. Share your gift with these people first, tell them what you are thinking about doing, and ask them to hold you accountable for everything you say.

One of the groups I meet with monthly consists of CEO's, owners like myself of various-sized companies. We each serve as the Advisor Board of Directors for each others' companies. If we want to benefit from these meetings as much as we possibly can, we tell one another our biggest problems and look for various ideas and inputs to find the best solutions. (Everything is kept confidential.) We discuss the past month, and the future, in three areas: personal, business, and family, all in an interrelated way for creating synergistic growth.

We all need a support system and/or group(s) of people to help us be our best. One way other people can help is to tell you when you are using your speech to edify and benefit, and also when you are shooting yourself in the foot due to what you say or even write.

Thank God for editors! I love to write as much as I love to speak, or so it seems. My fingers can get me into trouble typing e-mails to people more than my tongue these days, how about you? It is too easy to send off an e-mail to someone before editing it. We—some of us anyway—write things to people in such a way that we would never say out loud, even in a confidential one-on-one situation.

A good rule is if you are not sure how it will impact everyone you are about to say it to, don't say it. Or don't write it. Obviously, when you are speaking (or sending e-mails) for promotional purposes, you want to draw people to you and your message. If you offend a group of people—even unintentionally—don't expect to see your sales take off (at least not in the direction you're hoping!).

Rhetorical Questions

You can take almost any sentence and end it in with a question, can't you? Examples can go on endlessly to the point of nausea, so I will stop, okay? For speakers wanting to promote, market, and sell better, the point is that you are well advised to include many questions in your presentations to which you promptly provide the answer.

I write "promptly," thinking about one incident in a speech years ago. I asked the audience, or so I thought, a rhetorical question: "What is a mentor?" Before I could answer, a tall, thin man stood up to my right in the audience of about 100 people, and shouted out loudly for all to hear, "Mentor, why that is a city up on the lake east of Cleveland, Ohio." That got a big laugh—good thing I was practiced enough to not be thrown off and able to laugh and roll with the flow of the audience.

Using rhetorical questions engages the audience. They're paying attention, listening for the answer, perhaps ready to offer an answer themselves (such as what happened in my Mentor example). You always want your audience to be listening intently, but this is especially important when you are selling something!

Use Visual Aids Wisely to Promote

Many professional speakers see the value in using visual aids of all types to help deliver their message. Elsewhere in this book, we give you most of what you need to consider as far as visual aids go. But that is not slanted toward helping you to promote some product, service, idea, or image and make an immediate sale to the audience or create enough good will so that you'll get business down the road.

Consider some optional tools you can use for selling products. I have sometimes seen speakers pass out a copy of their book to all audience members and then quote from it, point to pages in the book, and get the audience so involved in the book that when the speech is finished and the speaker says something like the following, a higher percentage of the audience buys the book:

> "Oh by the way, if you like my message, and you like the look of my book, and what little bit in it you have heard and read while I was speaking, please consider purchasing a copy today before I leave. Ten percent of the proceeds go to a charity to feed homeless children, and for every 10 books sold today, one goes to your local library system. Please note I have already autographed each book in the front, and if you would like yours personalized, come forward. You can fill out the card in each book as to how you want to pay for it, and leave it at your place, or pass it in, or bring up front—I know you must get on to other things. The book is regularly $23.95, but today only it is $12. It makes a great gift if you don't have time to read it. I take cash, checks, charge cards, or IOU's. Please get your copy today, okay? Thank you. God bless you all."

You may not like this prior example. You may have other ideas on how to use visual aids wisely, but do give some thought to what you can use to help you sell more. By the way, it is helpful if you can get the person introducing you (and the person who also wraps up the meeting) to hold up whatever you are offering and promote it. (But make sure you have coached them how to do so! A poor promotional tactic is sometimes worse than none at all.)

Selling Solutions

The best of promoters are problem solvers, never simply pushing themselves or some product, service, or idea. You know this intuitively, yet sometimes people do the oddest things when they try to promote. I think it is mostly because they have not thought it out, prepared properly, learned other options, or been coached.

My research proves that you are as much as 50 percent less effective in marketing and selling anything if you push a product or service first. If you simply try to make friends with people and sell based on friendship first, you are 50 percent less likely to sell when compared to the professional problem solver.

Some people are technique-oriented; in other words, they have tried habitual routines (seldom do people admit they have these) that they feel comfortable using ... but if not focused first as problem solving, they are also 50 percent off.

Some retail salespeople are said to be the "take it or leave it type." What happens if you are attempting to sell to someone and you say something like, "Well, there it is.

If you like it, fine; if not, fine"? Most people are indecisive most of the time unless given enough reasons to part with their time or money. They need to be—often actually *want* to be—sold! So please don't believe that the product will sell itself—*you* and your techniques are an indispensable part of the process!

The Puppy-Dog Approach

You actually do people a *big* favor when you sell them something that will benefit them, even if they do not fully realize it when they encounter you. One approach to selling is what is called the "puppy dog approach." In the earlier example where the speaker provided a book to everyone and asked them to review it as he spoke, the puppy-dog approach would have been to let the audience members take the book home with them and then collect it from them in a few days if they did not return it.

You sometimes see this on TV with all the money-back satisfaction guarantees. They know statistically and historically only a very low percentage of people who get something and pay for it, even if it does not work or they change their mind, will return it and ask for a refund. Don't be afraid to ask for—and expect action toward—the acquisition of your products or services.

The Take-Away Technique for Speakers

Another famous technique! But more than a technique that works occasionally, this can be a secret weapon for a coy promoter. If used improperly, this method can really hurt people, so I hesitate to tell you much about it or even list it here. I do so because I care about helping everyone get better and do better, but only in ethical ways.

In the take-away, you actually can tell someone the bad things about what you have to offer, even yourself, and tell them not to buy the product or service unless they are truly serious about receiving the benefits and solution. You can see the psychology of this approach—you give it to them and take it away by discounting significantly the value of it—humbling yourself—before saying "On the other hand …"

 Words to the Wise

Please use all sales tips wisely and combine it with the Golden Rule. I am not talking about the one that some use, which is: "Those who have the gold make the rules." Take a new pledge to treat others the way you want to be treated, no matter which sales tactic you're using.

Involvement Tools While Speaking

Giving is always the first and best way to getting more. I could give a hundred examples to prove this assertion, but instead I will give you an anecdote. My 102-year-old grandmother, after 73 years of marriage, was asked by my wife, "Grandma, what is the secret to a long and successful marital relationship?" She wisely responded, "Honey, a lot of give and take, with the emphasis always placed on giving."

I love when I am given a handout as an audience member. I immediately think more of the speaker when he has given me some sort of outline or a synopsis of the message, don't you? Well then, if you are speaking, create and provide handouts every time. Put your contact information on each page with good, understandable, and valuable information—not just sales stuff, but real valuable info.

Use Involvement Tools Wisely

Giving some involvement-type tools that reach the tactile or kinetic learner in all of us helps you to connect with the audience. If you are not careful, however, you can hurt your presentation by scattering the attention of the audience. I recommend first and foremost a simple fill-in-the blanks sheet(s), something like an outline of your PowerPoint slides with the lines next to them for writing. This is one easy-to-create item for audience involvement and take-home value.

Can you think of other tools you have seen used successfully? I once attended a seminar where the speaker broke a board with his bare hands with a karate chop to make a point—that got everyone's attention! He asked, "Which of you who have never tried this would like to try to break a board today?" I still have the two pieces of the board I broke that day.

Borrowing from Trainers'/Facilitators' Secrets

Trainers, just like very skilled college professors, can so impact a person that they create permanent behavior changes. When promoting, you want some kind of change. Maybe you need a cash box to make change, but that is not what I am getting at here. You want people to do something—maybe part with something of their own or their company's money for what you are offering—but you want to be remembered long term.

Storytelling may be your best bet. Tell success stories in the third person about how others have benefited from what you are offering. You have seen these kinds of promotions all the time. Look around and learn. Years ago, I went into a women's-only exercise facility to set up a free speech in an effort to sell employees on coming to one of our open seminars. I asked the receptionist while waiting, "Tell me, Miss, do the services you offer here really work for people?" She responded, "Boy, do they!" With that, she stepped out so I could see what she looked like top to bottom, and then she showed me a picture of what she looked like 70 pounds heavier before she started her workouts and other treatments at this establishment. I looked at her; I looked at the before picture. I was instantly sold.

A picture is always worth many words, maybe at least a thousand. You can paint beautiful pictures with the use of your words—think of what you can do if, like this receptionist, you do the work and make your dreams come true and *then* serve others with your message!

Sale Is Not a Dirty Four-Letter Word

Selling successfully is a great thing to learn, something that will benefit you in many ways your whole life long. "Sale" or "sold" are four-letter words, but they're not dirty or offensive. They are the best words possible, first to the consumer, then to the salesperson.

Everyone loves something that is on sale! Don't be afraid to offer a deal (a great buy) to people who take action today and today only. We are all conditioned to the fact that things are discounted for a limited time. When using that platform to sell, you could say at the end of your message, "If you respond today, you will save the shipping costs." And if your product is motivational, you can add, "The best investment is always the investment you make in yourself—it pays the biggest dividends."

Ask for a Decision and Close the Sale

People are making all kinds of decisions while you are speaking. Therefore, structure your message (maybe using the vignette approach given in Chapter 6) in such a way that people never say "No!" to themselves while they sit with rapt awe in your audience. Every sentence or story or detail leads them to say a small "yes" over and over again to themselves, or "I can agree with that." At the end of your presentation, when you ask for one big "Yes!" they are glad to accommodate you.

Today is the best day for setting up your next speech (free or paid), making some phone calls, sending some e-mails, or promoting yourself in some other way. You can learn how to do this with perfect practice. Do so by applying the true Golden Rule, and I hope you will earn a great deal more gold. (After all, who knows what the regular currency will be worth tomorrow?) I hope that you will gain priceless contacts and relationships that serve you for years to come!

The Least You Need to Know

- ◆ Always look for ways to promote yourself or your offerings to groups of your best targeted clients.

- ◆ Promotional speakers should not take too many shortcuts; you want to make a great, long-lasting impression to sell *yourself!*

- ◆ Allow the audience some time with your promotional materials before offering them at a discount.

- ◆ Combine all sales tips with a healthy dose of ethical behavior. Don't take advantage of anyone just to make a sale!

- ◆ Offering discounts and short-term special promotions may increase your sales.

Chapter 9

Finding a Helping Hand or Two

In This Chapter

- ◆ Bookings through a bureau
- ◆ What speakers' agents can do for you
- ◆ Showcasing your talent
- ◆ Why to book yourself independently

You have heard about men who would rather drive 25 miles out of their way than stop and ask for directions, right? I once was speaking to an audience about this very topic, but before I could discuss the pros and cons of asking for help, a woman in the audience said, "I *used* to be married to a man like that!"

The biggest mistakes I have made in my 30-plus-year career in the speaking profession have come as a result of my forgetting to ask for help, another opinion, or some additional insight. Asking for help doesn't come naturally to some folks—those who see any sort of aid as a sign of weakness. Whether you are male or female, learn to think of asking for help as a wise use of your time. Finding a helping hand or two is one way to save you money. And you can make more money if you find the right help.

Personal Support

I have a friend named Alan who has been a big help to me over the past 10 years. I am thankful for his help and am sure to tell him so; I also do my best to reciprocate and help him in a variety of ways. Not long ago, Alan fell from a ladder and damaged his arm and one of his hands quite badly. He needed several operations and significant ongoing therapy on his hand.

Alan found that in order to make a full recovery, he would need a lot of helping hands. You may never be in that position (I hope not, anyway), but there are lessons to be learned from being humbled to the point of requiring a great many helping hands. Sometimes (especially in our youth) as young people we think I can do anything, or we think we must be self-made men or women.

Sorry to burst your bubble, but there is no such thing as a self-made woman or man. Without exception, professional speakers who make it to the top of the profession have had many helping hands over the years. And it is inspiring to hear these successful folks give a great deal of credit to their mentors, teachers, coaches, and so on who have helped them along the way. A great many people have offered me personal support during my career. Some may not be aware of how important their support was to me.

Most readers and audiences want me to get right to the point; they're always thinking, "Thom, what's in it for me?" It's important for all of us to stop and think about "what's in it" for the people who offer us their assistance. Are they helping us out of the goodness of their hearts, or might they expect a reciprocal arrangement (where we help them out from time to time)? Which arrangement do you think is better for both parties?

There is something that experts call the universal law of reciprocity. If you give of yourself to others each and every day, you actually set yourself up to receive more—including more personal support. It is in giving that we best set ourselves up to receive. What would happen if for the next 30 days you awoke and said to yourself, "Who can I give something to today? How can I be a great blessing to others today?"

In cranking up a speaking business, it is very helpful to develop a support system of caring people to talk over issues by phone, to meet with weekly (and monthly, at minimum). Family support is wonderful, and you should accept it whenever it's offered; however, there are certain times when you're going to need to "talk shop" with someone who's been where you are right now. That's when it's helpful to have friends in the business.

You are more likely to receive all the support you need if you stay focused on *giving* support to others in the form of love, appreciation, affirmation, ideas, hugs, and answers. You might want to make a list of what you need more of in your life (both personal and professional) and then start giving toward these goals. This is how I have survived and moved onward and upward in the world of professional speaking for all of these years. If I have a secret to success, this must be it!

Success Shortcuts _____

Giving people what they need in the way they need it—or can accept it—is a noble way to live. It's also a way that will be rewarded, guaranteed.

The Benefits of Bureaus

In Chapter 3, I briefly mentioned speakers' bureaus. Now let's consider all the benefits of building relationships with bureaus. The goal in doing so is not only to find a helping hand or two, but also to find more paid speaking engagements. As the owner of a speakers' bureau (Professional Speakers' Bureau International), I will give you the lowdown on working with bureaus, how they go about booking speakers, and what most bureaus require from speakers.

Speakers' bureaus are first and foremost focused on their clients, the people who purchase speakers. Bureaus act as the middlemen between speakers and clients. You need never work with bureaus; however, they can bring you business you would never get on your own. But do understand, please, that bureaus, especially the good-size ones, may have several new, aspiring speakers contact them each day of the workweek. Be prepared to answer factual questions, and try to keep the chitchat to a minimum, at least initially. Understand that the bureau is playing a delicate balancing game between serving clients and bringing in new, great speakers!

After speaking to a bureau decision-maker (usually the president) by phone, send a press kit by mail or by e-mail and direct it to a specific staff person at the bureau, keeping in mind that bureaus like material that is *bureau-friendly*, which means that it doesn't have any of your contact information on it. (More on the importance of bureau-friendly materials a little later in this chapter.)

def•i•ni•tion _____

Making materials **bureau-friendly** refers to removing any hint of how to contact you on the materials you send to a speaker's bureau.

Words to the Wise

If you are one of 100 or more speakers that a bureau offers via their website, please remember a bureau's first responsibility is the client, not the speaker. Be patient; you'll get your bookings in due time!

Follow up with the bureau by phone if you do not hear from them after they have had your material about a week (unless they've told you that you shouldn't expect to hear from them for a couple of weeks or by a specific date; then follow up at that time).

Having your material on file with a bureau or several bureaus is a benefit to you. Even if they don't have a current client who can use your material, you may be the perfect fit for a future client. Again, bureaus work on a 25 to 30 percent commission, but this can vary from bureau to bureau, so when you provide your fees, have this commission built into the fee that the bureau is to quote.

Bureaus do not want to offer speakers for 25 to 30 percent more than what you offer yourself for. Most bureaus claim you can get the speaker at the same fee as if booking direct. Bureaus bring you business opportunities you would never create on your own. Wise speakers realize it costs at least 30 percent of every fee they take in (when they book themselves) to generate each booking. When you book yourself through a bureau at the new, higher fee to pay for marketing costs (and the bureau's costs), you lose nothing, and you actually gain 30 percent! When a bureau books you and earns their 25 to 30 percent, you gain much more than you lose!

The client has many benefits in working with bureaus, so many that some large clients never work with individual speakers, but rather with the bureau nearly exclusively. Whereas most true full-service speakers' bureaus do not want to represent speakers exclusively, they would love to work with clients exclusively, meaning that the client would work with one bureau and only that one bureau.

Benefits to working with bureaus from a client standpoint can include the following:

♦ Saving the client time looking for the perfect speaker

♦ Negotiating a better fee from the speaker

♦ Giving the client several speakers to choose from

♦ Prescreening speakers and checking references of speakers

♦ Offering value-added services like free back-up speakers

♦ Payment by one check if the client hires all speakers from the bureau

♦ Saving time in securing a known or celebrity speaker

If you want to work with a bureau, call them in the mid- to late afternoon after they have taken care of their top-priority clients during the morning. And don't get bent out of shape if a bureau does not bend over backward to please you. Show consistent respect to bureaus and eventually they will respond and show you respect, too. This does not mean that a specific bureau will book you anytime soon. Be patient, and never be demanding.

Many bureaus prefer only to work with veteran speakers who thoroughly understand the ethics of working with bureaus. Let me tell you a little story to explain why: a bureau owner recently received a $2,500 cashier's check from an unknown person drawn on a Chicago bank. There was no way to identify who had sent the check or why, but the owner had a pretty good idea of what had happened.

The bureau had offered a *speakers' showcase* in Chicago nearly a year earlier, an event where speakers had an opportunity to present themselves and their material to meeting planners that the bureau had invited. (Some showcases have the objective of creating tapes for speakers or offering other educational services.) Because the bureau had set up this event, all bookings resulting from it were the legal and ethical right of the bureau.

def•i•ni•tion

> A **speakers' showcase** is an event hosted by a speakers' bureau, where speakers are able to present their material to meeting planners and other decision-makers in the hopes of getting booked for various events. Some speakers may use showcases as opportunities to videotape their performances or offer out-of-the-ordinary educational services.

Ordinarily at a showcase sponsored by a bureau, all materials handed out by speakers should be bureau-friendly and a speaker should not collect or give her business card. When bureaus take the time to bring clients and speakers together, they want to make sure they get the commission they have coming; to this end, they do not want any of your contact information on your material that you want them to send to their clients. Otherwise, you and the client could walk off into the sunset together, ignoring the people who brought you together in the first place. If the client attending likes a certain speaker and wants to book that speaker, they contact the bureau.

Now here's the nitty-gritty of the mysterious check story: apparently a speaker successfully stole a booking from the bureau—probably a $10,000 booking, otherwise why would a bureau get a check out of the blue for $2,500 from some unknown person? Now, if the bureau has to play Dick Tracy to investigate who did this and restore the client to the bureau, you can see this can be time-consuming. And of course, if the bureau finds out which speaker did this, the bureau would not work with that speaker again. I guess the speaker's guilty conscience got the better of him (or her) because he could have gotten away with keeping the $2,500 commission that rightfully belonged to the bureau.

Again, when you work with bureaus, the bureau does all the billing and collections from the client; the client is the legal property of the bureau. As soon as the client pays the bureau, the bureau deposits the check and pays you after deducting their commission from the total paid by the client.

As the owner of a bureau, I encounter all kinds of situations that make me cringe and wonder, "Can we really trust this speaker?" One day, for example, we had a voicemail message from a client requesting the services of one of our speakers. The client said they had heard Miss Speaker speak and thought she was great, and wanted to bring her in to speak to another organization. Well, because the client found Miss Speaker on our website after Googling her name, our bureau is entitled to the booking (and the commission). Had the client had Miss Speaker's contact information (without getting it from our site), they could have set up the deal with her directly. This is another reason why speakers should have the bureau commission built into their fee so you don't feel that under any circumstances you are losing money by working with a bureau.

Booking Speakers

Because they work on commission, bureaus want to book as many speakers as they can, so make yourself easy to work with—create a demand for yourself before expecting anything from a bureau. Again, a bureau is not an agent with whom you have contracted with certain expectations. A bureau is not your cure-all to a lack of speaking bookings. Bureaus field offers from clients; they don't go out looking for specific speaking engagements for you.

When a bureau books a speaker, there are several typical steps involved. First, the bureau will often offer several speaker options based on the criteria of the client. The bureau usually does not contact the speakers offered until the client says something like, "Speaker Z seems like a great choice; can you tell me more about her, maybe see if she is available?"

As a bureau owner, my response is: "I will be pleased to check, Miss Client; I'll call Speaker Z and get back to you ASAP." Now, this is where you can lose it with getting bookings from clients. I have actually had speakers not call me back for a week or more when I leave a voicemail message or send them an e-mail. That puts me in a sticky situation with the client. Is this what the client will experience when she books Speaker Z? Why would I offer a prime client an unresponsive speaker? That could hurt my bureau's reputation!

If you want to earn profits like a business, then you have to operate like a business. When you call a small business and leave a voicemail, you expect someone to get back to you—if not on the same day, then within the next two or three business days (at the very latest). Imagine how wound up you'd get if your local pharmacy just ignored your message, or if your dentist's office just didn't feel like calling you back. Bottom line, if a bureau calls you on a Friday morning, for example, they want a call back by Tuesday at the latest.

Now, once the bureau finds that the speaker is available, the bureau representative asks you, the speaker, to place a *hold* on your calendar and then contacts the client with the good news. When you hold a date, you're booking it on a temporary basis—until you hear back from the bureau as to whether or not the client has decided to go ahead and purchase you.

def•i•ni•tion _____

Speakers place **holds** on their calendars for dates that are potentially sold to clients; these are dates that are "in the works" and not yet contracted.

Sometimes clients can make immediate decisions about purchasing speakers, and sometimes not. Here is the important protocol. When a speaker places a hold on her calendar for a bureau (or an agent), she writes the name and phone number of the bureau. At this point, the bureau may or may not give you the name of the client. Some bureaus have strict policies about guarding the client's name; others will give you the name if they have an established relationship with you (and they know that you aren't going to run off with their client and commission).

If the speaker gets another inquiry for that same date, the ethical speaker will call the bureau, inquire about the status of the booking, and then hold the date for 24 additional hours. This in turn triggers the bureau to call the client and ask them to make a decision today or lose this particular speaker. Make sense?

When the client is ready to buy, a booking agreement is prepared and often faxed to the client for a signature. Simultaneously, the bureau calls the speaker and lets her know that the contract is being executed. As soon as the signed agreement comes back from the client, it gets faxed to the speaker for signing, and the deal is done. The bureau owner signs the contract and usually instructs the client to pay the bureau a 50 percent deposit. The bureau holds on to this money because if something were to happen to prevent you from holding up your end of the agreement, the bureau is often responsible for a backup or replacement speaker. Honorable bureaus will pay you very shortly after they are fully paid.

Note that bureaus want you to guarantee that you will let them know if anyone in the audience or if the client wants to book you again. This is called a *spin-off*, and because the client is the property of the bureau, the spin-off business is commission-able to the bureau.

def•i•ni•tion

A **spin-off** is when someone from the audience wants to hire the speaker after hearing him speak. It could also be repeat business from the same client.

Bureau Requirements

Okay, what do bureaus ordinarily require from speakers? It is rather standard; however, in our current world of electronic marketing and websites, some of the following may not be required by every bureau.

- Send a PDF or Word Document with your material, including your bio, by e-mail, addressed to specific person at the bureau.

- Make your material bureau-friendly for best results; this means remove your contact information on the one-sheet brochure and other materials you send to bureaus.

- Bureaus may require that you are already an established speaker, although some bureaus may be skilled at helping start-up speakers.

- Bureaus ordinarily require that the speaker's fee have the bureau commission built into the fee.

- Some bureaus may require a marketing fee from speakers.

- Some bureaus have a separate contract with a speaker that spells out policies like repeat and referral business.

- Bureaus want to preview speakers, so many will require a preview tape to be mailed to the bureau. The tape may be sent to the bureau's clients, so provide a quality tape.

◆ Another way a bureau could preview you "live" is for you to invite the bureau to preview you when you are in their city doing a program for one of your clients.

◆ Ask bureaus for any additional requirements.

Specialized Bureaus

There are bureaus that specialize in certain markets. For example, there are sports-marketing bureaus that only offer sports speakers; bureaus that only offer speakers representing directors, writers, producers, and so on; bureaus that only offer comedians or humorous speakers, and/or musical acts that "speak"; bureaus that only offer business speakers; bureaus that only offer speakers with disabilities; bureaus that only offer English-, German-, Spanish-, or French-speaking speakers; bureaus that only offer keynote speakers … and the list goes on and on!

Some bureaus offer all kinds of speakers and simply have a special emphasis or targeted niches like speakers who are media personalities or experts. Some offer more trainers than they do speakers; some bureaus (very few) may claim to be a "personal management company" for speakers, which is akin to their wanting to represent the speaker exclusively. For speakers who do not have the time or interest in doing their own marketing or administrative work, this "exclusivity" can be a beneficial arrangement; however, be careful to make sure you have an "out" in case you start picking up lots of business on your own.

Success Shortcuts

Want to find a speakers' bureau? Walters Speakers Services has published a directory of bureaus for many years, available for a $25 fee or with a subscription to *Sharing Ideas News Magazine for Speakers.*

Limitations

Just like anyone or anything, bureaus have their limitations. First, they obviously have only so many hours in each day and this limits how many clients they can handle for booking possibilities; of course, it also limits how many speakers they can respond to in any given day. (Again, be patient!)

Next, bureaus are limited by the number of clients they can book speakers with. This is a direct reflection of the quality of the marketing work or relationship-building work that bureaus do with prospective clients. We aim to please the clients, and spend most of our time doing so. In other words, there is just so much business available for paid speakers, just a certain size of pie each year. The bureaus individually and collectively want to help increase the size of the pie—increase demand for paid speakers—while also getting a bigger piece of the pie. Everyone's happy then, right?

Agents

Because many speakers may never be ready (or qualified) for the use of agents, you will find far less material in this chapter about agents than about bureaus. Many agents, if not most, work only with celebrity speakers and then only if the celebrity speaker is worthy of generating $50,000 or more for an appearance and speech. In cases like this, of course, the agent wants an exclusive contract with the celebrity speaker for at least a year.

A few bureaus like to do double-duty as an agency and offer speakers' services (like help in creating your marketing materials or contract administration) that entice the speaker to want to be exclusive with that bureau. Sometimes, depending on the reliability of the bureau, this is in the best interest of the speaker. Most of the time (and I'd go so far as to say 90 percent of the time), it is in the speaker's best interest *not* to be represented exclusively by anyone, whether they call themselves a bureau or an agent, or some combination of the two.

Where to Find Them

The best way to find agents is from other successful speakers. Get referrals. You might want to interview two or three established agents. An established agent will have more contacts in the business and thus more to offer; but on the other hand, a newer agent has the desire to make it in the business and may charge you a lower commission.

In addition to agents who simply market and book their few speaker clients, there are also literary agents. These folks are actually wonderful for the speaker! You may need someone who knows how to sell your book idea(s) to publishers.

Next … how about a publicist once your book is published? This kind of agent can get you on radio and TV shows, or so they claim. Where do you find a publicist? The same way you find a bureau or a speakers' agent or an authors' agent: ask around. Or do a Google search, go to an NSA meeting, or look in Appendix B of this book!

What They Can Do for You

Agents can open doors for you that you did not even know existed! But like bureaus, agents are *not* out there looking for you. You must reach out to them. So for your further consideration, I'll describe which agents can do what for your career. Then you can choose to concentrate on finding the type of agent that will serve you best.

Speakers' agents can advance your career by helping you make contacts. This is the most valuable aspect of speakers' agent services, along with closing bookings for you. Agents can nearly run your business for you, but be sure to keep control of what's happening with your career. Use them to do marketing mostly, and maybe also administration. They work on a percentage (possibly less than a bureau) and they can also make contacts with bureaus for you. But again, build their commission into your fees.

Authors' agents pitch your book ideas and proposals to established publishers. Some have built relationships with acquisition editors so they can save you the fumbling around, wasting valuable time, etc., that comes from trying to make these contacts on your own. They get a percentage (usually 15 percent) of your book's advance.

Publicist agents put you into the limelight quickly. Again, they have already established relationships with media of all types, so they save you time—and remember that time is money, a very valuable and nonrenewable asset. Publicists usually work on an upfront fee, and maybe an ongoing fee, too. You pay this fee whether you get any of the desired results or not.

Typical Contracts and Commissions

A speakers' agent typically requires a one-year exclusive contract, but may require or ask for a longer contract. An agent can work on as little as 15 percent commission or may want as much as 30 percent (or more!). There really isn't a typical contract for a speakers' agent because they tend to be customized and proprietary from agent to agent. I would recommend contacting your attorney before you sign a year-long agreement with anyone. Protect yourself and your interests first!

You'll need all the helping hands you can get if you are so ambitious to want to make it to the very top of the speaking profession. You may never want or need a speakers' agent, but don't overlook the value in getting helping hands from all kinds of people, especially authors' agents and publicists if you expect to create a best-selling book based on your area of expertise.

Before signing with an agent, working with a bureau, or committing yourself to anything more than a one-shot program, find out what you can do on your own. You'd be better off grooming someone to be your own marketing person and paying *them* 30 percent commission than signing with an agent who may or may not come through for you in the long run. At least that way you aren't tied into a legally binding agreement for a year or more! An agent can also force you to work at a pace you may not be ready for. In that case, the helping hand you might need most is someone to give you a massage to remove the stress.

Just remember: patience is a great virtue. Take the time to make sure you're doing things right, and at the right pace for yourself. Many huge companies were started in a basement, a garage, or at a dining room table, with the help of friends, family members, and business partners.

The best agents are your satisfied clients who become advocates for you. So work to create those relationships at all times.

The Least You Need to Know

- ◆ Speakers' bureaus represent the best interest of the client first, but also want what is best for speakers.

- ◆ A speakers' showcase can be an opportunity to present yourself to myriad potential clients or to create a demo tape, showcase before a bureau, or network with other speakers.

- ◆ Speakers' agents can be helpful with various marketing duties and create bookings for you; but try to groom your own salesperson first.

- ◆ Bureaus and agents work on commission—usually 15 to 30 percent of your booking fee. These percentages should be built in to your fee anyway, to cover your marketing costs.

Part

Cultivating Your Speaking Career

Whether you're working as a part-time speaker or easing into presenting your material full time, you must have your eye on a long-term goal. The best way to make yourself indispensable to clients is to make yourself memorable. Branding yourself as a speaker is an important part of finding success, and you'll learn how to do this here.

Chapter **10**

Full-Time Career, Part-Time Speaking

In This Chapter

- ◆ Balancing a job and a budding speaking career
- ◆ Getting organized
- ◆ Spending your time well
- ◆ Appealing to mass audiences

When it comes to deciding on this career path, one immediate (and logical) question that arises is, "How often will I be speaking? Can I really make a living doing this?"

Many speakers begin as part-timers. Some of these folks have a deep passion for their message and a need to share their wisdom with others. They may not be as concerned with money or professional gains as other folks are; they're driven by other factors. Other part-timers are building their careers to the point where they will be able to be full-time professional speakers.

If you have no desire to go full time, that's fine. Plenty of speakers are already ensconced in stable careers providing excellent pay and benefits, perks that they feel they'd be crazy to give up. You can decide what's best for you! I want you to have a balanced, happy life, no matter what you decide!

Striking a Successful Balance

Unfortunately, it's far too easy to bankrupt your life—and I'm talking spiritually, emotionally, and personally—while pursuing your dream of professional speaking. There are only so many hours in each day, after all. Working 40 hours a week at your present job and putting another 20 to 30 hours into your speaking career may seem like a necessity, but I urge you to take stock of what's important to you now and find ways to nurture those things, like your family, health, and friends, while building your career. Of course, short-term sacrifices can seem worthwhile when beginning, but gain the support of those who you want in your life five years from now when you start your journey.

Words to the Wise

I know a speaker who lives in South Florida and travels all over the United States for engagements, which isn't so unusual. For some reason, though, he has managed to pick up a lot of clients in Alaska and is constantly shuttling back and forth! I am doubtful this man has a balanced life.

This may sound contradictory—nurturing certain things in your life while making sacrifices and working on your career. I know it sounds difficult, but it's essential to find a healthy balance for yourself.

To me, balance means that you have established goals in eight areas of life and invest time to pursue some goals in each area each week. Doing so helps guard against burnout, bad health, and other unforeseen issues and problems. The eight areas of life are as follows (given in no priority of order, necessarily): career, family, intellect, health/wellness, spirituality, social life, recreation, and financial well-being. See these as eight spokes on a wheel—the wheel of life.

Here's a great example of how the wheel of life relates to the speaking business: Recently I spoke to a fine woman in North Carolina. She said, "I had a baby about six months ago, and I want to stay closer to home now. If you have any speaking opportunities closer to me, I will negotiate my fee. I may not be willing to travel far." She realizes that a big part of speaking can be the traveling time to and from engagements. And with as much as 50 percent of the airplanes late to their destination, and having to arrive 24 hours prior to the speaking engagement (a requirement for some clients), travel can take a big commitment on your part. This new mother simply isn't willing to give up that much family time right now. How would you handle the same situation?

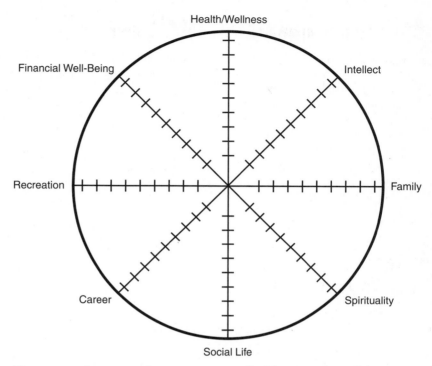

To ensure total success, make sure to nurture all of the areas in your life—not just your career.

Tips for Compartmentalizing Your Time

I want you to have written goals for all eight areas of your life so that you can see which areas need attention. When everything is in balance, you're more likely to sustain yourself long term as a professional speaker and create a positive and lasting legacy.

There are many tragic stories about established and aspiring speakers who neglected their families in pursuit of their careers and, in the process, lost the people they were working so hard for! If just one spoke on the wheel of life is weak (or nonexistent), you can have a bumpy ride through life. You may not even realize why you feel so off-balance, and that's why I want you to write

Success Shortcuts

You need balance in your personal and professional life so that you can persevere when things look bleak or when doors are not yet opening or people are simply not yet ready to accept you or your message.

Words to the Wise

Balanced living requires that you embody the message you deliver, sometimes in unexpected ways. For example, a motivational speaker who is 100 pounds overweight is obviously not motivated to improve her own health. She can't be an effective speaker if she doesn't "walk her talk."

down your goals and compare them to these facets of the balanced life. Many people, for example, allow spirituality to fall by the wayside, when once it was so important to them. Reconnecting with your higher power may be an essential factor to your success!

Once you've taken a long, hard look at your wheel of life and how it stacks up to the diagram in this book, you may have a better idea of where you need to spend more time and where you might cut back a little. If your focus has been almost exclusively on the financial spoke of the wheel, you're probably doing well enough that you could focus a little more time on the social aspect of the wheel.

Time Empowerment

Now let's talk about various ways to break up the hours in your day. We each have only 168 hours in the hourglass of our lives each week. Time has a huge effect on your success as a speaker. The numbers of groups and lives you impact may hinge upon your decisions about the use of time and how you compartmentalize your life. I teach time-empowerment in seminars and speeches (including one recently for the Supreme Court of Ohio's Judicial College). This material alone could easily be turned into another book (this is how speakers must think!), but for our purposes now, just consider how each of these tips can help you to become a successful part-time speaker:

♦ After having established goals for all eight areas of your life, determine how many hours you will devote to pursuing those goals, especially your goals to become a terrific and in-demand speaker.

♦ Now, delegate those hours to a planning calendar. You might have, as an example, a career position that requires your total focus 8 A.M.–5 P.M., so you have three nights a week open. During those evenings, you can devote two hours, plus six hours on Saturday and three hours of Sunday afternoon, toward your speaking career. That gives you 15 hours total each week.

♦ Next, determine how to best invest these isolated hours as you get into the rhythm of using that same block of time each week toward developing your speaking career. Think of all this time as an investment, not an expenditure. Some of these hours must be used for continuing your education, creating your speeches or seminars, doing the marketing, and so on.

◆ Consider that if you invest 15 hours a week for 50 weeks, you have invested 750 hours, and by that time, some great things should be happening. If they aren't, something is wrong! Maybe you have not targeted your marketing correctly or perfected your speech so that you create more sales.

◆ Some of this time may wisely be invested in writing your first book, as you may not be earning a lot with your first few speeches or seminars. But you can sell your book, notebooks, tapes of your messages, and so on, to get a return on your investment.

◆ Do not let interruptions distract you from your written goals. The benefits of establishing written goals are explained in the next section of this chapter.

◆ If you get off track and miss a night or two, make it up later! That is time you failed to invest toward your written speaker-development goals! You must be committed to making it happen!

◆ Just as it is important to exercise for a minimum of 30 minutes three to four times a week, and preferably at the same times each week, it's also important to plan the following week and set appointments by phone or e-mail with those you want to sell to and serve. (It has been proven that late afternoon or early evening on Thursdays, people are more receptive to scheduling things for the future.)

◆ As much as 60 percent of a speaker's time is invested in marketing (not simply in product development or in delivering programs). Continue to work with the marketing material in this book each week for at least a year in your start-up phase.

See? I haven't added time to your week; I've just empowered you to make the most of it! I've laid a lot of material on you here. Make sure to read and digest each of these points. I assure you that if you fail to commit the time to your career, it will never take off.

Time Goals, Commitments, and Tools

There are many tools (Blackberries, cell phones, laptops, and so on) available to speakers to help manage your time and schedule. But there's one intangible that you need to have with you at all times, no matter where you're headed or how long you'll be gone: a willingness to communicate!

We have voicemail, e-mail with automated response, personal assistants … all sorts of impersonal touches in our daily lives. These things are supposed to help us, and they do to a certain extent. But consider this from a potential client's point of view. Let's say XYZ Corporation wants you to speak to their new hires. The human resources director sends you an e-mail requesting your availability, and in return, she gets an automated reply: "I am out of the country until December 10th and will not be able to reply to you until that time."

Well, clients who want to book a speaker often want to book a speaker *now* (or very soon), and won't wait for you to return on a slow boat from China. They'll simply find someone else if you don't make yourself available. The best-paid speakers, whether full time or part time, are always available to text message, e-mail, or take important phone calls—even while on vacation!

I know, everyone is short on time, and I just told you that you have to learn to prioritize the important things in your life so that everything is in balance and your career doesn't kill your marriage or your spirituality, for example. However, as a successful speaker, you have to be willing to take calls and answer e-mails almost every single day. But don't panic: you don't have to be willing to take an hour-long conference call on the spur of the moment while you're sitting on the beach with your family. Rather, communicate with the client. Let them know that you're on holiday but that you're willing to work with them to find a time to talk. Not only does that give you time to alert your family, but it also shows the client that you know how to manage your time.

How and When to Reevaluate Goals

Think of your speaking career as a business, and review it quarterly. Are you meeting your goals? (You'll know for sure if you've written them down!) Which areas on the wheel of life are you struggling in? How are your part-time hours working out? Are you devoting 60 percent of your time to marketing, or do you need to step up your efforts a bit?

Again, write this information down—give yourself a real progress report! You may have needed to keep a log on your activity, including hours invested in some kind of planner or planning book like those provided from Franklin Templeton or Daytimers. Be honest with yourself, above all—how much time have you really invested in your goals?

Investing Your Time Wisely

For a speaker, investing time wisely, like it or not, means first and foremost thinking about marketing for your next booking. Yes, you must also invest time wisely toward writing a book or creating a new seminar or speech, but if you have no one to purchase your great new book or speech, it will all go for naught!

Web Contact

For a part-time speaker, the marketing-time investment can be particularly challenging, especially if you are only available to do that marketing effort at night or on weekends. Decision-makers are not always available at those times. Good news, however! More and more speakers are booked through websites, which means clients can take a look at you any time of the day or evening. It doesn't matter if it's your own site or an agent's or bureau site, you are wise to invest your marketing time promoting the website once it's created.

And if you haven't yet created your own website, what are you waiting for? It's essential to have a homepage in this day and age in order to be competitive. Find a good graphic designer (through word of mouth or the Yellow Pages) and get your face on the Internet!

Telephone Treasures

A telemarketing expert speaker reminded me recently that for those who know how to use the telephone effectively—and will make themselves do so—the telephone can provide a treasure trove of rewards for any speaker. How so?

Next to being face to face with clients, the telephone is your best tool and best investment for your time in cultivating clients, whether old or new. Your voice is a big asset. So … use it or lose it!

What does the client hear in your voice?

- Emotion
- Voice quality
- Pitch
- Intelligence

… all of which you expect to be paid for! Whenever possible, let the client see you in his or her office; if that's not going to work for practical reasons, make the call! I know e-mail is easier and faster, but trust me on this. It just doesn't have the same impact.

I know some veteran speakers who force themselves to make 17 phone calls each and every working day. They understand that you must smile and dial. They know that the more clients they speak with in an effort to identify needs for a professional speaker, the more bookings they can create for themselves. Successful speakers realize that, just like in baseball, it can be a numbers game: you gotta go up to bat to get a hit. Sure, you might strike out the first several times, but in my 30 years of experience, I've learned that if you persevere and keep calling people, you'll eventually create a booking, sell a seminar, or get some desired results. Hooray!

Face-to-Face Meetings

How do you make a professional sales presentation selling your services eyeball to eyeball in the proper psychological sequence for maximum motivational impact and closed sales? (Can you repeat that last sentence, please?) In other words, how do you get a client from point A (no interest) to point Z (closing the sale for your next booking as a speaker, preferably ASAP)? Follow these guidelines:

- Preparation: Research your topic, your client, and your audience thoroughly.

- Attention: Throughout the meeting, look for ways to catch and maintain the client's attention.

- Examination: A professional speaker, just like other professionals, is a problem-solver and never offers a solution without first thoroughly examining the client's needs.

- Prescription: Demonstrate that you understand and have listened to the client (by repeating key phrases or summarizing key points), and that your solutions are designed to solve problems.

- Conviction: Present the client with information about why you are the best choice to fill their needs.

- Motivation: Let the client know exactly what you'll be able to do for them; focus on using positive language.

- Completion: Share stories of your former successes with the client and leave them thinking, "Wow, I can't not hire this speaker!"

In my book *Become #1 in Selling!*, endorsed by some of America's top salespeople including governors, ministers, business CEOs, number-one sales leaders, and speakers like

Mark Victor Hansen of *Chicken Soup for the Soul* fame, they all agree that these are the proper seven psychological steps in face-to-face encounters where closing the sale is the objective.

Granted, times have changed significantly in the past 30 years, and we want to provide you with current, cutting-edge ideas and methods. However, if something cannot be improved upon—and these steps simply can't be improved—then stick with it!

Websites, Internet Interactions

The buying public is aware of how to access information through their own Internet searches, so why should they pay to hear a speaker? Even a speaker who delivers material via a website or some kind of interactive Internet effort?

Personally I would not trade my website for $100,000. It is worth at least that much money to me, in terms of my future and my company. Do I have your attention? Look at www.terrificspeakers.com if you have not done so, to understand why. Or look at any number of other speakers and especially speakers' bureaus website where lots of speakers are featured, to see what a great sales tool websites can be. I'm not a website designer, so I'm not going to tell you how to develop a website. I am simply writing that you must have one ASAP and then you must learn how to market that website. (More on that in Chapter 12.)

A few tips for your cyberspace interactions: be polite and never write something to someone you would not want your mother or most respected colleague to view. You can research further, if you need to, things like Internet etiquette to upgrade your communications skills via the Internet. Remember: you want to appear and behave like a professional. And of course, don't let your website take the place of face-to-face (or at least phone) communications. Your site is a tool to help you pull clients in; once you've made contact on the Internet, personalize it with a genuine sit-down meeting.

Webinars and Teleseminars

Offering what are now called *webinars* (a seminar delivered via a website) may require a significant paradigm shift for many speakers. *Teleseminars*, or teleconferencing, continues to grow in popularity due to time constraints, costs of traveling to seminars, and other factors. I won't get into trying to explain the pros and cons of offering webinars or teleseminars, because I feel that's a highly personal decision. I will, however, introduce you to the concepts and ask you to consider, "Are either or both right for me?"

I would suggest logging into a webinar that interests you. This is R&D (research and development), so pay attention! Take notes! Afterward, ask yourself these questions:

◆ What do I like most and least about this seminar given in this way?

◆ What can I do to improve upon this kind of delivery system?

◆ What is my best content to deliver in this way?

◆ Who will best purchase this kind of seminar from me?

◆ How will I market my seminar?

Make your answers to these and other related questions a part of your business plan. To find a webinar that you can offer, you may need to attend a few yourself and see how it is done. If you think you're interested in following this path, creating your own webinar is your best bet.

def•i•ni•tion

A **webinar** is a seminar offered via the World Wide Web and led by a professional speaker. People pay a fee for this seminar, just as they would for a real-world seminar. A **teleseminar** is a seminar delivered by a professional speaker via the phone. Clients sign up and phone into the event.

Educating Others Online

These days, people log on to websites to earn degrees, certificates, and educate themselves on anything and everything. Although it will never completely replace other kinds of traditional classroom or conference education or learning, online education is expected to continue to increase. Here's why:

Many professionals have an ongoing requirement to earn continuing education (CE) credits to continue their right to practice their profession. Three of my sons are medical doctors and have heavy requirements for earning CE credits. My daughter, Erin, is a Registered Respiratory Therapist with lots of CE requirements, even though she works part time. My son, Todd, is an excellent chef and has worked to help manage a catering business. This requires his continuing to learn about all kinds of food. He recently enrolled to go back to college and become a Physical Therapist. Now, collectively, my children are married to two registered nurses, one nurse practitioner, one librarian, and one Doctor of Optometry.

These people have very busy lives (there are also nine children thrown into this mix!). Between the 10 of them, they have at least 300 required CE hours each year. They would love to get this by some kind of Internet training without ever having to leave their home or office. Ask yourself, "Can I create something that could be accredited to offer to my friends, family, and acquaintances for CE credit and deliver it online?"

Consider, please, that each profession has set up, or at least has tried to, a governing body to regulate how CE credits are issued, and who can issue them. In the United States, you can check with your state regulatory bodies or agencies (the New York State Medical Association, for example); they can give you specifics for the areas of your interest of expertise. You can also ask the staff (perhaps a hospital human resource director, for example) of the clients you want to serve, "How do I get my CE course approved?"

Potential for Big Earnings

Yes, there is the potential for BIG earnings in webinars and teleseminars; however, you must be realistic while also challenging yourself to THINK BIG. I know of one woman based in San Diego whom I met with recently who claims she is getting rich offering teleseminars. Now, because I cannot verify this, I will simply say that recently I personally earned $5,000 from a California company for about 5 hours of my time (plus another 5 to 10 hours for preparation) to give teleseminars.

Often, teleseminars are sponsored by speakers or their organizations, but you can also find companies who have to train their staff but do not want to take them out of the office. For them, a teleseminar (organized almost like a conference call) can be a great option.

Now, why would a company want to pay you such good money when they're trying to cut corners by not sending their employees out of the office? Consider that the cost of bringing in a speaker is relatively small when the other option is 100 salaried employees taking a day or a part of a day off work to attend a seminar or training. If each of these people earns, to be very conservative, $150 a day on average, this is $7,500 in payroll costs. So getting people into teleseminars or webinars during off-hours makes sense to managers.

Elsewhere in this book I work to motivate you to think big and yet be realistic. Those who are number one in their topic area with unique and high-demand, problem-solving content can be paid big bucks. Is that you? If not now, it can be if you target and look for unique ideas and solutions presented in the most effective targeted ways—maybe by offering teleseminars or webinars, or maybe by developing another presentation that helps your audience make big changes in their lives.

No matter which path you follow in your speaking career, try to keep your strong desire to make a positive difference in the lives of other people. The people who eventually make it from part-time to full-time speaker are those with a deep level of commitment. Make that commitment because you have a message you have to share, not just because you are frustrated with your past career or current job, or simply because you want to be like So-and-So, or to earn more money.

You must be better, unique, different, and make a significant difference with your messages to move from part-time to full-time speaker. These words and those preceding provide the pathway to the next level of speaking success. The next chapter will help you take some bigger steps into the world of professional speaking.

The Least You Need to Know

◆ Balancing a full-time career and part-time speaking takes a lot of effort.

◆ Every so often you need to reevaluate how your career is developing and make any necessary changes.

◆ Make the effort to talk to clients; if not in person, then speak to them on the phone.

◆ Speakers are educators, and have many opportunities to help others learn through webinars, teleseminars, and online courses, to name a few.

Chapter 11

Full-Time Speakers

In This Chapter

- ◆ Characteristics of full-time speakers
- ◆ Affirm yourself!
- ◆ Knowing your audience
- ◆ Living a life worthy of imitation

In Chapter 3, I talked about a day in the life of a professional speaker; here, I'm going to share in more general terms the various tasks of the professional speaker.

Most professional speakers work in the solitude of a home office. You are your own boss, responsible for your own work. No one is going to check up on you and make sure that you're towing the line, so to speak. You need to be motivated and prepared—emotionally and financially—for the good times along with the bad.

Working Alone

Working alone as a professional speaker is not like that movie, *Home Alone*. No one has left you alone for the wrong reasons. But like the small hero in the movie, you should learn to use your time creatively and wisely.

Here are a few things I've learned about professional speakers during my years in this business. Full-time speakers are without exception …

♦ Self-motivated people. Some report that they wake up and go to work at 2:30 A.M. to finish a book or write a proposal or send out an e-mailed monthly newsletter to their contact lists.

♦ Self-confident people. They know they can solve any problem and make their desired results a reality. Some report that this very confidence is apparent to their clients, and it's what keeps them in demand.

♦ Goal-oriented people. They plan their work and work their plan every day. They know hard work is key to success.

♦ People with a positive mental attitude. Because of their positive self-talk and belief in themselves, they can believe in and affirm others without being sidetracked by negative happenings in life. Working alone can be dull and depressing for some folks, but professional speakers tend to keep their chin up and muddle through even the dullest days.

You need all four of the characteristics to make it long term as a full-time paid professional speaker, trainer, or seminar leader. Learning to be productive while working in solitude can be a tough transition, especially if you're coming from a very structured office environment. In this section, I'll give you some tips for making the most of every workday.

Daily Tasks of the Professional Speaker

Once you decide to become a full-time professional speaker, you are self-employed. You're now 100 percent responsible for your business, your earnings, and the direction your business moves in. How can you make this the most positive experience possible?

Thoughts determine your actions and actions will develop your habits. Great speakers boost themselves daily with positive self-talk and affirmations, like the following:

♦ I can and will succeed as a speaker.

♦ I will be as productive as possible today.

♦ I am terrific! (This is my personal favorite!)

Your beliefs about yourself and your capabilities will shape your daily behavior and contribute to your positive or negative outcomes. So task number one is to put yourself in the right state of mind to achieve your goals for the day.

A full-time professional speaker is also focused on preparing for upcoming clients. A pro realizes that future business success can come from repeat and referral business, so doing a great presentation for each and every client is of paramount importance. Task number two, then, is to focus on your presentation and consider what you can do to make it better, more informative, more entertaining, or otherwise more appealing to your upcoming audience.

After you have considered what you must do to serve your existing and potential clients, you'll invest a great deal of your working hours in marketing yourself, like it or not. You can't rely strictly on creating patrons from referral business. Build your own custom list of prospects and go after them! Work this list daily, by making calls and/ or mailing out material (see Chapter 12 for ideas).

Each day, you'll have to sleep and eat. Even these traditional "down times" can be turned into effective time investments. Great speakers realize that the mind is never fully asleep, so some go to sleep (and wake) to uplifting, inspirational music or taped motivational messages. I usually try to schedule client meetings during mealtimes, but if you must eat alone, use the time to read something that educates you on your topic or inspires you to be the best speaker you can possibly be.

Managing Your Time

Effectively managing your time can sometimes feel like managing gelatin outside the bowl. And like that gelatin, if your time slips through your fingers, you'll never get it back.

Success Shortcuts _____

I start each day at a 6:30 church service, and I know many other speakers who do the same kind of thing. Not only does this help establish a morning routine for us, but it's also a chance to hear a great speaker (your priest, rabbi, or minister) in action and get motivated for the day!

Time is one of your most valuable assets, and as with any asset, you want it to grow in value. Speakers who earn $10,000 for a one-hour keynote speech often think considerably differently about the value of their time than a speaker who never earns beyond, let's say, $1,000.

Most people live their entire lives simply exchanging hours for money. That doesn't cut it in the speaking world. If you want to be a highly paid speaker, you have to get past the mindset of billing by the hour. Your time is simply too valuable to put a one-size-fits-all price tag on it. The best way to free up time for more productive work is to charge more per speech and then have the operating capital to not feel so pressured to earn so much more each hour on the hour.

Consider: Would you prefer to give one speech a month for $10,000, or work hard for 100 billable hours at $100 per hour? Or maybe 40 hours at $250 per hour? See the point? Now, many speakers give three or four speeches or seminars a month for $10,000 and some never get to that plateau. Of course, usually you cannot start out asking $10,000 per speech or seminar unless you have created some kind of demand for yourself, either by word of mouth or by publishing a best-selling book or motivational DVD.

Part of managing your time well is justifying your worth. No point in accepting $5,000 for a presentation when you could charge twice that amount. Because you're earning more, you've freed up some time in your schedule—time that would have been spent booking engagements just to make what you've earned from one presentation. You now have more time to book other events or to cultivate new clients … or both!

Research Tips

Speakers have to enjoy the game of research. In this profession, we not only research our topic, but clients and audiences as well. The speakers who refuse to cut corners during this process routinely deliver a knock-'em-dead presentation.

I know many speakers who invest 40 hours of research for every one-hour speech. They send out surveys to audience members, and they talk to key players on the phone; they might even research the entire industry, including a competitive company, before they give their speech. In seminars and workshops, in particular, some speakers have found it's absolutely essential to research the demographics of the audience population. The more you know about the people, the thinking goes, the more effective you can be at relating the material to each audience member.

In researching your audience, it is wise to find out if you will have any potential troublemakers in the group—someone, for example, who has a reputation for talking more than usual. A dominant audience member can throw an unprepared speaker off track and totally ruin a seminar or even a speech. Years ago, I was speaking to an audience in central Ohio and I asked what I thought was a rhetorical question, "What is a mentor?" Before I could answer my own question, a man stood up and shouted out, "A mentor? That is a city on the lake, east of Cleveland!" Fortunately, everyone had heard of the Ohio city named Mentor, and it got a big laugh. (It also was an opportunity for me to clarify further what I meant by the word mentor.) Fortunately, I was practiced and skilled enough to laugh with the audience and not get thrown off track as I proceeded to make my planned points.

Words to the Wise

Research indicates that audience members want speakers to use well-defined words. Clarify any unfamiliar terms in language that's easy to understand. That way you'll keep your audience tuned in.

Shifting into High Gear

The price of entry into the world of professional speaking is far more than a $20 book (like this one, for example). To shift into high gear (full-time speaking), you have to plan ahead. Allocate a certain amount of time and money each week and month toward the desired goals. Hopefully you have saved some money to live on and have some to invest as you move into full-time professional speaking.

Operating Capital/Cash Flow

Obviously, it's very important to have an adequate amount of capital in reserve before you begin a full-time speaking career. How much do you need? Probably six months' income (minimum) that you can live off while you invest your time cranking up your contacts, finding bookings, and so on. If you're already a part-time speaker, you don't need to worry so much about saving up half a year's pay; your part-time earnings should be able to cover your expenses. Your main focus should be on establishing more and more contacts.

Before you go into a full-time speaking career, make a written master list of exactly what you will need to spend money on in the first 6 to 12 months. Consider everything and anything, from office supplies, equipment, phone and Internet bills, to food, and healthcare for yourself.

I recommend that you don't primarily operate on borrowed capital. Sure, it's good to have open lines of credit (just as in any business), but usually all a speaker needs is a few charge cards. Keep track of what you're spending and try to pay all your debts in

Words to the Wise

I can't urge you enough to keep your finances under control during this initial startup period. Don't go spending your money on a fancy car to impress clients. Very few will base their opinion of you on the type of material possessions you have.

full on a monthly basis. (That's why you've saved up six months' income, remember?) If you can't keep up with the payments and you find that your reserves are being depleted, it may be time to consider going back to an employment situation and developing a part-time speaking career.

The first lesson about cash flow is a simple one that always applies to everyone: spend less than you receive! If you go through your reserve money, do not simply go into debt or borrow money to continue the climb up the mountain of your speaking career. Look at what you are doing and try to understand why you are not yet achieving your desired results (including the cash flow you want and need).

Here's another tip for keeping the cash where it belongs: pay yourself first! Many entrepreneurs don't do this, and burn themselves out of the business as a result. By setting 10 percent of your earnings aside, you're creating a great big safety net for

Words to the Wise

Cash flow for some speakers is low at certain times of the year—near Christmas, sometimes, or maybe in the summer months. Anticipate this and plan accordingly. Save some money for these so-called rainy days. Of course, let's hope you never have any rainy days, but just in case, plan ahead.

your future—just don't touch it! This money isn't for a night out on the town or a trip to Honolulu—it's for your retirement. Pretend that you have absolutely no ability to liquidate that cash; you're just acting as the caretaker of the account.

If you can pay your expenses (personal and business) with 60 percent of what you earn, then that leaves 30 percent to reinvest in your business or your other personal interests. If you invest wisely, you will create more and more cash flow, and eventually you can pay yourself more than 10 percent of gross income—maybe much more!

Conserving and Using Energy Wisely

You can feed off the good energy of others, can't you? Well, people who hire you want to feed off of your positive energy. Make sure you have plenty to give! Your health of mind, body, and soul are like launching pads from which you energize the world around you, including your audience members. This makes your energy level an important part of building your career.

What drains your energy? If you do not know the answer to that question, please find it now. Some common energy leaks include smoking, drinking, drugs, or any sort of addiction. Get rid of these things (through professional help, prayer, or the support of loved ones), and you'll find your energy level skyrocketing!

Other common energy drainers include a poor diet, lack of exercise, and sleep deprivation. Fractured personal relationships can add to the mix. Investing your energy in cultivating and nurturing meaningful relationships can pay huge dividends in both your personal and career lives. Get your priorities in order and place positive relationships at the top of the pecking order if you want to increase your energy.

Nurturing and Expanding Your Contacts

Once your career gets cranking and you're entertaining offers from big-time benefactors, it's easy to forget about the smaller clients who gave you your first bookings. Here's what I have to say about this: it's all right to move on to bigger and better opportunities, but don't ever burn your bridges! You never know who knows whom, who might be able to help you in the future, who's connected with which corporations, and so on. Plus, it's just not nice to bite the hand that once fed you.

Nurture every single client as if they may be your last. Many client decision-makers can lead you to others, sometimes within the same organization, and within the same industry for sure. Think of all positive contacts as relationships worth treasuring, not simply as steppingstones toward your "real" success. People—clients—are too important to think of as something to be used. You want to be treated with respect, right? Then treat others how you want to be treated—it's the golden rule in action.

Finding Your Motivation

The best type of motivation comes from within you. Internal motivation provides drive for truly terrific speakers who are intent on making a difference in their audiences' lives. What really gets you moving, ready to take significant action and never give up? In this section, I'll address the main motivating factors for many professional speakers.

Money

It is never the money that truly motivates you (or anyone, for that matter). It is what you can do with the money that motivates. Money in and of itself, even the accumulation of lots of money, is only a means to a desired end. What is the "end" you have in mind? If you don't know, think about it now. Sometimes, having a specific goal in mind is the only thing that keeps you going during the slow times (and I think this is true for any career field, not just professional speaking).

Love of Topic

The love of a topic has propelled many speakers to great success, acclaim, and the money that follows. I could give you dozens of examples of topic experts who simply love their subject and do very well as a result, but I've narrowed them down to just a few. I hope these folks motivate you.

- ◆ Bill Driscoll inspires people to deal better with stress and create "Peak Performance Under Pressure." Willy, as his older friends call him, was a Top Gun pilot, the ultimate example of someone who succeeds because failure cannot be an option. Either shoot them down or be shot down. Bill uses his experience as a Top Gun pilot, and instructor of other Top Gun pilots, to teach as well as inspire people about performing under pressure-packed situations, dealing with stress, and balanced living.

- ◆ Marilyn Manning, Ph.D., CMC, covers a number of topics and is a strong expert in areas including conflict resolution, change management, strategic planning, developing teamwork, and creating people skills. Her background is conducive to working with many different types of groups. Marilyn loves her topics and loves her audiences. She is committed to helping people improve.

- ◆ Randy Snow might at first seem like a motivational speaker and nothing else, but upon learning about his background, you quickly conclude he is an expert in topics including diversity, overcoming adversity, and so on. Randy is the only athlete to compete in three different sports in three different Para-Olympics summer games; he also won a gold medal. He has an amazing story with customized applications for his audiences.

Now, how can you benefit from their love of their topics? Search the Internet for topic experts in your field. Do these people inspire you? How do they do it? Improve on their offerings, even imitate a little, and do what it takes to share your love of your topic with others! (Just don't ever copy or plagiarize.)

Love of Teaching Others

All other things being equal, people tend to respond best to someone who communicates that they care. Do you care? If so, show it and prove it! If not, find out why not and change!

We have all been exposed to teachers who absolutely love what they do. Even if they aren't the best teachers skill-wise, their love of the subject gets you excited and your learning experience is of much more value to you.

Speakers are teachers; never forget that you are teaching something of great value to other people. What you do is very important, because you're opening minds, imparting wisdom, and, in the process, making a difference in a great many lives.

Words to the Wise

You may have heard the saying, "Those who can, do. Those who can't, teach." I have not found who to attribute this quote to, but that doesn't matter, because this assertion is simply not true. In fact, the opposite is true: those who teach master their topic!

Visualizing Success

I can think of few things more important to your eventual success as a speaker than consistently and persistently visualizing the success that you hope will one day be yours.

Now, I am not talking about visualizing success in a general way, like saying to yourself, "Well, I guess when I am well-known and booked two years in advance, I will be driving a very fancy car and eating at the very best restaurants." I'm talking about visualizing who you truly want to be, both professionally and personally, and then making it happen.

Too often, in the pursuit of a dream, we lose sight of what inspired us to begin with. Here, I ask you to take a moment to evaluate what's most important to you right now and to find a way to take those things with you on the road to success.

Vision Statement

In business, a mission statement (which you'll read about shortly) is very much like a vision statement. Both define the terms and goals of the company. But when I talk about a vision statement, I'm talking about envisioning the life you want to lead and the example you want to set for the most important people in your life.

Years ago, I was delivering a motivational presentation in southern Ohio, which was very well received by the audience. Afterward, an elderly gentleman approached me and said, "Thom, I want to buy two of your books for my grandchildren. They don't listen to me, but they might listen to you."

I was very flattered, of course. As I opened the books to sign them, I asked the gentleman his name, as I wasn't sure if he wanted the note inside made out to himself or his grandkids. He looked a bit surprised, and said, "I am Bob Evans!" Yes, *the* Bob Evans, the restaurateur.

Well, what really struck me about this story was Bob's devotion to his grandchildren, even though he admitted that they didn't always want to hear his advice. This incredibly successful (and I'm sure very busy) businessman wanted to make sure that his loved ones were following the right path in life! Bob had a vision of what his life should be, and I believe he achieved it: he struck a balance between his work and his family, and never lost sight of the people he was so devoted to. This is what I want you to do! Envision yourself reaching the pinnacle of success. Who is with you? Are they the same people who mean so much to you now? How will you ensure that they will still be with you in the future?

Many children and grandchildren cannot envision themselves following in the footsteps of their fathers or mothers or grandparents, yet to do so is a blessed thing. To carve out a life that is worthy of following is a most outstanding life. Speakers often inspire others. Don't be surprised when someone in your audience comes to you after your program is complete and asks, "How do I become a terrific speaker like you?" Consider this a great compliment, and do your best to help this person reach his or her vision of speaking success. It's by helping and mentoring one another that we continue to learn about ourselves!

Mission Statement

Most professional organizations, corporations, or any sort of national group has a *mission statement*. This statement usually amounts to a few sentences explaining the goals and acceptable practices of the group. Speakers also need to have a mission statement; it helps to remind you of where you're headed and how to stay on track.

Mission statements tend to be best when they are short and to the point. They typically are well crafted when they have several short statements that begin with the word "to." For example, your mission statement might read, "To teach others; to be honest with clients; to strive to be my best; and to put my all into creating a successful career."

def•i•ni•tion

A **mission statement** is a series of short sentences highlighting your goals and intentions as a professional speaker.

When and How to Change Your Outlook

When do you know if you need to change the way you're approaching your speaking career?

- When your attitude is getting sour.

- When you're discouraged enough to quit.

- When you can't find any motivation.

How do you best change your outlook? Some speakers habitually listen to other speakers—especially motivational speakers—who can provide a "check-up from the neck up" (as famed speaker Zig Ziglar always said). Listening to the words and tones of people who can help you believe in yourself, your future, and your potential, is important for speakers. I believe that to become a great speaker, you need to listen to other great speakers as often as possible. Many speakers like to do that at least once weekly in their local church, synagogue, or mosque. The added benefit of this is that you may find it spiritually uplifting and motivating!

Above all else, believe in yourself and help others to believe in themselves. You have the power to change so many lives for the better. As you work on booking clients and perfecting your presentation, think about your audiences from time to time—and suddenly you'll realize you're far from alone!

The Least You Need to Know

- Full-time speakers thrive on daily routines.

- Self-affirmation is one way to boost your attitude during the workday.

◆ It's essential to acknowledge and save for any possible expenses before you begin a full-time speaking career.

◆ Visualizing a successful career is a great way to keep yourself motivated.

Chapter 12

Making Yourself a Brand Name

In This Chapter

◆ Being unique is vital to your success!

◆ Marketing materials that work

◆ Setting up shop in cyberspace

In Chapter 5, I talked about the value of expertise. But consider this: what good is it for you to be an expert speaker if no one remembers you when they have a need for you, your products, or your services?

Differentiating yourself from others who might offer similar services or, in the case of speakers, similar topics cannot only make the difference between whether or not you are hired, it can mean the difference between being underpaid, fairly paid, or paid twice or more what others are paid for similar services or speeches!

If you don't present yourself in a way that says, "I'm worth more than other speakers!" you won't be paid more. In this chapter, I'll talk about ways you can help potential clients to know—right off the bat—if you're worth their time and money.

Branding Yourself and Your Presentation

Branding is a marketing method that's used to make yourself instantly recognizable to your clients and the public. You are the product that is for sale. You offer services that can be branded with a great book, seminar, logo, and so on. Register or copyright your brand. Use your brand everywhere and on everything you produce, if you can.

def•i•ni•tion

Branding for speakers is a way of turning your name (or what you offer) into a memorable product (or service) that creates a demand for you as a speaker.

For example, when people think about the book *The One-Minute Manager*, they instantly think of the one-minute speaker, Dr. Ken Blanchard. When people think of baby-boomer health or the book *The Age Wave*, they think of the guru on aging, speaker Dr. Ken Dychtwald. These men have successfully tied themselves to their topics and, as a result, their topics are synonymous with their names! Putting this marketing trick to work effectively can mean the difference between a ho-hum career and one that exceeds your wildest imaginations!

You've probably never heard of the speaker David L. Hart, but as I write this, I have his materials in front of me. Now please realize, I have looked at materials from several thousand speakers. I know a unique speaker when I see one. I know when people have invested some time and money in branding themselves, and when they have not.

Mr. Hart is CEO/Founder of the Jump Institute. He provides a presentation called "Leaps in Organizational Performance & Teamwork, A Skydiver's Perspective." His material shows him jumping and free-falling from planes, some with American flags; in one shot, he's right over the Statue of Liberty in New York harbor. He also offers t-shirts and hats promoting the Jump Institute.

This is all very well and good as far as marketing himself goes, but one error he makes is that he hasn't tied his name to the Jump Institute and the programs he offers—not yet. In other words, there's not enough in his marketing that makes clients recognize him as David L. Hart and as someone better than some other plane-jumping speaker. So I suggested he add the word Hart to his pictures and other promotional materials, which in his case is as easy as adding a heart-shaped icon to his image. And as easy as that, a brand is born!

Making Yourself Recognizable

Why are some speakers successful while others are not? In many cases, it doesn't come down to expertise, talent, or timeliness of their topic. It's how they brand themselves to be remembered as distinctly different and, of course, to be perceived as a great value to potential clients. Let's consider what some other well-known speakers have done to brand themselves:

◆ Jim "Basketball" Jones does programs about project management for adults and kids as he twirls several basketballs simultaneously. He gets your attention, he keeps it, he's memorable, and he has as many bookings as he can reasonably handle.

◆ Kinza is a speaker based in Wisconsin. She is a performance pro, vowing to "make your best better" and offers "Wow!" keynotes. She is memorable for many reasons, but more so because she brands herself and her programs with her name, introducing them with "Kinza or Kinza Presents ...."

◆ "The Boomerang Man" is Chet Snouffer, a part-time speaker (and full-time owner of a fitness business). Chet won the World Championship in boomerang throwing. His message, "What Goes Around Comes Around," is very memorable (and in some variation could even be trademarked) as he demonstrates with boomerangs by throwing plastic or Styrofoam boomerangs around the room. You remember him and his main point, which is to send out what you want to come back.

◆ More recognizable perhaps than these last three is Dr. Ken Dychtwald, best-selling author of books including *Age Power, Age Wave,* and *The Power Years.* In this last book, he provides "A User's Guide to the Rest of Your Life." He is the number-one expert in marketing to baby boomers and is paid big bucks. He brands himself through his books and TV documentaries.

Now do you get the idea about branding your presentations? Take your topics (and your name, too) and craft a memorable (preferably trademarked and copyrighted) title for speeches and seminars (and eventually a book) that people will remember. You're selling yourself when you sell your brand or anything branded that you create.

Speakers can't be shy; you must be willing to be recognizable or you'll be lost on the road to success! Find a branding technique that announces to the world, "I have

Success Shortcuts

Working with consistent colors is always a good branding idea. Look at any top college and you will see some consistency to all of their branding. The University of Michigan uses blue and gold, for example, while Ohio State University is scarlet and gray.

arrived! You need to hear what I have to say!" A speaker friend of mine who knows how to make herself recognizable is Gayle Zinda, or as we call her, the Pink Lemon Lady. She has branded herself in various ways, including driving a 31-foot pink mobile home (christened the Motivator) that has 6-foot-tall lemons on its side, and owning an SUV (the Mini-Motivator) that is also wrapped with her branded lemons. Her son (who works for her) told her years ago, "We need to go *big* or go home." Gayle says, "We realized we had to make ourselves different and recognizable. It has worked out very well for me!"

Years ago, I had a hard time coming up with my own logo or slogan or branding. After years as a speaker, I remembered that my mother had given me the nickname "Tom Terrific!" as a child starting in first grade (Tom Terrific was the name of a cartoon that played during the Captain Kangaroo show). Having this unique nickname built my self-esteem and taught me even at that early age that it was important to be willing to be different—which is essentially branding oneself, making that strong impression on other people so that they don't forget you. The word "terrific" has become a big part of my branding technique. An easy example is that our company website is www.terrificspeakers.com.

Don't take as long as I did to come up with your branded message! You *must* be willing to stand out and stand up so people notice you favorably if you are to be a super-great and highly paid speaker!

Marketing Yourself Pays Off

Branding a product is to marketing like a husband is to a wife—ideally they are inseparable forever. Branding yourself as a speaker is like seeing the desired end result and claiming it now in your marketing. The simple example I gave above was claiming I was Tom-Terrific long before I was. You may think and feel you are not the best yet, so you hesitate to brand yourself accordingly; however, to not do so is a *big* mistake. Of course, I am not recommending you claim to be the world's greatest at something right now, but you can position yourself so you look like the greatest, and that is all you will need. Greatest what? As in the example of Gayle Zinda, the Pink Lemon Lady, the bigness of her brand makes you think and feel as if she is the best at turning lemons into lemonade, the idea she presents.

Once you've branded yourself, you have to get out there and let people know who you are and what you're capable of! Marketing yourself to the media is, for some speakers, as important—and maybe more so initially—than marketing themselves to clients who have budgets to hire a speaker, trainer, motivator, or expert.

Your worth as an expert can be enhanced if you can show you have been interviewed or featured some way on TV or other media. You must know a career can be made, as an example, by appearing on the *Oprah Winfrey Show*. But don't hold your breath waiting for that invitation. For every person who makes it onto Oprah's couch, 10,000 more have sent her proposals asking to be on the show. Your odds might be better playing the lottery, and I'm not advocating that.

The 80/20 Rule of Marketing

In Marketing 101, students learn about Pareto's Law, which in a nutshell says that in any industry (including professional speaking), 80 percent of the marketing effort put forth is wasted. The other 20 percent brings in most of your revenue. The good news is that the 20 percent that does pay off can pay off big—big enough to fund your entire budget! The not-so-good news is that you still have to put 100 percent effort into every marketing attempt.

Think of it this way: the farmer knows that he must plant the seed before a harvest can be had months later. He's not concerned with which seed will bear the biggest crop; he nurtures all the seeds once they're planted. And of course, the seed must be planted deep into the soil, not just dumped on the surface for the birds to come and eat.

Words to the Wise

Don't waste or invest too much time or money with nondecision-makers or by marketing to nondecision-makers. Don't be afraid to ask, "Who makes the decision to hire outside speakers in your company or organization?"

Branding through things like logos and key phrases are like planting seeds that can find deeper soil; if pushed, the seeds take root and bring about a harvest of results. It goes without saying that creating a memorable logo and slogan(s) is a great idea. Find other speakers by doing a web search and see their logos for ideas. Certainly do not copy—that is not allowed—but do get ideas from them.

Your Best Clients: 80 Percent of Revenue

It's all right if just a few of your clients provide 80 percent of your revenue. But you can't depend on those few clients signing your paychecks indefinitely. If you concentrated all of your efforts on just a handful of clients and then lost them (and it happens—sometimes through no fault of your own, but because of economic changes or shifts in information needs), you'd be in pretty big trouble. In fact, you'd find yourself right back at square one.

Diversify your client base. This includes expanding your message (see Chapter 7) so that it can apply to various groups. And no matter who you're catering to, always keep marketing to bring in new clients. A good idea is to look for new clients who fit the profile of your best clients, even if you have to market yourself outside of your local area.

Credentials Are 20 Percent of Earnings

In addition to most of your earnings coming from just 20 percent of your efforts, there's another small item I'd like to talk about for a moment … your credentials.

It may be hard for the person who's just finished his doctorate or for the person who's clawed her way to the top of the corporate ladder to believe, but your credentials are only about 20 percent of what's important in creating paid speaking engagements. Think about it this way for a minute: even though credentials are important, they mostly speak to your past accomplishments. Unless and until you translate your credentials into benefits for your potential clients, they don't carry nearly as much weight as you'd like them to.

Success Shortcuts

Clients want the answer to the question "What's in it for me?" or WIFM. Tune into this frequency and always ask yourself what's in your presentation for the benefit of the client. And then you can add your credentials to the 20 percent of your marketing that's paying off for you!

You can be sure that there are plenty of other professional speakers who have your level of education, work experience, and so on, so clients really want to know what's unique about you and your offerings or services: "What's in it for me?"

Making an Impression—Extending Your Brand

In making yourself into a brand name, take into consideration that the best-quality products often generate the most profits. For example, because they're both manufactured by Toyota, a Lexus and a Camry may share many of the same body parts. However, because the Lexus contains higher-quality engine parts and a more luxurious interior, your monthly payment on it might be double what you'd pay for your Toyota Camry. For Toyota, this is terrific. They put a high-quality product out there, and people respond to it, even though there may be very little difference in factors like reliability and mileage. Some buyers want the Lexus. They're willing to pay for it. They buy it.

How does this relate to speakers? You may share some credentials with your competition; you might even be neck-and-neck as far as the quality of your presentations go. But making a great first impression on potential clients can be the thing that gets you in the door to give the next seminar. Just like that Lexus, though, you have to be able to show that you're high quality. I'll explain how in this section and later on, too.

Press Kit

Press kits are also sometimes called media kits. These are portfolios including information about you and your services or product(s)—maybe a new book or seminar announcement—and are not just sent to the press or media, but to all potential clients. They're designed to market you, brand you, position you, and sell you to your ideal clients, complete, ideally, with color coordination.

def•i•ni•tion

A **press kit** (or media kit) promotes a speaker to prospective clients. It contains information about you and your products or services, presented in a way that makes you memorable and worth hiring.

The word "kit" implies some kind of package with enclosures. Ordinarily, people use a two-pocket portfolio with a place to insert a business card. Speakers with bigger budgets sometimes have their pocket portfolio preprinted with their names and branding logo.

Here's a list of things (in addition to a business card) that may be contained in a speaker's two-pocket portfolio press kit. In one pocket would be the following:

◆ Preprinted material that might include your one-sheet brochure (we'll talk about one-sheets momentarily).

◆ A sheet of paper (quality paper that matches your portfolio ... remember those branding colors!) featuring your client lists and a long laundry list of testimonials in a summary format.

◆ Color copies of reference or testimonial letters from current and former clients.

On the other side of the packet (to balance things out) are the following:

◆ Copies of articles you have written that add to your credibility.

◆ Press releases about books you've written (addressed to the media) and maybe a flyer about your book(s) if you have one.

- Speakers sometimes include a glossy photo, but with the advent of easily sending photos online, this isn't truly necessary. But do include a current photo of yourself on some of your inserts.

- Enclose a demo DVD if you have one. Whether or not you send a DVD, include a full page with your bio written in the third person ("Mary Winters is a NYC firefighter with a degree in psychology …") listing your credentials, past speaking engagements, and personal info.

Ideally, your materials for all of your press kit are top quality or at least glossy stock for the cover pieces. Rather than print these one at a time in your office, it is best to go to a printer. Press kits are sent directly to your best prospective clients but not until you contact them, usually by phone, and they agree to review what you send them.

In addition to mailing materials in a nice press kit, speakers will have the same material on their website, branded in much the same ways (same colors, same font, and so on). It's customary for speakers to include a cover letter on some nice (also branded) stationary. The letter is tailored to your client with a respectful greeting and references to their specific needs.

Now some speakers will say, "I have a website. Why should I send all of this stuff to a client?" Sending a complete, high-quality press kit about you and your programs by mail, UPS, or FedEx can be much more impressive than asking a client to log onto a website. The press kit also has staying power: it can be left on a desk for daily review or circulated among a committee of people who are making the buying decision together. Yes, many decisions for hiring speakers are a group decision.

One-Sheets

One-sheets are 8.5×11 brochures or flyers featuring all the key details about a speaker and her topics, titles, and so on. The one-sheet can be included in a press kit, but it can (and should) also be used all be itself when you're aiming for prospective clients with iffy potential. If and when you have a website (which I'll discuss later in this chapter), you can post this same material on your homepage.

Minimum components of a one-sheet brochure include the following:

- A photo of you, preferably in color.

- A banner headline that sells your brand or umbrella topic area.

- A list of your various offerings with a brief paragraph about each.

◆ Some quotes from your best, satisfied clients or prior audience members.

◆ A couple of paragraphs about your background, written in a way that supports your primary offerings.

◆ Your logo or an attention-grabbing image.

◆ Colors that coordinate with the other components of your marketing materials.

def•i•ni•tion

A **one-sheet** is an important marketing tool for speakers. As the name implies, it's one sheet of paper listing pertinent details about the speaker and her offerings. It may be printed both sides, ideally on glossy quality paper.

Good news! These days one-sheets do not need to be printed 1,000 at a time like in the "old days." Nowadays, you can print them out as you need them. Here are a couple of tips: again, glossy paper is most desirable. To get the best quality, you may need help and a graphic designer (at an inexpensive print shop) to start. If possible, collect sample one-sheets from other speakers before printing your own. That way, you can get ideas of what might work for you, and what you'd definitely like to steer away from.

Previewing Tapes Creates Bookings

Buyers, especially those who have bigger budgets, usually like to *preview* speakers before hiring them. Sometimes a meeting planner is responsible for choosing the speaker, and their job is on the line if the speaker is a flop. You can understand his reluctance to hire someone sight-unseen. Once in a great while, references or referrals from prior engagements will offset the need for a *demo tape*, but that's definitely not the norm, unless you are a highly branded speaker, the author of a great book, or you've been seen "live" by someone on the buying committee. You need a demo tape if you want to play in the big leagues, so stop procrastinating and create one!

def•i•ni•tion

A **preview** or **demo tape** is a short 5- to 15-minute video that contains the best clips of who you are and what you offer.

How does one create a top-quality preview tape? This is a question that is often asked by aspiring speakers. Some speakers invest way too much (or way too little) money creating demo tapes.

First things first. On a demo tape, you want to include …

- Footage of you in action during a presentation.

- Clips of you speaking to diverse audience groups or in unique locations. Or one great clip of you at your absolute best.

- Any media appearances you've made.

- Testimonials from audience members or your best clients.

- Consider wearing the colors that look best on TV; and pay attention to all your nonverbal communication. Make them all more emphatic, bigger, or bolder for the taping.

Whether a professional videographer, a friend, or a client is creating your master demo tape, discuss the following beforehand: staging and backdrop (what's in your shot?), adequate lighting, microphones (for you and the audience, if needed), and whether you want close-up shots.

The tape doesn't need to be Hollywood-quality, but it must be clear, both in picture and sound. Lighting must be adequate so your potential clients aren't listening to a voice that seems to be coming from a dark stage. If you aren't handy, hire an editor to remove things that knock you out of consideration. For example, edit out things like too many "you know" or nonresponsive audience members. These things don't make anyone look good!

All of this builds your value and credibility in the eyes of the client so that you get the booking! And keep in mind, a preview tape can pay for itself easily if you get just one booking from it, so it's usually worth the investment (somewhere between $500 and $5,000, based on your target market and the fee you typically earn).

Website Marketing of Services and Products

There's no use beating around the bush on this one: you must have a website featuring you and your program offerings to succeed in this business. It can start out simple (just a page or two), but design it in such a way that more and more material can be added to your site to educate people about who you are and what you offer. Of course, you want some "hooks" to keep people on your site once they come to your homepage.

You want people to call you or e-mail you, so have your phone number (preferably toll-free, in addition to a regular toll number) and a link to your e-mail address on every single page.

Because you are selling yourself and your programs, use your name in your website address—and in your e-mail address, too. This is better than infofromspeaker@ greatspeakertoday.com (bogus site) or some other kind of hard-to-remember or unprofessional-sounding e-mail address. Don't be shy or wrongly humble in this regard: put your name forth and work to brand it!

Here's a checklist for your website. Ask yourself these questions:

❑ Have I branded myself and my presentations with consistent images, colors, logos, slogans, memorable and attention-getting pictures, and so on?

❑ Have I made my homepage short and friendly, positioned myself as a problem-solving expert, and presented my brand quickly and succinctly?

❑ Do I motivate people to contact me as a result of the headlines, offerings, and interactive devices on my website?

❑ Do I keep people from leaving my website too quickly? This is not easy to do, but make sure you answer the question that everyone has: "What's in it for me by staying on this page?" or "Why is she/he better than other speakers?"

❑ Do I provide information on my site that my ideal type of customer would really appreciate and benefit from?

Marketing your website is more important than simply having a website. After all, what good is it to spend money and time building a website if very few people end up considering booking you to speak as a result of looking at your website? You want your website to be a great investment, not simply an expense. So market it with keyword search tools to search engines through Google and Yahoo! Many wise speakers use postcards to get the word out about their website. Billboarding your great website on the side of your car is okay, too. I think it's better to overdo the promotion of your website than not promote it enough.

Other Impression-Making Tools

You've read about many kinds of tools that help speakers get noticed, remembered, and hired. Here are some other impression-making tools that have caught my attention and made me remember a speaker:

◆ Pens or other promo items with logos or memorable branding slogans—a slogan that's too good to throw away.

◆ Several books authored by the speaker, presented in a bag marked with a slogan like, "Greatness is never an accident."

- A preview tape that comes with a bag of popcorn and a challenge to "Have fun watching me on TV—see the star your team needs to win big!"

- A box of the best chocolates sent to the client with a kind thank-you note saying, "You are better than the best—thank you."

- An autographed poster of the speaker with a saying or slogan that truly motivates people to be their personal best or to remember key aspects of the speaker's message.

- A calendar with photos and quotes from the speaker's books or seminars for each month, and of course the speaker's contact info on the bottom of the calendar.

- Magnets from the speaker with the info that makes him memorable.

Remember to make other people feel needed and appreciated as you attempt to get them to think about and remember you. You might think you are the star … but really your client is the star. Treat them accordingly!

The Least You Need to Know

- Branding yourself makes you memorable and easily recognizable to clients.

- One-sheets and press (or media) kits are marketing tools sent to potential clients. They contain information on your latest gigs, your credentials, and your services and offerings.

- A demo tape is usually well worth the money; it enables potential clients to see you in action.

- Websites are a must for aspiring speakers. Potential clients expect easy access to your information.

Chapter

Write It Down!

In This Chapter

- ◆ Solidifying thoughts through writing
- ◆ Finding the right publications
- ◆ Tracking down editors
- ◆ Marketing your writing

Speakers are, above all else, amazing communicators. This excellence could simply be a type of giftedness—even so, gifted people have to exercise their special abilities to maximize their potential. Speaking as often as possible is one obvious way to achieve this, but have you discovered the great value and benefits of writing down your thoughts?

You are a professional speaker, or soon will be, so you want to be clear, concise, and wise in all of your communications. Many great communicators have discovered that writing out a speech helps them to think of better word choices that enhance their speech, seminar, workshop, or presentation.

Writing also helps to crystallize thoughts and helps perfect your effectiveness as a communicator. One of my mentors used to say, "You don't really know it if you can't write it down."

Being published is a shortcut to success as a speaker. Even if you aren't paid for your work, get published anyway. You can use published material to help promote yourself and build credibility.

Articles Sell You and Your Ideas

Veteran speakers collectively agree: aspiring speakers must learn to get published. The best (and easiest) way to begin is by writing articles.

As a general rule, you want to be recognized as an expert so that you can be hired and paid to speak on your area of expertise. One of the best ways to prove your mettle is to write articles that will be read by prospective clients. In addition, writing articles in your area of expertise is a great public service. Articles sell you and your ideas while establishing you as a credible, expert source.

Success Shortcuts

At the start of your speaking career, you may have plenty of time to research and write articles. But even after your career starts picking up and you're extremely busy, it's still important to write. Articles—combined with your experience—can be the starting points for a book.

Hundreds of established speakers can attest to the importance of publishing your work. The visibility and notoriety that come along with having your name in print are important building blocks in your career. Not only are you more recognizable to clients, but as a "published expert," you can also start raising your fees.

As a speaker, you want the stage. You must make great use of both the spoken and written word to be your best. If you are rejected the first few times you attempt to have something published, don't give up. You may simply need to learn how and when to approach the people who can publish your materials and ideas. Or perhaps you need more to strengthen your written communication skills. Take some more time if you need it, but don't dilly-dally! Someone else may be poised to steal your spotlight!

What to Write About

It's best to have a long-range vision, mission, and purpose in mind so that you'll be less likely to go off on tangents, wasting time researching any old subject that someone wants you to write about.

Having said that, I have to note that it's also important to be somewhat open-minded about what you're willing to write. I once wrote an article for the monthly magazine *Meeting Professionals International.* Before I began, I asked the editor, "What kind of articles do you need? What topics?" These questions opened the door for two articles that went out to their 20,000 members.

Success Shortcuts

To serve their memberships, many national associations publish a monthly or quarterly magazine or newsletter—and they all need material to publish. Do an Internet search for the publications that interest you, and don't be afraid to contact them!

First and foremost, write from your current level of expertise. By writing articles for one market niche or industry at a time, you brand yourself as an expert in those areas. This is far different from writing a book covering a lot of general information. By writing niche-specific articles, you're appealing to a specific audience and position-ing yourself as their go-to person. A professor of classical music, for example, might be able to write an entire encyclopedia on stringed instruments. But if he narrows his focus and writes articles on playing the fiddle, he's appealing to a very specific group. He may not get a lot of feedback, but when he does want to move on to writing books or giving presentations, he can use those articles to get his foot in the door with clients.

One way to expand your niche audience is to stay focused on your area of expertise while finding related areas to write about. What do I mean by related areas? Think in terms of an umbrella topic, under which you have several related areas. As an example, health and wellness is a strong and in-demand topic. But nutrition, exercise, diet, positive thinking, sleep, balanced living, lifestyle, and several other subjects are related to health and wellness and could certainly be discussed (in writing or in a presentation) by an expert in the health industry. Get the point? You could write about all these subcategories but ideally, you tie it back to your main topic and brand yourself, in this example, as the health and wellness expert.

Success Shortcuts

Writing articles in your topic area saves you a lot of time and money that you'd other-wise invest in marketing. Once your name is published, you'll become well-known rather quickly for your branded expertise.

How to Get Your Articles Printed

Which comes first, writing articles or finding publishers for your articles? Like many things in professional speaking, it depends on some variables.

If your goal is to get published, you need to create a list of the publications that are closely linked to your area of expertise and are likely to publish your work. Once you create this list, prioritize it. Which publication is the best venue for you? Which is second, third, fourth, and so on? I would like to tell you to go after your number-one choice from the get-go, but it's usually better to get some articles published in lesser publications first.

Words to the Wise

Keep a few copies of your published work on hand. Some can be sent and used to help you get more articles published; others will go into your portfolio to be shown to clients to build credibility; and others could be shared with friends and family or other VIPs in your life.

Just as with speaking, it's best to practice the art of writing articles in the "minor leagues" before moving to the "majors," or your top-targeted audiences. Besides, top publications are likely to ask, "Where has your work been published?" If you're able to produce a list of smaller magazines, websites, newsletters, and so on which have displayed your writings, you'll be taken more seriously by the bigger companies.

Once you've published some smaller articles, then you can move on to the bigger magazines. But where will you begin this process? Do a Google search for magazine editors. If your topic is women's issues, for example, look for editors at women's magazines. My files are filled with material from women speakers who have published their articles in national publications. (Naturally, when I see that a woman has her article in a well-known publication, I conclude "She must be an expert!")

Here's a good example of how writing an article can lead to great success: I recently had a two-hour meeting with a pioneer in homeland security, Randall J. Larsen, Colonel, U.S. Air Force (retired). Randy clued me in on some of his ongoing efforts to write articles. He showed me his full-page article in *U.S. News & World Report*. Because this is a major publication, it may sound like he got a lucky break, but I can tell you, he works hard to make contacts with editors everywhere.

This article has led to some amazing opportunities for Randy. Because many news anchors on TV are not true journalists, but are instead talking heads reading scripts, there's a real need for experts during news broadcasts. Editors review the possible news stories the night before a morning broadcast. If there happens to be a story concerning terrorism or homeland security, Randy's name inevitably comes up, and many times he's contacted to share his views with America. Although the article was a great marketing tool in and of itself, it's led to an even better opportunity for Randy to market himself—on national TV! In addition, Randy has gone on to publish a book, *Our Own Worst Enemy.*

Do you see how articles can help you gain recognition for yourself and your expertise and help you move forward in your career? You can easily make a list of editors to sell your material to, just like Randy did. Have confidence! Do it now!

You Could Write a Book

I like to think that each speaker must write a book, but I haven't yet been able to convince everyone that they're capable of doing so. You may think, "This is not for me!" or "I could never write a book—at least not a best seller," or "What would I write about?" If you have enough material to give a one-hour speech, then you're on the right path to writing a book. Plus, you can expand your well-researched and well-written articles to write a short book, for starters.

One of my great mentors, Carl Stevens, co-authored a college textbook years ago. Carl had a lot more life experience than I had at that point, and I was sure he had a lot more to write about and say than I did. (So my natural reaction to his writing setup was, "If *he* needs co-authors, how could *I* ever write a book?!") But I learned from his example: get some co-authors to lessen your load the first time around. Once you know what goes into writing a book, you can decide for yourself if you'd like to author the next book on your own. Another idea is to simply publish an essay in an anthology. In 1980, *Those Marvelous Mentors* featured my material in one chapter of a 16-chapter book.

Don't say, "I don't have time to write a book." Most authors are experts in their fields—they're incredibly busy, just like you are! You just need to allocate time for this project. Record your ideas on your long commute to and from work. Purchase voice-recognition software (which does all the typing for you) or hire a typist. You can also find a ghostwriter to help you along the way.

If you are looking for a step-by-step formula on how to write a book, that won't be given here. But I trust that you are self-sufficient enough to find those resources. Check online for books to guide you along this path, or go to the local library. More important, go to stores where your kind of book would be sold. Study every book that might compete with yours. If the book you envision is not quite right for the bookstores, you can always self-publish it and market it to specific markets, either through your website or during your presentations. (The *Chicken Soup for the Soul* series was self-published, and millions of copies have been sold!)

Words to the Wise

There are people out there who could take advantage of your naïveté in regard to publishing books. Some authors find when all's said and done, they made less than minimum wage on their book project. Take the time to calculate what you're spending (in time or money) versus what you expect to earn. Regardless, it still might be worth the effort for many reasons.

It's hard to explain all the advantages to the speaker who writes a book. One great benefit you may not think about until the book is complete is the self-confidence you gain due to simply being published—that self-confidence carries over into your presentations, and that's priceless.

If you're still undecided, make a list of the pros and cons of writing a book. If the reasons for writing a book outweigh the reasons against writing by a factor of three to one, I recommend you clear time on your schedule in the next nine months to work on your first book. Make it happen! Give birth to a great book.

Success Shortcuts

To get a major publisher to take a look at your work, you'll probably need a literary agent to help you put together a proposal and pitch your book idea. Agents usually take 15 percent of your advance for the book, but it may be well worth it if you're able to get your name out in the public domain and earn royalties.

Great Tools for Motivational Speakers

Published books of any type, even the co-authored or anthology variety, are great marketing tools for any speaker, but perhaps especially for the motivational speaker.

During a seminar, a motivational speaker will present nine or more major points and emphasize and reemphasize them. These are take-home applications that the speaker (and buyer) expects audience members to practice long after they've left the presentation. After all, what good is temporary motivation? Buyers want motivational speakers to shake things up so that positive change occurs.

Therefore, anything a speaker can offer that will reinforce or enhance the message, making it more memorable and actionable, is of huge value. Historically, motivational speakers sell books to 50 percent of any audience. At an average of $15 each and an audience of 800 people, a speaker could reasonably expect to earn $6,000—on top of what she's being paid by the buyer! And because those autographed books are going out into the world to be read, reread, and passed around, the speech also has lasting value.

As a motivational writer (and speaker), don't be afraid to use a little humor! One of my early mentors, Cavett Robert, used to say that presenting heavy subjects "on the wings of humor" made the topic much more palatable to audiences.

Success Shortcuts

Humor is one the best tools for almost any speaker or writer. Going to work as a speaker without the use of humor is like a surgeon going into an operation without his anesthesiologist.

Tips for Selling Timely Ideas to Publishers

Publishers are always on the lookout for valuable information to publish. They also keep their eyes peeled for new writers, authors, and experts. As you must know, some of the big New York–based publishers and others are hard to get to … but not impossible.

As I already mentioned, when you want to publish a book, you most often need an agent. However, if you're bound and determined to do this on your own, I recommend buying a book that lists editors and publishing houses (*Writer's Market* is a good source). From this source, you can find out who you need to contact and how to approach them. Your main goal in doing this is to ask what their current and future needs might be, and how you may be of help in fulfilling those needs. If you have some unique ideas that seem to fit with their needs, write a proposal and e-mail it to the editor you're in contact with. Be prepared for rejection, but also be prepared to get to work—the publishing industry needs hot topics published now!

Ideas for Marketing Your Book

Once your book is published, you may think you're going to sit back, relax, and reap the profits. Well you may reap profits, but you're certainly not going to do it by relaxing. You need to get out there and sell your book!

Do not depend solely on any publisher, not even the biggest and the best of them, to market and promote your book. The big publishers may not take much interest in your book even if they publish it. A publisher is a for-profit company, in most cases, and they direct their resources toward the books that will earn them the biggest return on their investment. If your book doesn't happen to fall into that category, then it's up to you to get the word out!

def•i•ni•tion

A **press release** written by speakers is used to alert media outlets about new books, appearances, awards, trips abroad, difference-making activities, and the like. It's written in the third person.

Getting your book into the media is one of the best ways to sell it. To do this, you need to write a *press release*, a fictional news story written in the third person, using any hook that you can think of. The press release has to be primarily about you, not your book! This may sound counter-intuitive, but what you're aiming for is a journalist or writer to read your personal story and say, "Now, this person is interesting! I'd love to interview her and hear the full story!" Of course, during that interview, you'll plug your book.

The cold, hard truth of the matter is that there are so many books out there (many written on the same topics) these days, it's difficult to make yours stand out among the millions. That's why making a personal connection to potential readers is so important. People are also fickle and busy. Few will sit and read an article about a book, but many will read a human-interest story about an author. See the difference?

Here are some things to consider while writing your press release:

◆ What's so unique about you? (Why would people want to read about you?)

◆ Is there some adversity or challenge you had to overcome to become a speaker or author?

◆ Do you have any famous clients? Don't be afraid to mention them (after you get their permission, of course)!

◆ Keep your press release on the short side—no more than one page.

◆ Customize your story to each media outlet you contact. If writing to a woman's magazine, for example, play up the fact that you were a stay-at-home mom for 12 years before becoming a speaker.

◆ If you're sending a hard copy (as opposed to an e-mail), include one of your marketing tools, like a pen, a flier, and so on. (It's acceptable to send a press release about yourself [and your book, of course] via e-mail.)

Whether you send your press release via e-mail or through the mail, make sure you've tracked down the right person (spell his name correctly) and his correct address.

Also don't be shy about contacting bookstores and setting up book signings. Most stores love the "local author" angle and will be helpful in assisting you. You will need to give a brief talk about your book, but because speaking comes naturally to you, this shouldn't be a big issue. You can also contact organizations that might benefit from your expertise, and ask them if you might put a link to your book on their website. A speaker who covers conservation as her main topic, for example, might do well to hook up with a local or national eco-friendly group.

Self Promotion Do's and Don'ts

One of the most important things a speaker can write is an e-mail newsletter. But before you begin sending this out to clients and prospects, you have to have some kind of website presence, such as your own website. When you send your newsletter, position a link to your website under your signature. Also post copies of links to all the articles you've written, whether or not they've been published.

Always be truthful about your background. If a reporter does pick up on your blog or site and requests an interview (and you hope she will!), she will check the facts—all of the facts. Save yourself time and embarrassment later. Make yourself sound interesting without reaching into untruthful territory.

Words to the Wise

Some speakers only publish their own material on their website or blog, only to find that no one ever reads them. Sending newsletters to your clients is a great way to make sure your writings get read!

If and when you do end up speaking with a journalist, establish the ground rules of the interview before the tape recorder is on. Request to have any and all quotes read back to you, and feel free to have some topics that are off-limits. If, for example, you're thrice-divorced and have written a book on how to make a marriage last, you may not want the interview to veer onto the topic of your failed relationships. You can certainly negotiate that point with the writer.

Do not claim at any time, especially in writing, that you are America's greatest or the world's best this or that. It is always best to let others promote you in this way, so use references and testimonials from those you have served to help promote the most wonderful product and service in the world (you).

Be prepared to do the legwork to promote yourself, your writing, your blog, or your website—and be prepared for what you hope will follow! Success means that you will be thrust into the public eye. That means more marketing in terms of giving interviews, making appearances, writing follow-up books or articles, and so on.

The Least You Need to Know

- ◆ Publishing articles on your area of expertise boosts your credibility as a speaker.
- ◆ You can contact magazine editors directly with ideas for articles.
- ◆ Ask editors what their needs are, and be prepared to meet them.
- ◆ Book writing is a considerable time investment, but well worth it for its marketing potential.
- ◆ Be prepared to market your own book to your best audiences.

Chapter 14

A Gold Mine of Presentation Guidelines

In This Chapter

- ◆ Make audiences remember you!
- ◆ Using stories in small doses
- ◆ Dressing the part
- ◆ Body language for the speaker

Presentation skills focus on delivering the spoken word in a way that will make a memorable goldlike impression on the audience. And while verbal skills play a huge part in a successful presentation, nonverbal communication is also an essential golden skill that the professional speaker must master.

Whether you are male or female, look at yourself as others would look at you. Is what you are wearing appropriate and professional? How about a better choice of words? Or are you in need of better timing in your delivery? Do you come across as someone who is truly enthusiastic about what you are presenting? Asking these questions of yourself can help you become a gold-nugget presenter.

How to Make Yourself Stand Out

One day when in San Diego County, California, where I was doing work for some clients, I decided to take a drive and see some of the beautiful view of the country-side. What Mother Nature presented to me along the coastline near the Pacific Ocean was awesome, especially in places like La Jolla, Delray Beach, and so on. When I headed inland I saw the tropical vegetation of Balboa Park, and the farther I went east on Route 8 away from the ocean, the higher the temperature and the fewer palm trees I saw. Finally I reached the desert with lots of rocky hills, mountains, and an arid environment—and I saw all of this within 60 minutes! Suffice it to say that Mother Nature's presentation changed dramatically but held my attention throughout my drive.

Most speeches are anywhere from 20 to 90 minutes, averaging around 45 to 60 minutes. (Anything longer is often considered a short or mini-seminar or workshop.) Like my drive that day in San Diego County, the best kind of speech paints pictures that take you from the heights to the depths, and often back again, appealing to your emotions while also presenting you with the facts—regardless of the topic. Words that bring golden sunlight of day to the darkness of midnight help embellish and enliven a speech while keeping an audience's attention.

During that same drive I was just describing, after taking a road off the main freeway, I entered an area where a sign directed me to what "was once the most productive gold mine in Southern California." The mine was once owned by the governor, but it went bust in about 1888. An entire community at one time bustled with activity when the mine was in its heyday, but not today—it's a ghost town with no signs of the prosperity that once must have existed. I went away from the area with a feeling of sadness, but as I realized that prosperity exists in many other places, and "gold" is whatever is precious in one's own life, my spirit began to lift. No use crying over a long-gone town; how can people today work hard and make something of themselves?

Just as my realization recharged my spirit, your presentations (of any type) need to always hold a gold mine of ideas or solutions or inspiration for your audience members—and the meeting planner who booked you to speak.

Making the Point

Now go back and take note of the examples of useable guidelines for your presentations provided in the preceding story:

- Be specific as you paint a picture in your presentation. Use descriptive words and comparisons.

- Appeal to emotions, both positive and negative.

- Always remember why you were hired in the first place, who hired you, and what your objectives are.

- Remember that people can relate to places and people better than to things.

- Realize that words can mean different things to different people.

- Action words (like "bustled") can help people accept the actions you are recommending.

And now, think about this:

- Only 7 percent of the lasting impact of a presentation comes from what people hear you say.

- Within 24 hours, people will forget 25 percent of what you said.

- Within 7 days, the average person will forget 60 percent of what you said.

- Within 16 days, most people will forget 95 percent of what you said.

So it's important to give yourself and your message some "staying power" in your audiences' minds! The use of colorful language, anecdotes with broad appeal, and realistic solutions are all important aspects of any successful presentation!

Some experts in presentation skills, as well as in media relations and training, like speaker Brad Phillips, would tell you to make a maximum of three points worth remembering, in any speech of 45 to 60 minutes. You can (and maybe must) emphasize your points with anecdotes or stories, which go down easy with audiences and always make a presentation more memorable.

Words to the Wise

Because many people will forget most of what they hear, audiences need to be encouraged to take notes. Suggest to them, "Write it down, please; take notes. Writing helps to crystallize thought; you don't know it unless you write it down."

You'll note that one thing I don't encourage is including the work of other experts in your presentation. Sometimes speakers feel as though they have to offer up opinions of other experts, either to prove a point or to demonstrate their expertise or to simply fill up the time allocated for the speech. Remember: as the speaker, you are the expert. You need not quote a dozen sources to prove your points or your expertise. That's just overkill in most presentations. Phillips says, "The more you say, the more you stray." Keep the information on target and to the point.

Sharing ... a Little

To have long-term success in this business, you have to make yourself stand out so that clients and audiences recognize you as a unique presenter who can offer what no one else can. This is not easy for some people. Many of us were taught to conform as children; worse, many of us were taught that standing out in a crowd was akin to being a show-off! Well one thing is for certain: to be a successful speaker, you can't be just like everyone else. You have to cultivate a willingness to be distinctive.

Sharing your personal experiences as they relate to your topic is one way to make yourself a unique presence. But don't do it unless the story will benefit the audience, and even then, keep it to a minimum. People don't want to walk away from your presentation feeling as though they just relived your life.

Success Shortcuts

Skillful speakers always remember the line, "People don't care how much I know, or what my experiences have been, until they know how much I care about them." Show them you care, and they'll listen!

One reason speakers skillfully don't overuse personal pronouns (and never without a direct point of application for the audience) is because people just aren't that interested in how the world affects the speaker as a whole—they want something that relates to their lives. If I tell you a story about how I learned the lesson about being willing to stand out by changing the spelling of my name to "Thom," and not Tom, Tommy, or Thomas, you probably wouldn't be interested unless I tell the story quickly and for your benefit.

Change Is Good

When considering how to stand out and above the crowd, whether in marketing yourself or in giving your presentations, please consider these points:

- ◆ You are an expert. Act like one, dress like one, and present like one.

- ◆ You are different. Don't be worried about what others think.

- ◆ You are unique. Continue to upgrade and perfect your uniqueness.

- You are better. Continue to compare and contrast your presentation skills with other speakers' abilities, and set incremental goals to improve and be better.

- You are a great communicator. Never stop perfecting your use of language and upgrading your nonverbal skills, too.

You must believe these affirming thoughts if you are to succeed as a professional speaker! Identify what, if anything, prevents you from buying into these beliefs and working on changing the way you see yourself.

The only person who loves change, it has been said, is a baby with wet diapers. But I have seldom in my 30-plus years heard a speaker—and I have heard thousands—who could not improve with a small change to some aspect of his or her presentation, speech, or seminar. You must learn to look at change as a skill! You'll be asked to change your presentation for various audiences; you'll be given suggestions on how to better appeal to the groups you speak to; you may even want to make a change from being a keynote speaker to becoming a professional coach or consultant! Life is all about change, and those who fight it end up being quite unhappy. Embrace change! It is a fun way to live!

Verbal and Nonverbal Guidelines

A crowd gathering to hear you give a speech has every right to expect you, the speaker, to be a model of communication excellence. Your attitude during a presentation may determine how you view your audience and whether or not you connect with them. Try throwing a net of love out to the audience and see what you get back.

This caring principle applies in knowing which skills to exercise at which times. If you care, you will not forget to look each person in the eye and smile warmly, for example, as you present. A speaker once asked his audience, "How many of you like to be around people who smile at you all the time?" Every person's hand went up. "Do you do your best when people are smiling at you or acting as if they are happy to see you?" Every hand went up again, saying, "Yes!" Then the speaker wisely encouraged, "Well then, will you please notify your face right now that you are happy to be here?!" The audience laughed and agreed.

This speaker's ploy demonstrates several points for how to make skillful presentations:

- Use a series of questions to get and keep attention.

- Interact with your audience (and specific individuals in it) even if giving a keynote for hundreds of people.

♦ Use humor every few minutes to make points and keep the audience's attention.

♦ Show empathy for your audience and cause them to empathize, too.

♦ Asking questions of the audience where you know the response will be "yes" (nodding their heads in agreement, for example) helps set a positive tone.

♦ Don't put any one person in your audience on the spot.

♦ Nonverbal communication can tell you if an audience is with you, and often is a reflection of your expectations.

♦ Use nonverbal skills to prompt audience response (in the previous example, the speaker might raise his hand first in answer to his own question).

Words to the Wise

Speakers are often their own worst critics to the point of paralyzing themselves with fear of failure. Evaluate, set goals for improvement, and then say to yourself "Who is next?" Seek out new clients and continue to work on your presentation skills. That's really the best thing you can do!

In this one-second example, you can pull out several techniques that any speaker can use. For example, you can practice methods like rhetorical questioning so that you are truly skillful in moving your audience to a great experience. Also this gives you an edge on anticipating problems during a live performance and correcting them right off the bat!

In addition to winning the audience over so that they like you personally, you also have to know how to appeal to their brains. Research from various sources (too varied to mention) tells us that every single person has his own dominant learning style:

♦ Auditory: Learning through listening

♦ Visual: Learning through watching or reading

♦ Kinetic: Learning by performing a task or interacting with others

Now what does this mean to you? Because most people learn by either hearing, seeing, or doing, you must find a way to make your presentation appeal to all three styles of learning! Use colorful language, engage your nonverbal skills (which we'll discuss shortly), and use those rhetorical questions to hook everybody into your message!

There's another learning issue to deal with: women's brains versus men's. The brain is made up of two hemispheres, the left and the right. The right side of the brain controls emotion, creativity, and things of that nature, while the left side is concerned primarily with logical thought. Women tend to be "emotional" learners, meaning that they go with their "gut feelings" and are deeply affected by how an issue or topic makes them feel. Men, on the other hand, tend to be more logical, seeking out the facts and little else aside from the facts. So it's also important to customize your presentation for both sides of the brain. If you are speaking to an all-male audience, for example, most of your speech should appeal to the logical left side of the brain. (You can wrap your facts in anecdotes, but make sure you have plenty of factual information to give!)

In regard to your movements, remember that it is called "body language" for a good reason. Have you ever seen people whose bodily movements didn't match the words coming out of their mouths? Someone who says, "I'm happy" but doesn't smile, for example, or "I'm not scared of the boss" but is cowering behind his cubicle wall? This happens in the general population, but it should never, ever happen with the professional speaker! Communicating effectively with your words and movements is part of your job! In other words, if you're excited, it's not enough to raise your voice—start using your arms to demonstrate your point. Use those legs to move yourself from one end of the stage to the other. Show some passion when passion has its grip on you!

Integrating all aspects of yourself (body, soul, attitude) into your presentation makes for a more exciting work life for you and a more exciting presentation for your audience. Your body can communicate volumes through the nonverbal, including feelings that are transferable to audience members. If you are feeling and looking sad, for example, don't expect your audience to be feeling inspired or uplifted after your message. You can prevent this by learning everything you need to know about verbal and nonverbal presentation skills. There are countless body language books out there; one that I recommend is *Let Me See Your Body Talk* by Jan Hargrove (Kendall/Hunt Publishing, 1995).

There's also a way to use body language to draw in an unresponsive crowd, and it's called mirroring and masking. Master salespeople are pros in this technique, because it really works. When someone is giving you a negative face, mimic it (subtly, of course) for a short time. Then (just as subtly), shift your movements in a more positive direction. The other person will start mirroring you without even knowing what's happened! Of course, this is much easier to do in a small group or one-on-one. When presenting to a large group, locate the sour-looking faces in the bunch. Make eye contact with them (without obviously singling them out). Show them the face that you want to see looking back at you!

Success Shortcuts

Practicing your presentation skills is important. Practice in front of the mirror and in front of family or friends who will honestly critique and advise you.

Body language is also important to keep in mind when you're working with different cultures. Asians, for example, generally don't use a lot of broad gestures or loud exclamations. They also don't use eye contact the way we do. On the other hand, some Middle Eastern countries expect what we'd consider to be an uncomfortable amount of eye contact and are immediately suspicious of anyone who doesn't provide it. So whether you're offering a presentation to a group of foreign businesspeople or working with different ethnicities during a workshop or seminar, brush up on your body language, not only to get your point across, but also to make sure you don't offend anyone!

Makeovers and Makeup for Speakers

One of my children, Todd, was given the nickname "Toddy Toad" when he was a baby. (The way he hopped around made him appear to be amphibianlike to my mother-in-law.) When he was in elementary school, Todd had a hard time focusing on anything for long periods of time. He "hopped" from one activity to the next; hence, the name "Toddy Toad" stuck and he may have begun to think of himself as a child without academic focus.

Well, Todd brought home a bad report card in third grade, and I decided that things had to change. I sat him down one night and told him that he was to have a new nickname from that point on: "Mr. Brains." I told my wife and others that there was no more Toddy Toad; he had been replaced with Mr. Brains. Todd started to think of himself as an intelligent kid, and guess what? The next report card was decorated with A's!

Almost every speaker has a flop performance, especially during those first couple of years. It's not the end of the world or the end of your speaking career, but you may need to reevaluate the way you think about yourself, your public persona, and your presentation. Even though you can't go back in time and redo a bad presentation, you can make yourself over completely and take your F performance to an A+ in the process.

We can all use a makeover of our persona once in a while. This is another aspect of change that you have to embrace. If you change the way you dress or do your hair, for example, you may change the way you feel about yourself. (The opposite is also true—changing the way you feel about yourself may lead to a new wardrobe and a whole new look for you.) It's amazing how powerful the mind is. If we think we can succeed, if we think we look the part, if we think we're great at what we do … then all of it becomes reality.

Whoever said, "The clothes make the man" knew what he (or, more likely, she) was talking about! When I was about a year into my speaking career, I went into a fine men's store and purchased a very expensive executive double-breasted power suit with faint pinstripes. I was told the suit was made in Italy. It was three times as expensive as any other suit I had in my closet. I would only wear this suit, and did so for at least five years, when I gave a speech or seminar. In some ways, this suit, complete with the red power tie and wingtip shoes, helped to brand me as a powerful speaker. Somehow I spoke with more confidence in that suit. Know what I mean? Try it; you may like it and find this kind of makeover makes a difference for you, too.

Makeup is another issue altogether, and I would never advise others on how to beautify themselves. However, I do know that when speaking in front of an audience, speakers need color in their face, just like they need descriptive words in their use of language. And when you are creating a demo tape, you'll want to use face powder to remove the glow or glare. You want to be the picture of health so that everyone is focused on your message, not your frail appearance!

Let's talk about attractive colors for clothing to bring out the best of your attractive features. Flesh-colored makeup to remove bags under eyes may be necessary; or extra rouge on the checks, even for men, so those in the back of an audience see that you have a little glow about you. Consult a makeup expert if you feel you have a problem or want to improve in this area of appearance.

Success Shortcuts

Internal makeovers start with your belief system about who you are now and who you can become. Of course, you may also need to rework some of the material you have been presenting so that it is more acceptable to your target audiences, but when you feel good about yourself, you can do almost anything!

We can relate the issue of appearance to a tangible business example. Successful companies use some of the most refined or advanced presentation skills in getting you to pay more for their products than other options. Think about Starbucks, for example. What is it that makes you go into their store and pay almost $4 for a cup of coffee? They pull you in with all sorts of presentation tricks (the lighting, the chairs, the windows, the cups). You're paying for the great feeling you get when you walk through their doors. The deli across the street might have great coffee and pastries, too, but somehow, you just don't feel they're up to the higher standard set by Starbucks.

You have to think of yourself as a premium-brand speaker. If you present yourself as an inexpensive brand, you'll also act like one and attract bargain hunters. And in terms of your bargain-basement brand presentations skills (such as very few or ineffective presentation skills), you will be limiting your appeal and longevity.

Speakers often start out charging inexpensive fees. That's all right; that doesn't make you low quality. Think of this as a time when you're handing out samples of your wares, letting people know about your product. Even during this warm-up phase of your career, it's very important to present yourself (and think of yourself) as someone who's already a great success. If you believe it, others will, too.

Odds and Ends

In making and enhancing presentations, there are a few other odds that are important to consider. Because they didn't fit neatly into the other sections of this chapter, I've included them here:

- Show and tell to sell. As you are selling ideas to your audiences, you need to remember that my research indicates up to 87 percent of the mental impact comes from the visual. So, using a variety of visual aids along with handout material is always a good idea.

- If you don't use your speaker skills, you'll lose them. Speakers need to speak, make presentations as often as possible the first few years, and critique themselves and ask others to do so. Continue to upgrade those skills!

- Read as much as you can about giving successful presentations, watch DVDs on the subject, or take classes to learn more about presenting to groups and communicating better.

- Find speaker role models and study their presentations. Incorporate the best ideas, especially in the areas of nonverbal communication, from other respected and established speakers.

- Never, never, never tell a lie during any kind of presentation. If a story you tell is not your original material, do your best to give credit where credit is due.

Embellishing stories and material within your presentation to make it more appealing to audience members is okay (within reason).

Two more for you: The opening and the closing of the speech or seminar are usually the most important moments to set up and recap your golden message. Speakers often open with appropriate attention-getting humor or visual aids or strong questions (or all of these); speakers work to keep attention throughout, and close with a summary of the three major golden points of the speech with a golden dessert, like a memorable anecdote or brief story or poem as a recapping reminder.

Never, never say "In closing …" more than once! Once you say it, wrap up your presentation quickly always, before it tarnishes the message and your image.

Close any speech or presentation on time even if you were delayed in starting … otherwise people might leave the gold you provided and never use it. Please respect the value of your audience's time. Time is like gold to many people.

I give *you* a standing ovation (always better than a sitting ovation). You are truly golden! As our U.S. Presidents say at the end of most speeches, "God bless you and God bless America!" (How can you top that?!)

The Least You Need to Know

- ◆ Descriptive words help audience members envision what you're saying.

- ◆ Encourage audiences to take notes.

- ◆ Your nonverbal communication should reinforce (not contradict) your message.

- ◆ Appealing to the three dominant learning styles (auditory, visual, and kinetic) helps to ensure that all audience members are engaged by your presentation.

Part 4

Financial Fundamentals

You'll never make money in this business if you're underselling yourself. In this part, I'll tell you what you can reasonably charge for your services. I'll also advise you on where to find clients who can write big checks, as well as talk about client-speaker business etiquette.

Chapter 15

Client Basics

In This Chapter

- ◆ Treat your clients well!
- ◆ How to establish long-term relationships
- ◆ Phasing yourself in with a client
- ◆ Using your contacts to find new business

Established speakers love to point out their client success stories, especially if the client has some prestige associated with their name. Are we just a bunch of braggarts trying to one-up each other? No! In landing new clients, it's almost a necessity to tell how you've served your established clients in the past. Your success stories are truly attention-getters, and because you need to be constantly looking for new clients, whether you're a part-time or full-time speaker, you need all the attention-getting ideas you can use!

In this chapter, let's look at the three most important areas of client relationships: acquisition, service, and retention.

Your Clients (a.k.a. Your Bosses)

Clients are not just insignificant people signing checks with your name on it. Your clients are your bosses while you're preparing to serve them and when you're actually giving your presentation. Of course, you must pay attention to their wants and needs, to all they might say, or even what is not said, as all of these factors can give you clues about how to best provide your client with the services they need most.

Kings and Queens for More Than a Day

Even if you are a very laid-back and casual kind of person, you would stand and bow if the Queen of England entered the room. Imagine all the people you speak to in client or prospective client companies are queens or a kings (or at least princes or princesses; they are simply keeping their royalty a secret).

Words to the Wise

Not every client will be a prospect for ongoing services. Many organizations only hire a speaker once a year for an annual event. They want all their experiences with the speaker to be pleasant and meaningful to their objectives.

Have you ever stayed in a four- or five-star hotel and experienced the amenities and extras that make you feel very special? The staff leaves candy on the pillow, comes to turn down the bed sheets, picks up after you, and rushes to your every request and need. The best hotels anticipate your every need and make those things available to you—not always for free, mind you. When you have every amenity at your fingertips, the theory goes, you're bound to spend extra money on something—and indeed, you probably do! This is more than branding, it's an experience being sold to you, and at the heart of that experience is the feeling that *you* are, indeed, a super-special person.

This is exactly what you need to do for your clients—make them feel as though they are your only client, and the only client you would ever want to have! Remember the names of the people you deal with; remember personal facts about them; don't ever make them feel as though you don't have time for them. Ask questions while demonstrating an attitude of service. Clients want speakers who will go beyond the extra mile to get the job done successfully. Demonstrate this kind of attitude whenever you speak with your client VIPs.

As a cautionary tale, I'll tell you about a speaker I booked one time for $20,000 whose ego got in the way of treating people properly. It became obvious that neither the client nor the bureau (which brought him business and cut his checks) were his kings or queens—he treated all of us like we were his royal subjects! I really still believe that the reason he had such a high fee was that he must have known no one would hire him a second time.

Fortunately, most speakers are not like this! They realize that they are fortunate to have a gift for speaking and the opportunity to make money while at it. When you combine true talent and dedication with humility and gratitude, clients will remember you—for all the *right* reasons.

Success Shortcuts

Through my speakers' bureau, I have worked with hundreds of different speakers, but I especially recall the few who have acknowledged what we have done for them in memorable or unique ways. Anything done with class can make people remember you (and often hire you again and again). Send thank-you gifts or cards!

Repeat Clients

Repeat clients are those who will hire you again and again, but they can't necessarily sustain your career. One repeat client might hire you every year to talk about yearly sales and profit objectives, as one example, but you won't have another contact from them for almost another full year (when it's time to discuss the particulars of *next* year's meeting).

But some clients are so large (with so many varied departments and employees) that you could create a strategy for working with them fairly regularly if you can offer seminars or workshops to benefit all of their divisions.

In these cases, shoot for the moon! Bend over backward in your attempts to serve them, and no matter what they ask of you, be willing to at least mull over the request before saying no (and only say no if there's absolutely no way it can be done). But also be realistic and do not promise more than you can deliver. As I've said before, a client will be sorely disappointed if they feel as though they haven't received what they've paid for.

You may want to say to your clients: "I want to earn the right to become the number-one speaker on your list of speakers forever! How can I do that?" Well, in reality, this is not always possible. Many organizations need to have a different speaker personality at each annual meeting. So guard your feelings and don't take it personally if you're not invited back. This happens to almost every speaker, and it's just the nature of this business.

Ongoing Clients for Ongoing Revenue

Speakers love the idea of having ongoing clients providing ongoing revenues. I can think of masters of this strategy who have sustained themselves and made millions in the process: Nido Quebin, Thomas Winninger, and Ty Boyd are three who come to mind. I've known these men for almost 30 years, and just like great athletes who strive to be better when a challenge is presented to them, competitive master speakers improve by considering the details of what other master speakers are doing. It's not that we steal from one another—we simply build on each other's great ideas with the objective of serving and retaining clients.

Phasing In

Many speakers try to sell themselves to clients in phases. Phase One might be the speech, Phase Two might be a seminar, Phase Three might be a series of seminars, and so on. This strategy has been important to the long-term success of many speakers who have survived long term in this business.

When I first entered the business of pro speaking full time on March 1, 1977, I was asked to focus on my mentor's past clients in order to generate more business; I was also to focus on new clients to create new business. I was told that associations were great prospective clients in many ways, so being based in Columbus, Ohio, a state capital, I focused on all the members of the Ohio Society of Association Executives. There were associations of every kind in this group—you name it, from A to Z—but I had no idea which of them hired outside speakers and which did not. I began to phone all 500 associations while my mentor Carl Stevens, was off traveling the country and the world.

I honestly believed (and still do) that my mentor was the right speaker for about 80 percent of those associations, and as long as their budget was sufficient to cover his fee. If their budget was too low, I would say, "We have another great choice at half the price. Which speaker would you prefer?" The clients rolled right in. I ended up booking Carl at a big annual convention for the North American Heating and Air-Conditioning Wholesalers Association (NHAW) in New Orleans that December. Doesn't really sound too impressive, does it? Well, he was paid about $2,000 for that presentation, and this was when hardly anyone was paid as much in those days!)

Our strategic plan including this speech was Phase One. The plan for Phase Two was for the association to sponsor one of our two-and-a-half day seminars—but only if Carl's speech at the big convention was well received. The hope was that we'd be sponsored in Chicago, and that this seminar would open us up to more clients from all over the United States.

Carl wowed the client in New Orleans, and so we moved on to Phase Two, the seminar that we both presented. We had 43 people attend at $295 each, and we grossed about $13,000. Today we would get at least two or three times that amount for that kind of seminar, which, by the way, went so well that the client agreed to sponsor about six more seminars around North America. Because Carl's book was also released that year and we were able to sell copies at the back of the room, some of these seminars produced much more than our first seminar in Chicago had. So you can see Phase Three was a success, and through our association with this client, several large companies contracted with Carl's company for him to do in-house seminars in their home cities. In other words ...

One $2,000 speech resulted in well over $100,000, maybe $200,000, in gross income for one speaker's company over a one- to two-year period. This method is used over and over again—and at *much* higher fees these days!

Success Shortcuts

You can create dozens of clients in some niche markets through an effective phased-in plan for client acquisition. Start with one simple speech that positions you as an authority in your field, someone who has much more to offer than the competition.

Establishing Ongoing Relationships

As an independent speaker (or a coach or consultant who is on retainer with a company), it takes real brainpower to create that ongoing client relationship; and sometimes being an expert isn't enough. There are other experts in your field, as you well know. Being personable, being willing to work with the company to meet their budget (while also making sure they're meeting your minimum fee), interviewing the decision-makers to find out what the client likes best about your presentation and what they like least ... these are all good ways to go about showing your loyalty and dedication to the client while establishing an ongoing relationship. Here are other ideas:

◆ Don't wait for the client to call you back. If you know their annual meeting is coming up, call them well in advance and let them know you'd love to serve them again.

♦ Go the extra mile. Even if it's extremely difficult to meet the needs of the client, you should strive to do so if it's at all possible. If you have a presentation in Phoenix on Monday morning and your ongoing client wants you in NYC on Monday evening ... go!

♦ It's all right to disagree with a client, but don't be disagreeable, no matter how long you've worked with them. Speakers are not on retainer usually, so you are not entitled to additional business automatically.

Keep in mind that in business relationships, you often do not get a second chance if you mess up the dynamic between yourself and the person who has the power to invite you back again. You may get a standing ovation from the audience, but if you fail to please the big cheese, you may not be back. It's that simple. Your job is a balance between pleasing the powers-that-be and the people in the workplace trenches or the audience. It's not easy (but then, I never said it would be, did I?).

Words to the Wise

People are stretched and don't have time for idle chit-chat (at least not during the business day). Find out what the decision-makers want and give it to them—quickly. And make sure you're speaking with a decision-maker—your time is valuable, too!

What efforts seem to pay off best for speakers in establishing ongoing relationships? It is the little things that make you memorable. Sure, you can provide extra marketing memorabilia or thank-you gifts, but connecting with people must always be your first priority.

Speakers have found that getting decision-makers out of their normal business environment works best for building relationships for ongoing business. This can include something as simple as a breakfast or lunch meeting where you can talk about family or personal interests or hobbies. This finding of mutual interests can be a true bonding experience. But just remember that you are not being paid to speak at the moment; be a good *listener!*

Over the years, I have participated in many client-sponsored golf outings. In this kind of setting, we seldom talked business. We discussed everything else, or so it seemed. If golf is not your game, you could suggest using your concert or opera or baseball game tickets. In these kinds of settings, never forget that your personal traits are on display and are fair game for your client to judge. If you cheat at golf, don't be surprised if you don't get more business. If you treat the usher at the opera badly, don't be surprised if your client begins to treat *you* badly.

It is always a good idea to remember what those you serve care about, and comment on it in appropriate ways at appropriate times. I know some corporate CEOs who have wanted to do more business with me because I sent a condolence card when a father or mother died, or because I told them I would pray for his family when I learned that they were facing some difficulties.

Success Shortcuts

For 25 years I have believed in and talked about what some experts have labeled The Law of Attraction, which says that if you expect great relationships (and act accordingly with love and respect) you will attract what you expect.

There may be nothing new under the sun about building great relationships, but I still like what Dale Carnegie wrote in the classic book, *How to Win Friends and Influence People*. At the heart of that thinking is the Golden Rule, "Treat others the way you would want to be treated." Simple!

Using Your Contacts

Years ago, before I entered the world of professional speaking, I won some quarterly awards from one employer. I can see one of the cups in my executive office now—it is *The Bird Dog Award*, showing a picture of a dog with his nose to the ground, sniffing for the game bird. I was sniffing out the prospects and bringing home, so to speak, the big game. This is exactly what you need to do to bring in new and ongoing or repeat customers.

So where are you going to find these long-term customer relationships? Use the relationships you already have! You may have hundreds, even thousands, of business contacts. Be humble and ask those contacts for help. Keep in mind that no matter how many bookings you need to pay your mortgage, you want to come across as professional and upbeat (as opposed to down on your luck and desperate). Send an e-mail to your contact list detailing your area of expertise and your speaking services. Add a link to your website and ask contacts to keep you in mind or to forward the e-mail to prospective clients who might need you. You might want to categorize or customize your contacts by prospect or industry type and send specialized material to each group.

Success Shortcuts

Many speakers who have sustained themselves in the speaking business long term have become experts in one industry at a time. In other industries or niches, the speaker is unknown, but in his or her "home niche," the goal is be the world's number-one guru.

Once you get some feedback from your first-line contacts, make sure to follow up on the information they've given you! Don't be shy—remember that this business depends on you selling yourself. To do that, you have to have a long list of clients to sell yourself to (which is why you've asked for help in the first place). If the new prospects turn you down, that doesn't mean you never contact them again. (That's no way to sell yourself!) Call them back at a later date and offer your services again … and again … and again.

Joining a group like The National Speakers Association (NSA) is another way to establish and use your contacts. The NSA was established in the early 1970s in an effort to build the professional speaking business and to get speakers networking with each other. The result is a group where information sharing and referrals are the norm. (You can accomplish similar objectives by joining a group like Professional Speakers Bureau International, as this bureau acts like an association for speakers, in addition to booking speakers.)

Now take another look at your list of contacts. Is there anyone there who might be able to help you in another way? Do you have a friend who's a graphic designer, for example, or who's a whiz with website design? Is there anyone on the list who can help you to find a trustworthy personal assistant? Are there community leaders on the list who might need a speaker for a rally or other event? Is your rabbi or minister on your list? Might he or she be interested in your services at a reduced rate (or can this person of influence offer referrals)? Are any of your friends writers who can help you get published?

Remember: the point of "using" your contacts is to expose you to new, repeat, or long-term clients, and you may end up with a lot of new prospects and offers. An easy method for weeding through the good and the bad is discussed in the following section.

Accepting and Rejecting Clients

One of the most difficult things speakers, or for that matter anyone, will have to do is to reject certain clients. Of course, when you don't have much business, you want to accept almost any client you can find. But your hunger and neediness can backfire on you if you are not careful. Obviously if a prospect needs a speaker in a topic area that is totally new to you, and at the same time you can hardly make your monthly home or auto payments, you are extremely tempted to say, "Yes, I can do that!"

I know speakers who have been in this position and then completed some research in the topic area, and pulled it off successfully because they were excellent presenters and took the time to prepare. On the other hand, other speakers have done this and nearly got booed off the platform and may have never quite recovered from the devastation of that experience.

The best policy for rejecting clients spins from the policy of determining who your best clients are. Envision a bull's-eye target with some rings around it. The bull's-eye (client A in the following figure) is your ideal client.

Success Shortcuts

Have *written* criteria for who your ideal clients are or might be, and what their needs might be. When you locate these clients, you'll be very likely to recognize the good fit between you and them, because you've put time and effort into matching your skills to prospects.

- ◆ A clients: They can hire you not just once but many times, and there may be many more in the audience who can hire you; A clients can all pay your realistic requested fees. These clients are in your comfort zone. They do not require new topic research. They allow you to sell your books in the back of the room after your speech or seminar if you ask.

- ◆ B clients: They aren't perfect, but they're still a good-enough fit for your skills, and they can hire you at least once at your regular fee; you may find people in the audience who can pay your regular fee. B clients may require more preparation than an A, so in reality you may earn less.

- ◆ C clients: They may not have many client prospects in the audience; it might be all employees for the same organization. You may be able to create ongoing business with C clients, but the fee is so low that it's not all that appealing.

- ◆ D clients: They are worth considering only when the others are not yet ready to buy you. D clients give you a hard time about your fee; they do not appreciate your expertise enough; you have to continually prove that you are an expert who can really benefit them.

Another reason to avoid D clients is that they're a poor fit, usually: you'll end up spending an inordinate amount of time researching and preparing your presentation for fairly lousy pay. And while you're suffering through all of this, you won't be closing deals with A, B, or even C clients.

You get the idea! If you can't hit the board and come up with a couple of winners, guess what? You would be better off getting a full-time job and using your skills now in-house with an employer who appreciates you properly.

Partnering Policies

There's an old saying, "Behind every successful man is a terrific woman." While times have changed and it's now just as likely for a man to be supportive of his successful wife, the point of this adage is that partnerships are often important to success. We've been talking a lot about finding and pleasing clients in this chapter. Now let's discuss actually working with clients.

Too Much of a Good Thing?

Perhaps the greatest compliment of all is when a client wants to keep you on retainer—in essence, they want to make you an employee (an employee who will have a lot of freedom as an independent contractor). In this relationship, you'll work side by side with the client, determining and anticipating their needs. They'll pay you a considerable sum in return for your attention and loyalty. And while this seems to be a great setup on the surface, think carefully before jumping into a contract situation. The reason you entered the world of professional speaking, most likely, was to share your gifts—not to find another employer or a client to put inordinate demands on you.

Now if you do accept a retainer, don't feel as though you're abandoning your dream to become a famous full-time speaker. It may very well be that this retainer creates a relationship in which you'll best be able to serve and help others! So go ahead and do so if all seems right, but get a written agreement with a severance clause that includes enough money for time to get your independent speaking career up and running, just in case things don't work out with the company. And make sure your client knows you are continuing to speak for pay even if they have so many needs that they pay you for 40 hours a week. The client will want your loyalty to be first with them, but you have a right to pursue your own goals in addition to the company's goals.

Always keep that client's loyalty-mindset in mind. If your client gets the feeling that you might take what you are learning and help out their competitors (either directly or indirectly), you'll be out the door, and in truth, this might be the very reason why client decision-makers may resist hiring you on retainer. So as any great salesperson knows to do, anticipate the possible objection. Write a clause into your retainer agreements that you will not work for competitors for one full year after you stop working for your great client. In doing this, you further demonstrate your commitment to your client's success.

When and How to Fire Clients

Not long ago I had to fire a couple of clients, and I admit clients have fired me (so to speak), or more accurately, my company. It's not pleasant, but this is business, and it happens. Because I've advised you to ask clients how you can best serve them, it may seem as though firing any client—for any reason—is unacceptable. Think of dropping a client as self-preservation: it's one thing to serve them; it's another to sacrifice your career (or worse) for them.

So … when do you fire a client?

◆ When nothing you do seems to please them

◆ When you are consistently not being paid on time

◆ When the client is headed for bankruptcy

How do you fire a client? Very nicely. Although it may seem like you are burning a bridge, it's possible to leave part of that bridge standing. People and situations change, after all, and down the road you may come together with this client again, under different circumstances. For example, if you can't work well with a client because one of the decision-makers is impossible to get along with … he or she may leave the company in a year or two. If all other factors in your relationship with this client were amicable, then you may be able to completely rebuild that proverbial bridge.

Drop a client in writing, but use an excuse that does not offend anyone! Something like, "Due to other client demands, we are unable to give you the quality and quantity of time you deserve. Effective at the end of the month, we will no longer be available to serve your company. Attached please find our final invoice; you will see the standard due date. If we can be of assistance between now and the end of the month, please let me know. Thank you."

We have discussed a treasure trove of ideas and guidelines. Don't fire me! Keep reading and applying what you learn, inch by inch, and you will see, your success in speaking is a cinch.

The Least You Need to Know

◆ Going above and beyond the most basic speaker expectations helps you to establish a long-term relationship with clients.

◆ Repeat clients may invite you back year after year.

◆ Ongoing clients may provide you with steady work year around.

◆ Clients come in four categories: A, B, C, and D. A clients are the most desirable; D clients are usually a waste of time and energy.

Chapter 16

Clientele with Capital

In This Chapter

- ◆ Big business, or profitable businesses, have money to spend with speakers
- ◆ Creating a demand for you as a speaker
- ◆ Benefactors and patrons for your success
- ◆ Keeping yourself visible to your best client prospects

There's a lot of money in this country. People and organizations with money to spend or invest are everywhere. To find them, you need only be looking for them.

In America, we have a tendency to think of success only in terms of money and possessions accumulated. Who has the biggest net worth at the end of life or the most toys during life? Is that the only kind of way to measure success? I think not!

However, if you are an aspiring speaker wanting to locate people who work in big-budget organizations, you may need to study executive types (in other words, the organization decision-makers) so that you can attract them to you. And never underestimate the power of surrounding yourself with such people. In big cities, where big corporations are plentiful, you'll have a much better chance of landing a presentation with a Fortune 500 company than if you're waiting in Podunk, USA, for a corporate bigwig to breeze past your home (on his way to a meeting in a big city, mind you).

Big Business: Who'll Hire You, Who Won't

Certainly people or companies with the most capital or profitability are thought to have the biggest budgets for speakers or outsourced professionals. However, whenever *any* organization is at a crossroads in their development, they may be more likely to hire a speaker expert to help guide the company toward more productive days and a brighter future. Companies that are growing and expanding use more speakers than companies that are downsizing. Keep this in mind so can you target the winners and win speaking opportunities.

Some speakers have found they can create opportunities to speak with small- to mid-size organizations that may have never used an outside pro speaker. Every organization has problems begging for solutions. Every organization has people who need to work together better as a team, overcome stress, sell more, manage better, stay motivated, etc., etc., etc. (Some topics are so broad in their application that nearly any organization is a prospect!) Not every company has the budget to hire a speaker, but almost all companies, even the smallest, with 1 to 10 employees, have people who need to go off and learn more so they can earn more. These employees will often go to seminars, and who do they listen to once they're there? You, the professional speaker!

Success Shortcuts

Because the backbone of our society is small business, you need not focus only on big business. However, if your plan is to become, as one example, a $5,000-per-booking speaker (or higher), your market is big business or big organizations.

Big business speakers like Pat Williams, the author of several books and full-time VP General Manager of the Orlando Magic NBA organization, asks for and receives $10,000 or more per speaking engagement. So who can and does hire a Pat Williams type of personality? Obviously some company raking in big bucks. Public corporations with stockholders and a board of directors have nosey people like auditors scrutinizing what they are doing and why they are doing it. These companies may need to justify the expenditure of big sums of money spent on speakers. If you can prove how your programs or presentations have a positive impact on increased profitability, you will be well received by the decision-maker who is concerned about the quarterly profit report! And when these organizations are losing *millions* of dollars, they'll think very little of paying you several thousand to stem the bleeding.

Private, but also for-profit, corporations are most receptive to speakers who can demonstrate how and why their message is a great investment. Think about it this way: if I have 250 employees in my for-profit private company (not truly a big entity) and I as the sole owner had a gross profit of $250,000 last year (or $1,000 per employee), one of my goals is to increase that to $2,000 per employee. I must increase sales in the

Success Shortcuts

I purposefully use the word "personality" to describe Pat Williams because clients look for and hire speakers who not only offer solutions, but do so in an entertaining and memorable way.

process. I am wondering, "How can you help me with these things?" You must learn to think like the top decision-maker in the organizations you are targeting if you are going to win business from those organizations.

If I am the CEO of a nonprofit hospital system with 3,000 employees, I have many departments and many managers, all of whom need to be motivated to work together as a team, to stay focused on our goals to deliver the best medical services possible while also fulfilling our published mission and vision statements. I am also accountable to a board of directors, some of whom are wealthy doctors, some of whom are community leaders, and all of whom want balanced books, great publicity, fully educated and motivated employees, and a growing enterprise.

I could give you a dozen more examples, but you get the idea. The ultimate decision-maker is the top executive in every organization. The closer you get in the decision-making chain to that person, the greater the likelihood you will be paid more; you are dealing with someone who cares a great deal about the success of the organization and will be genuinely interested in your return-on-investment proposition, because his career may be on the line (unlike, say, the receptionist, who has relatively little to lose or gain if the company succeeds or fails—her head won't roll if profits are down, and if worse comes to worst, she can probably find a comparable job elsewhere without much difficulty).

Creating a Demand

As I did research for this book, as well as reflect on more than 30 years of experience in professional speaking, I have found many instances where speakers created a need for their speaking services. A few examples?

Many times a speaker shares so many ideas and so much enthusiasm and energy during a presentation that audience members think to themselves something like, "Wow! The people I work with *really* need to hear this message!" So through the speech itself, more opportunities are created. (These new bookings are called spin-offs, something we talked about in Chapter 9.)

Taking a Risk

Speakers write books and create a demand for their services. They also write articles presenting solutions to problems. These are all great ways to get others to take notice of you and your ideas and say to themselves, "Gee, I have to hear more of what this person has to say!" Speakers join associations of all types so that they can network (inform people about their services) and create interest. Speakers will also showcase themselves in all kinds of venues, sometimes by giving free presentations. A buzz is created, people take notice, and the speaker is booked by a meeting planner. Here's another example of creating a demand: many speakers teach, either full-time or part-time, often for adult learners (say, MBA students). They form trust and relationships inside the classroom that carry over into the real world.

If you cannot learn how to create demand for yourself, you may never make it into full-time speaking. Recently I met a headmaster of an all-boys high school. This man was obviously a very intelligent, dynamic, and caring person. I could easily see him as a speaker addressing teachers and students, and eventually all kinds of business people. He also had a strong athletic background (a theme that's often useful in motivational programs), but his dream to become a professional speaker may never come to pass. Why? He is not a risk-taker.

As a speaker, you must take risks, and in doing so, you set yourself up to help others take risks. You can't sit around and wait for a demand for your presentations to just happen; *you* have to create a demand! Of nine speakers I interviewed while staying in a city many miles from my home base, this headmaster was the only one who didn't have a business card or anything that promoted himself as a speaker ... no brochure, nothing that could create interest. And bear in mind that some of the other speakers were only part-timers, but they had learned the lesson already: sell yourself! Make people want to hire you! It won't happen any other way!

Your Expertise Is Needed!

In this last example, the man was very talented—he was dripping with expertise—but he did nothing to help create a need for himself as a speaker. It's such a shame, because his expertise is needed in the broader world far more than he realizes.

Likewise, your expertise is probably in need than you now know. Remove your blinders and get some peripheral vision—look around at all the possibilities. Consider that some of the knowledge you take for granted, believing that "everyone knows this," may not be so simple at all. Sometimes when things make perfect sense to us, we can't even imagine how other people couldn't understand. So for example, let's take a CEO who spends his days looking at spreadsheets and talking about profit margins. He's a very smart man, obviously, and you might not think that you have anything to offer to his kind. But this man is stressed beyond belief and simply doesn't know how to relax. If you're a holistic healer of some sort, this man needs *your* expertise!

Years ago I heard a speaker say, "Find out what your fastball is, and then get yourself in a position where you are pitching your fastball(s) as often as possible each day." This indeed is a master key to success in all human endeavors! How can you do this so that you are a speaker in demand?

> **Words to the Wise**
>
> Career experts often tell speakers to do an assessment of all their skills. There are assessment tools (like the Myers-Briggs Inventory) available to help you take a complete inventory of your skills, interests, temperament, weaknesses, and so on. Do all you can to know yourself, even if it hurts a little to acknowledge your shortcomings.

Marketing Yourself Directly

In Chapter 12, I gave you lots of ideas for marketing yourself. Now read this: you must market yourself *directly* to the best prospects for your expertise! This seems like common sense, but this involves a two-step process: knowing your area of expertise and knowing who needs it. If you were a rocket scientist looking for a career position, you would not market yourself to restaurant operators; you would find all the rocket manufacturers or those who may need to launch rockets, and send your resumé to them only. (And if you really want to get the job, you best not sit on your duff and wait for the phone to ring. Follow up with anyone you send your resumé to.) It is not much different in marketing yourself as a speaker. You pick your best target markets for your presentations and follow up repeatedly until some good things happen. Let me give you an easy but powerful example.

One time our company booked a speaker, Janet Sue Rush, to speak to the Ohio Funeral Directors Association (OFDA). She did a great job, so we booked her again to the same group, but this time for a leaders' retreat out of state. After that program, the meeting planner was very thankful for the great job Janet Sue had done, and we got a letter of reference from OFDA. Then we put together 49 brochures about

Janet Sue along with a cover letter (49 copies with custom salutations) and sent them (along with 49 copies of the reference letter) to the 49 other state funeral directors' associations in the United States, introducing Janet Sue as a speaker. She was marketed very directly to this niche in a very effective way.

Big Benefactors

Recently my wife and I went to a one-woman play, which we enjoyed immensely. Because we paid $40 for each ticket, you would not call us big benefactors of the show, but there were some deep-pocketed folks in the audience who not only paid a higher price for their seats, but who could also bring this woman into higher-paying venues.

def•i•ni•tion

A **patron** is someone who's willing to support a speaker professionally and/or back him or her financially.

Speakers can also benefit from having clients with connections—both financial and business. *Patrons* with deep pockets and great contacts are desirable for politicians, artists, nonprofits … why not for you, too?

Your best patrons can become your biggest benefactors. A great patron need not be a client, but ideally these people can lead you to paying clients. Your best patrons may believe in you so much that they help fund your business expansion.

Your first best patrons may be your family. I have known many speakers who would not have made it to full-time speaking and sustained themselves had they not had a patron spouse who stood behind them, often with a checkbook, to help make the dream a reality. (Your significant other need not have deep pockets, but any sort of financial support helps during the start-up phase of professional speaking.)

Words to the Wise

Some members of an advisory board or board of directors may be looking for an immediate return on their investment; others may be in it for the long haul. Make sure you know the needs of these folks before entering into an agreement with them!

Speakers can also sell shares in their business in an informal way. Why not?! Consider creating a board of directors or an advisory board. What would happen if you had 5 to 10 board members who each invested $10,000 to $40,000 in your business success? What would you have to give them in return? Maybe just meeting with you once a month for the next 12 months is enough, or maybe they want a 10 percent ROI (return on investment). Either way, you can make this happen!

Where to Find Them

Here is an idea about how to find big benefactors or patrons: get involved in charity work. At one time I was on the board of directors for United Way of Central Ohio. As the campaign coordinator trainer that particular year, I met some deep-pocketed CEOs of various organizations. The other board members also saw me in action, and some of them could have easily become my life-long patrons had I merely approached them in the right ways. However, I was too naïve and too busy at the time to convert these folks to my cause.

People love to donate time and money to good causes, and you could be one of those causes—you just need to develop an idea that other people can support. Get your cause down to a 25-word *elevator speech* that you can tell people about anywhere and everywhere you go. This mini-message could be a spin-off of your mission or vision statement, but it is stated in a way that makes people want to support *you*.

You can find big benefactors or potential patrons anywhere and everywhere. Be on your toes at all times and be unique—this is the best way to get people to notice you!

def•i•ni•tion

An **elevator speech** is no more than 25 words; it captures who you are and what you offer, and it motivates someone to want to learn more or to support you.

Etiquette of the Patron/Speaker Relationship

You must admit you want to be needed and to feel important, recognized, and appreciated, right? Speakers have these needs, often in greater abundance than the average person, but to bring these needs to fruition you need to make others feel important! To that end, the best way to win someone over so that she becomes your ongoing patron is to ask that person to help you reach a worthwhile and worthy goal. Get that person to want to do you a favor.

The more influential or more prosperous a person, or the higher a person is on the corporate ladder or in the community, the greater need this VIP has for recognition and appreciation. These VIPs never need your criticism; rather, they will always respond to your admiration for them.

If you are so very needy that you cannot affirm and appreciate and make others feel great, you may never create ongoing clients and patrons. Now, consider that this is actually a win-win situation. You make the patrons feel great, and they want to help you. Following is an example of how to approach this relationship.

"Mr. or Ms. Big Shot, I so admire you! You do a great job and are so well thought of; just to know you is a privilege. Your organization is blessed to have you in service." Maybe pinpoint something specific about the other person or her work that you admire. Then tell her ...

"My goal is enhance your success—may I ask you a favor? My mission is to make a lasting difference through my messages, a true impact that helps organizations and people reach their full potential. For me to reach my goal to be the best speaker possible in my areas of expertise, I need your help. Any ideas from you on how I can improve will always be welcome, and if you can refer me to others who may need my service, I will be forever in your debt. A referral from someone so great as you would go a long way in helping me with my mission to making a lasting difference with others. Will you help me?"

With this kind of dialogue, your potential patron will almost always say, "Sure, how can I help you?" or "I will be glad to recommend you." Now if they say something to the effect of, "What's in it for me by helping you?" then you either have not buttered the patron up enough or you're dealing with a cynical or self-absorbed person who won't be moved to assist you. It's best to write this person off right away.

Words to the Wise

Some speakers and bureaus do pay finders or referral fees to people who refer business their way. In most cases, this is perfectly ethical and okay to do. After all, that is a small fee to pay for a hot referral from a patron.

Again, great patrons need not be your current or past clients. They may simply act as a headhunter of sorts, introducing you to important prospects and helping you to make other business contacts.

Clients with Powerful Payday Potential

What has been your best and biggest payday ever? Okay, now double or triple that number—you can achieve *these* types of paydays! But it will not happen if you do not think it can and will. As the great philosopher and business success Mary Kay Ash (founder of Mary Kay cosmetics) used to say, "If you think you can, you can, and if you think you can't, you are exactly right also."

Surprisingly, the Fortune 500–type organizations are not always the best speaker patrons. Industries like pharmaceutical companies, for example, will usually pay big bucks for speakers, but restaurant industries usually will not. Through our speakers' bureau, some of the biggest-paying patrons have been new companies I hadn't yet heard of!

Here are some other examples based on averages and a historical perspective of payouts.

These have big payday potentials for speakers:

- Profitable high-tech companies
- Financial services industry
- Federal government (biggest agency meetings)
- National associations
- Large manufacturers
- Professionals, like large law firms
- Large universities and large school-district teacher training
- Fortune 500 for an annual leadership conference

These have low payday potential for speakers:

- Unprofitable companies of any type
- State or local government agencies (low budgets, bidding)
- Local or state associations
- Wholesalers selling to retailers
- Hospitality industry
- Small colleges and primary and secondary school assemblies
- Small companies with 70 to 100 employees or less

By big payday potentials I am thinking that, on average, the client can pay $5,000 (and sometimes much more) for expert speakers for a keynote. By low payday potential, I am thinking that the client pays far less than $5,000 for a keynote speaker, if they even use outside speakers.

Identify the best big payday/patron organizations and concentrate most of your marketing efforts on them. Realize that establishing one beneficial patron relationship allows for the potential for cross-marketing within the same industry. You give a successful seminar or speech to one profitable small- to mid-size company, and a similar company may want to hire you based on your reputation!

Keeping in Touch with Big Clients

Any client that has the potential to pay your top fee more than once should be considered a big client/benefactor. These clients have the potential to invest so much money for your services that you would be smart to follow up with some of their team members every day or even every week. The goal is to become a speaker on retainer with these folks so that your earnings are steady and substantial.

One of the most unfortunate things for many speakers is that they never figure out how to generate more business from the same big clients. Of course, the principles of quality customer service say that you should follow up with all clients, but you want to look for unique and memorable ways to keep in touch with your best clients. Some ideas include:

- Newsletters
- Legitimate phone calls, voicemails, and e-mails (not calls just to say "hello")
- Sending material by regular mail (more and more of a rarity these days, and therefore, more unique)
- Face-to-face meetings over lunch or dinner
- Video conferencing with clients who are out of town

In short, strive to be highly visible to your best potential clients, especially those with deep pockets and great contacts. Let them know that you are available to serve them and to take care of their needs, no matter what the day or hour. This is all part of building your business and ensuring your ongoing success!

The Least You Need to Know

- Create and focus on goals that are personally important while gradually upgrading your clients.
- Financial success comes from clients who can pay your regular fees.
- Patrons may be individual folks or businesses who are great clients or those who refer you to clients.
- Some of the best-paying clients for speakers are mid-size profitable companies, or at least growth-oriented organizations with good funding.
- Keeping in touch with big clients reminds them that you are ready, willing, and able to serve their needs, time and time again, while you cultivate long-term relationships.

Chapter 17

What You Can *Really* Charge

In This Chapter

- ◆ How clients compare you to other speakers
- ◆ Developing (and adjusting) reasonable fees
- ◆ When and how to discount fees
- ◆ For-profit or nonprofit? Which is more profitable for you?

As the owner of an international speakers' bureau, an association of terrific speakers, the one question I receive possibly more than any other questions is, "What fee can I really charge?" Speakers rightfully do not want to leave money on the table that could have been theirs by expecting and asking for too little. Conversely, asking for too much could backfire and result in your losing speaking engagements.

You must justify your asking fee first in your own mind and heart. If your self-esteem and self-image scream out that you are a $5,000 speaker, then it is okay to start at that fee level, or even higher, but keep in mind that most speakers do not. Fees are based mostly on your perceived value and your comparable value, but there are a couple of other things that can influence your asking price, too. I'll cover each of these factors in this chapter.

Your Perceived Value

You may have heard it said, "Perception is reality." I must admit that when someone drives up in a high-end Mercedes, my tendency is to think that this speaker is worth more money than the person driving the beat-up Honda Civic. That being said, most people considering you as a speaker will not know what kind of car you are driving. They can (and will) judge the quality of who you are by the quality of your business card or other marketing materials you send to them, or the quality of your appearance and personality when you meet.

Consider these scenarios:

- How is a person with a nearly totally clean desktop perceived compared to someone with a messy desk and office environment?

- How is someone who is 50 or more pounds overweight perceived compared to someone who is slim, when considering a person for a leadership position, all other things being equal?

- How is someone who is very well dressed in executive garb perceived by decision-makers when compared to someone with a sporty type of outfit?

- How is someone who is giving a seminar at a Hyatt or Ritz Carlton or full-service Marriott perceived, compared to someone giving a seminar at a Holiday Inn?

- How is a man perceived compared to a woman (or vice versa) when the meeting planner is looking for the perfect speaker for his annual convention with all men as attendees?

- How is a woman in a flowery dress perceived compared to a woman in a dark navy business suit when deciding on who is best for an annual women's leaders' conference?

As consumers, we all tend to associate certain things with value and higher prices. So before you go any further, ask yourself if you're positioning yourself as a high-end speaker, a mid-range speaker, or a bargain speaker. Base your answer on the quality of your appearance, the quality of your marketing materials, and the quality of your prospective clients.

Experience Affects Perception

If you have worked in a billion-dollar corporation before entering the world of professional speaking, your view or perception of the possibilities for your professional speaking career would be different than that of an aspiring speaker who, for example, has worked in the military or a state or federal government agency for the past 20 or more years. Or maybe you have a background in academia or in small business or have worked in a hospital setting for years. Your perception of both yourself and your markets will, initially at least, determine how you think about and set your fees.

Success Shortcuts

Ask yourself, "What are my high-end and low-end fees?" Most of your business for paid speaking will probably be on the continuum somewhere between these two extremes.

You can establish any fee you want for your services; however, those fees must be based not only on your perceived value but also on the reality of what your markets are paying. If state or local government agencies will seldom pay more than $2,500 for a speaker, you may have to be satisfied with that if you intend to work with these agencies. On the other hand, if you are going after multi-billion-dollar Fortune 500 companies, a fee of $10,000 may be comparatively easy to justify.

Realistic speakers realize it is better to get $1,000 or $2,000 from a client who's offering it than to hold out for a $10,000 client. It is one thing to garner $10,000 one time as a speaker, but is there enough of a market for your message to garner that again and again and again for years to come? Most speakers must build their business at lower fees where more clients are available, by establishing a *fee basis* and *base fee*.

When you start out in this business, the basis for your fee is based more on what your clients or prospective clients can and will pay than on what you can justify as a result of your total quality. You have established the right base fee if it is received (and paid) by clients consistently without much hesitation. If you establish a base fee that always requires you to adjust your fee downward, then either your fee is too high or the market niche you are serving needs to be changed or upgraded, if you want to earn more.

def•i•ni•tion

A **fee basis** reflects what your clients are willing to pay. A **base fee** is that minimum that you are willing to accept.

Realized Value

What do we mean by *realized value* for a professional speaker? It's the fee that a speaker expects and can reasonably earn from a client. Now, just because a speaker expects a fee doesn't mean she'll necessarily get that fee. If a speaker encounters a prospective client who has never in their history paid a speaker more than X, and the speaker wants X + $2,000, then obviously the speaker has a serious problem. Either her expectations are too high or she's barking up the wrong tree—or both.

def•i•ni•tion

Realized value is the fee a speaker expects and can reasonably earn from a client.

Now if your asking price isn't working out, there are certain ways to encourage clients to pay a bit more. Writing a book or having some other noteworthy accomplishment will increase your perceived value among clients and can help justify your realized value. Reference letters and testimonials (which you'll read about in Chapter 19) can also help to convince a client that you're worth more than they initially thought.

Realized value can be a burden for some speakers who come to think that anything less than their expected fee is not worth their time. A speaker may want $5,000 for a speech and be worth every penny of it, but if a client can "only" offer $1,000 (this is still a lot of money, let us not forget), then why not be satisfied with that, especially if this is a relationship with potential? (In other words, a situation where you may be able to earn your realized fee, and then some, down the road.)

Comparative Analysis

Recently, we had a phone call from an employee in a city in California who was considering purchasing a high-quality speaker to do a custom mini-seminar for her company's stressed-out employees. The employee inquirer said by phone, "Because we are a government agency, we have to have three proposals before we contract to hire the speaker we are considering now. Can you provide at least two more optional speakers and two more proposals?"

This agency had already made up their minds about the speaker they would hire, but they needed to have evidence that they had shopped around. I asked this California inquirer the sometimes all-important question, "What is your budget for the speaker?" She said, "$5,000 to $10,000." We offered her three speakers, one whose regular fee was $5,000, another at $7,500, and another at $10,000. Each had materials and expertise that helped justify, at least to some extent, the difference in their fees.

If she had not already known the first speaker, she would have been basing her decision purely on her perceptions, the realized (or expected) value that each speaker could deliver, and the relevant references and proven skills of the speakers before her. *This* is how clients compare and contrast you to other speakers. Fee is certainly an issue (everyone likes to stick to their budget, after all), but it's not always the *main* issue. If the budget has some wiggle room, a client would most likely choose a higher-priced speaker who has glowing reviews and years of experience over the less-expensive speaker who doesn't have the best reputation. So strive to be and do your best, and present yourself as the best at all times, and the money will follow.

Remember: fees are neither high nor low; they are able to be justified or not justified to your prospective buyer. That's the key. You cannot expect some organization that has never paid more than $50 for a speaker to pay you $1,000, can you? After all, they are comparing you to other speakers from the past and the payment those speakers accepted. Other clients suffer from faulty comparisons, believing that because their best employees earn $30 an hour, it's outrageous to pay you to $1,000 for a one-hour speech. In this last example, they are not comparing apples to apples at all; they are comparing you, the juicy plump apple, to one grape.

Standard Fees

Many speakers do have so-called standard fees, like a retail price, for their speeches, for half-day or full-day workshops, and for seminars for the for-profit corporations. How is this structured? A common way to price yourself is to have a fee for the local market, another higher fee for outside your local market (due to the extra time needed), and yet a third fee if you must travel cross-country or internationally.

For example, if you are a speaker in the first five years of your career and you were to give a presentation in your hometown of Chicago, you might ask for $2,000, depending on your topic and client. If you were to take that presentation to Los Angeles, you would charge $4,000. And if you were to pack up and move the presentation to Smalltown, USA, or do this for a nonprofit entity—both within driving distance of your home—you might expect to earn $1,000, again depending on who the client might be.

You can always turn down engagements if the fee is too low (or for any other reason). Let's say your small-town booking for $1,000 is a three-hour drive from your home and will take place three months from now. A lot can happen in three months—and if there's any chance you could book that same date at a higher fee, then the smart thing would be to say, "Thanks, but no thanks."

It's common for speakers to have a different fee for nonprofit organizations, whether they are corporations, associations, or other kinds of entities. These nonprofit fees may be as much as 50 percent less than the for-profit fees, and they are structured based on the travel distance. So to be specific, the for-profit fee might be $5,000, and the nonprofit then would be $2,500, depending on the organization in question. (We'll talk about nonprofits in more detail at the end of this chapter.)

Because more and more meeting planners realize that a speaker's fee might be higher if they must travel by plane and stay overnight before an event, they of course first look for local speakers. This is where it is important to compare and contrast your fees with others in your local market place. Be competitive in your pricing, but don't try to undercut everyone else just to get an engagement. That will hurt you, because you simply won't be earning enough to reinvest in your business. I'll talk about discounting your prices (why and when it's appropriate to do so) later in this chapter.

 Words to the Wise

I have known speakers who traveled for seminar companies who were contracted to give the same seminar five days a week in five different cities each week. They earned less than $1,000 a day, made a small commission on back-of-the-room sales, and within a year, were burned out on the speaking business. So be careful about grabbing just any opportunity!

The following figure displays a sample fee schedule. "Miss Teresa-Terrific Speaker" is established, not yet a number one expert, but not a beginner. Remember, this is a sample only; some speakers may be more or less.

Fee Schedule Sample for Miss Teresa-Terrific Speaker	
For-Profit Organizations	**Nonprofit Organizations**
Keynote Speeches	**Keynote Speeches**
30 to 90 minutes: $4,000	30 to 90 minutes: $2,000
If more than 1,000 miles and/or requiring two nights stay, add $500 to each quote above and below.	
Breakout sessions or short seminars up to 90 minutes at any conference same day when giving keynote speech, add $X for each session (usually 10% of keynote fee minimum).	
Seminars/Workshops	**Seminars/Workshops**
1 ½ to 3 hrs: $5,000	1 ½ to 3 hrs: $2,500
Stand-alone programs without a keynote speech. These fees are considered a ½ day program and could include a meal with attendees and customization in advance.	
3 to 7 hrs: $6,500	3 to 7 hrs: $3,250
May include more customization and prior preparation work along with handout materials provided for the client to duplicate or handout materials may be sold as an add-on.	
Multiple Programs	**Multiple Programs**
Two to seven seminars/workshops or trainings booked for the same client on the same booking agreement may receive a **discount** which varies from 10 to 30% per booking depending on whether multiple consecutive dates are contracted or whether significant travel is expected.	
EXCEPTIONS: Exceptions to the above fees can be made when travel of more than 500 miles requires more time or more overnight stays. Also, fees out of the home country of the speaker are marked up further in some cases.	
DISCOUNTS: Discounts are available only for local engagements or additional multiple bookings.	
EXPENSES: 100% of all expenses are reimbursed direct to the speaker within 10 days after the event. An expense statement will be provided. The speaker agrees to minimize expenses. *If you want to fly first-class, on the other hand, you would note that here.	

This is a sample of one speaker's fee schedule for both for-profits and nonprofits.

Fees for Speeches, Seminars, Workshops

Fees for speeches can vary from those of seminars and workshops. Because speeches take less time to deliver, this isn't to suggest that the fee is less than for a half-day or full-day seminar. Veteran speakers will confirm that the preparation and on-site time as well as travel time can be more, not less, when delivering a keynote speech compared to a longer seminar or just a breakout session at a conference.

The keynote speaker is the star of the show and is paid accordingly! It does not mean this speaker is more important or really has more relevant information for that audience, but it does mean that the keynote speaker has created some kind of justification (perhaps he's a published author or a celebrity) or buzz to justify the fee. As a matter of fact, at many conferences when the keynote speaker is paid, let's say, $5,000, the person giving a longer breakout session or maybe two breakout sessions is paid $250 for each breakout seminar.

Fees for workshops are sometimes lower than those for seminars. This goes back to perceived value. People often think a speaker who gives keynotes and seminars may be more skilled and experienced than a workshop leader. Look around you and you might find this belief confirmed, at least in some ways. Seminars typically have more bells and whistles associated with them than workshops, more extras to justify a higher fee.

Sometimes speakers do a series of in-house seminars for a client. Both CE-credit seminars and workshops often pay far less than other seminars. But there is good news: if you organize, host, and promote your own seminars or workshops, you can charge whatever the market is willing to pay. You won't get rich on your first open public seminar, but if you persevere and figure out all the angles on how to market yourself and your services, you may find this is the best way for you to make the most money.

Here are two high-end examples: my wife and I have attended a number of seminars together in a number of settings over the past 17 years. One time we attended a 40-hour, one-week seminar/workshop given by Nick Koon, a real estate investor and broker. We learned a great deal, sure, about how to "buy real estate with little or no money down" as investment properties. Nick charged each attendee about $1,000 to attend, and this included all materials.

Another time, my wonderful wife and I were giving one of my company-sponsored showcases in Dallas, so we decided to go to the Hill Country of South Texas outside of San Antonio and attend the three-day *Successful Life Seminar* given by Ed Foreman, a former U.S. congressman. We were 2 of 43 people in the seminar at $1,500 per person. (Most of the other attendees were management employees of big corporations with their employer footing the costs.) Figure the gross on that (43 × $1,500 – expenses = gross profit)!

In terms of producing revenue, the extreme low end of the seminar/workshop business includes speaking in places like churches and synagogues, or for nonprofit groups like political organizations. You're doing pretty well if you get $25 to $50 and the standard free chicken luncheon or dinner. Some of these people from these nonprofits will hit you up for complimentary presentations; this is when it's good to know how to say, "Sorry; can't do it." You have a right and a need to get a return on investment for your time and effort. And while it's certainly within the norm to donate some of your time, you do have bills to pay.

Some speakers look at using their gift of communication as a stewardship and give up to 10 percent of their working hours to charitable organizations. Many speakers have also found future clients in the audience while giving free, short seminars or workshops. This should obviously not be your main goal during an otherwise charitable act, but sometimes everything just comes together and everyone winds up profiting!

Consulting and Coaching Fees

Some consultants and coaches earn $100 or even several hundred dollars per hour, depending on the client. Many consultants do not charge by the hour; instead they are on retainer with a client. So some consultants might have a $1,000-a-month or even a $10,000-a-month retainer with four clients simultaneously and still spend most nights at home in their own bed.

This type of work has a lot of perks: not only are you under contract to the client (ensuring a certain amount of ongoing pay), but if you are efficient, you won't be locked into a 40-hour workweek with the client. I worked for one client as a consultant for 50 percent of my workday hours for nine months while writing books 20 percent of my time, and devoting the other 30 percent to my professional speaking business and speaking goals.

Now it can take some work to build these high-paying relationships. One Friday morning several years ago, I dropped my daughter Erin off at her school and then began driving, and driving, and driving. Before the day was over I had driven 1,100 miles. My destination was Orange County, then San Diego County, California. Because I left from Columbus, Ohio, I was not yet even halfway to my destination for a consulting assignment.

Why was I driving instead of flying? I knew that the client didn't have the money for an airline ticket, but I also knew it was the right thing for me to go and work with them anyway. Sometimes to create and then serve clients, you have to make unusual or "going the extra mile" types of sacrifices. This client saw my level of commitment

Success Shortcuts

Please consider that even if you are in your auto driving 2,500 miles, you can be on the phone many of those hours speaking to clients and prospective clients; and sometimes those hours on the phone can be billable. Also you can listen to books and various learning programs on tape while in your auto—thus you have a classroom on wheels.

to their success, and eventually they ended up giving me the most lucrative year of my life!

It is amazing what is possible and what some consultants are able to pull off. I actually know one consultant who works only with CEOs in major Fortune 1000 companies who has yearly retainers of $200,000 a year—and he has 10 such retainers! He still has time for his family, his community, and golf, and his speaking (part time) at $10,000-plus per speech. As a matter of fact, a speaking fee of $10,000 is insignificant to him at this point! I assure you he did not start out this way, but this is well within the realm of possibility for seasoned, professional consultants.

Pricing Books, Tapes, and Other Take-Home Items

Pricing items like books, tapes, and other take-home items sold at speeches, seminars, training programs, and so on can be as easy as understanding wholesale and retail. But to be as wise as possible, please do some research in the following ways:

Sometimes a $20 book can cost a speaker $4, and sometimes $10—be careful. If you self-publish, you can make much more money than from most large national publishers, but of course there may be exceptions. Your books and other items must be fairly and competitively priced. At some events, people think nothing of investing $20 for an autographed book; at other events, they may pay $100 or much more if the speaker is super-meaningful and has specific materials they feel they must have to compete or reach their goals. At still other venues, you are doing great if you can get 20 percent of the audience to fork over $10 each for a book.

Bottom line: know your market and what they will pay.

The same holds true for other marketing materials. How much did it cost you to make that motivational DVD, for example, including the cost of the cameraperson, the editing, the production, and so on? In order to come out ahead of the game, you have to aim for a particular profit margin.

What might be reasonable? You do not have a retail store where making 40 to 50 percent gross is the standard. As in the example above, you ideally don't want to pay more than $5 for a book you sell for $20. So your profit margin is about 400 percent, and you'll reinvest much of this profit in your business.

Discounting Fees

As veterans of this business will tell you, fee integrity is an important issue in the speaking profession. And the truth is that most of these same speakers will discount their fees in certain situations, as they help the client realize they are getting "a special one-time offer." The discount may be in lieu of some special consideration and is confidential.

Some speaker experts will tell you that you should never, under any circumstances, discount your fees. I estimate maybe 10 to 20 percent of the veterans in the industry hold to this policy; it is understandable why this no-discount policy can be a good one, for these reasons:

- Once you start discounting, where do you stop?

- Others can find out that you discounted your fee and this could hurt your reputation or create other issues.

- Someone in the audience might want to hire you—or the client may want to hire you again—and they may expect the same lower fee the next time around.

- You could hurt your own self-esteem and your image of yourself if you don't handle the discount with justifications that are valid in your own mind and heart.

On the other hand, the no-discount policy can be a bad policy for these reasons:

- You might believe that "sale items" are cheap and unwanted.

- You may have a jealous attitude that prevents you from ever accepting less pay than what other speakers get.

- Your ego and silly pride might be in your way of allowing for discounting.

- If you need income, some income—even discounted income—is better than nothing at all.

- You may be missing out on creating lifelong clients who will pay you more later on.

So I've given you two sides of the same coin: which side do you agree with? I think there's something to be said for compromise. Even if you firmly believe that discounting is not the best policy or that discounting is the best policy, evaluate each and every case individually and ask yourself whether you're doing yourself more harm than good in the long run.

Retail vs. Wholesale

Before I entered the speaking industry full time, I worked very successfully for two different, very large manufacturing companies where, as a branch sales manager (number one in the United States twice by age 27), I sold products at wholesale prices to retailers. Of course the manufacturer still made a handsome profit even though we had slashed the price of the product by 40 to 50 percent.

Retail prices are often inflated for many products and services to increase profits for those who offer them; the inflated price also allows for discounting. You undoubtedly have been in wholesale stores like Sam's Club where you're supposedly cutting out the middleman in order to get some great buys. We're all programmed to find the best deals out there, so why not let your client think they're getting one when they book you?

Of course, I've already said that price isn't the first deciding factor when clients book speakers; in fact, it isn't always a factor at all. But when all things between you and another speaker are equal, offering the client a lower, one-time "wholesale" rate might be the thing to sway the decision in your favor. Make the client feel as though *you're* aching to serve *them*, and then wow them with your presentation. Chances are, they'll be more than happy to pay your asking price the next time around.

Profit and Nonprofit

Earlier in this chapter, I mentioned that you may need to charge different fees for profit and nonprofit companies. If you don't know whether an organization is for profit or nonprofit, *ask*. Generally speaking, a *nonprofit* organization works to serve the public in some capacity; nonprofits include charities, religious organizations, hospitals, trade organizations, and so on. *For-profit* companies, as the title suggests, are working to make money. Fortune 500 companies, for example, are for-profit organizations.

Even if all of the organizations you work with are nonprofit, *you* can still pull in plenty of profits. *Do not* buy into the idea that all nonprofits have little budgets for speakers just because they tell you that. Some of the highest-paid executives in the world are people who know how to raise money for nonprofit charities! And some of the best-paid speakers work in the same field. Think about it this way: if one speaker

def•i•ni•tion

A **nonprofit** organization's main focus is serving the community, not making money. **For-profit** companies are answerable to stockholders and must make a certain amount of money each year.

can help an organization raise millions of dollars a year, isn't that speaker worth a substantial amount of cash? Even if you're paid $100,000, the organization has still earned a great return on their investment!

Like a speaker in a nonprofit, somehow I expect to earn an additional million dollars just as a result of writing this book because I know I am going to help thousands of people earn thousands more—many millions, collectively, due to this book. And like that speaker, I expect my value to increase: I am worth at least a million dollars more in the next five years than I've earned in the past five years. What about *your* value? Where do you expect it to go?

The Least You Need to Know

- ◆ Clients often base their pay on their perceptions of you; strive to come across as professional and intelligent.

- ◆ Be willing to negotiate a lower fee if the potential for an ongoing relationship with the client exists.

- ◆ Don't ever feel obligated to accept a fee that's unacceptable to you or to work for free for a charitable organization.

- ◆ Working for nonprofit groups can actually be very lucrative.

18

Collecting (and Preventing) Your Debts

In This Chapter

- ◆ The importance of written agreements
- ◆ When to bill your clients
- ◆ Expenses you may incur
- ◆ Don't spend all you earn!

Recently a speaker complained to me that a government agency had taken six months to pay him his fee. Not only did this make him mad, but it distracted him from creating new business and serving his existing clients with adequate preparation.

You know that old saying, "An ounce of prevention is worth a pound of cure." Lots of collection issues can be avoided with preventative methods. In this chapter, you'll read how to present payment options to your clients and how to follow through on getting paid. We'll also cover the issues of reimbursement and reinvesting in your business.

Getting Paid

Written contracts (or as we called them earlier in this book, agreements) are the most important aspect of getting paid on time and as agreed. No matter how well you know someone or how many times you have served a particular organization, remember, this is business, and good business dictates having written agreements, preferably signed by the decision-makers on all sides. Too many misunderstandings can take place with verbal agreements. A short pencil (or pen, or typed e-mail) beats a short memory every time.

Words to the Wise

Even after you receive a payment (whether by check or credit card), the payer has the ability to cancel the check or charge. Checks may take up to a week to clear even though the deposit may show up in your account the day after you deposit it. So be wise; don't spend the money you deposit for at least one week, as you never know what might happen.

Feel free to ask for half of your payment as soon as the agreement is signed. Few organizations will balk at the idea of paying 50 percent in advance; getting a 50 percent payment deposit today for a presentation you will do months from now is a common, nearly standard practice in the speaking profession, both by individual clients and by speakers' bureaus. One reason is because you have weeks (or months) of preparation ahead of you—as soon as that agreement is signed, you're working for the client! Another reason why the 50 percent upon signing is standard is because speakers sell their time. Once a speaker promises a date to a client, she can't sell it to another client; therefore, the speaker usually will not refund the 50 percent payment if the client cancels the booking.

Let me tell you that setting up a merchant account for my business was one of the smartest things I ever did. Not only can we process payments for booking fees, but also for the sale of books, taped learning programs, and other speakers' products or services. We would prefer to be paid by check, because the processing bank or credit card company charges us 2 to 5 percent just to process the charge, but the processing charge is worth the small deduction because we receive our payment very quickly.

"Batching" is the payment process that takes place each night, at about 10 P.M., and all charges of the day are posted to your account.

Some companies have sprung up that help with processing payments like PayPal. Basically, once you register as a recipient of funds with this online organization, your customers can pay you through a secure site, transferring money directly into your account without their needing to issue checks and without the risk of giving you (or others) a credit card. You can Google this company and/or ask your local bank for information and possibly other options.

You probably will never be paid in cash for a speaking engagement, but when you're selling books and products at the back of the room after a presentation, you will often be dealing in cash transactions. It's a good idea to have products priced in such a way that you don't have to make much change, although you should be prepared to do so. If you expect to do a lot of speeches or seminars where you offer products continually in the back of the room, you may want to pick up a cash box or bag (rather than stuff money in your pockets or purse).

> **Success Shortcuts**
>
> Back-of-the-room sales can be a great value-added service offered by a speaker. The objective is to offer your books and other products that will benefit the client and their attendees.

How and When to Bill Clients

To avoid payment issues with clients that drain your energy, test your patience, and take your focus off serving other clients, plan ahead and set up a billing system. Don't be intimidated by this; it's easy to set up a prototype invoice and save it on your computer for repeat usage.

Truthfully, how you invoice clients after they have signed the booking agreement (or you've executed a letter of agreement to which they have agreed) is really not a big deal. Many clients will actually send you the 50 percent deposit without your having to ask for it, if they have signed an agreement; hence, billing some clients may be unnecessary.

On your invoice, it is a good idea to include these items in this order:

♦ Date of invoice.

♦ Client's name: person and name of organization.

♦ Name and subjectly: for example, invoice for Susan Speaker speaking on December 12.

♦ Fee: first list the total fee that will be due; on the next line, list the 50 percent deposit payment that is due upon receipt; then list when the final payment is due.

♦ Expenses: note on the first invoice that expenses will be included in the final invoice, or that a separate invoice for expenses will be provided after the event.

◆ Provide the name of who to make the check payable to and the address where to send payment. (You could mention whether credit cards are acceptable for payment.)

◆ At the bottom of your invoice, list some of your other services and your contact information: phone number, fax number, website, e-mail address, mailing address, and so on.

◆ Thank you. You can never thank people enough—add it to your invoice. "THANK YOU!"

After the invoice for the 50 percent deposit payment, make sure to put the speaking engagement on your calendar, or program your calendar software to remind you to invoice the client about 10 days before the event. Some large organizations (including government agencies) will not process an invoice until the event actually takes place; however, you still can invoice the client a few days or weeks before the event for the balance due, like so:

For balance due for speech on December 12

Total fee: $2,500

               50% paid

Due: $1,250

Terms: Net due day of event, December 12
               [Or within five days after the event]

E-mailing an invoice as an attachment can also be a very effective approach. Your cover note says something friendly, letting the client know how excited you are about being with them in a couple of weeks. Let the client know that you are preparing your presentation, and with this e-mail, ask for any other materials they can send you about the event to help you prepare. End with "Attached, please find an invoice for the balance due for the program. I hope to do such a great job for you that we will work together again and again after this event."

By requesting it in writing in advance, clients will know to prepare the final payment. Many will pay you the day of your program if you simply send them the invoice early. Please do not ask a client to pay you before you speak, or demand they pay you immediately after you speak. Trust them. They *will* pay you.

Expense Reimbursement

You need to get 100 percent reimbursed for your expenses in nearly every speaking situation. If you don't, then perhaps you have an *all-inclusive* fee arrangement, and then you must at least keep your expenses in a file, on a log, or somewhere in an orderly way so that they can be accessed later on if needed. (Heaven forbid that you would need to participate in an IRS audit of your business or personal tax filings!)

Expenses are just that: an actual accounting of what you incur for serving each client. What can be included? Let's consider an example. You live in Columbus, Ohio (like I do!), and you have a booking to speak in California at the Disneyland Hotel in Orange County. You will give a keynote speech on one day, and the next day you have agreed to give (at an additional fee) two 90-minute breakout-session workshops for this national association client. What are your valid reimbursable expenses?

def•i•ni•tion

> **All-inclusive** fees are structured so that anticipated travel and lodging expenses are built in to the fee.

- ◆ Roundtrip airfare. Don't travel first class and expect to be reimbursed for your prime seat unless you've had prior approval from the client to do so. Book as early as possible for best rates.

- ◆ Travel expenses to and from your home airport and parking at your home airport.

- ◆ Tips for porters at all airports can be lumped into the "miscellaneous travel expenses" category.

- ◆ A cab to the hotel from the airport (and back again) is a reimbursable expense, as long as the hotel doesn't offer a courtesy shuttle from the airport. If it does, the client may expect you to use the shuttle.

- ◆ Meals. You should eat with the client whenever you can; this means that you may have few meals to pay for out-of-pocket. However, when you're traveling long distances, you'll have meals on the road, and those are reimbursable.

- ◆ As you know, gas is quite expensive these days, so if you drive more than a few miles to and from the airport, total that mileage up and report it like this: "Round-trip mileage to and from home airport = 50 miles × 50 cents per mile = $25." (50 cents is the current IRS standard for mileage reimbursement.)

◆ Hotels. In this example, you'd be staying at the host hotel for two or three nights. Clients often have a master account, and your hotel room is billed directly to the client's account; so in this case, you would not list any hotel expense. You would pay your own miscellaneous charges called "incidentals" in the hotel, like Internet service, long distance calls, movies in the room, etc.

Type up your expenses and keep a copy for your own files. Send the original in an envelope addressed to your client or meeting planner and enclose your receipts. Or give this to the appropriate person before you leave for home. Last choice is to send it by e-mail, as receipts may be needed to document expenses. (Keep copies of those, too.)

Sometimes clients will offer to make airline reservations for a speaker and prepay this expense; however, there can be problems with this kind of arrangement, so ask to make your own airline reservations. You know best where you need to be before and after the event. You might want to stay a couple of extra days, at your own expense, to see some friends or do some sightseeing or to work to drum up more business. In the preceding example, you might book an event in California six months or more prior to your arrival. If other bookings during the same week come along in neighboring states in the meantime, you want to be able to alter your travel arrangements to suit your client's needs.

def•i•ni•tion

A **per diem** fee is the amount of money the speaker figures he will spend on food and travel each day that he is working for a client.

There is another alternative to listing each expense as we have in the preceding. Rather than list meals, tips, mileage, taxis, etc., you can ask for a *per diem* flat fee. Some speakers simply ask for a $75-a-day travel per diem in addition to hotel and airline (or auto) reimbursement, and then they provide no receipts. There are no reimbursements to be made for things like meals, cabs, and tips, so this kind of arrangement can be easier on the client and the speaker. Even though this is becoming more common, it's best to ask the client well in advance of the event if this is acceptable, or better yet, simply have your "per diem" allowance spelled out in the agreement.

Important Points to Include in Contracts

In Chapter 4, I talked about the finer points of contracts, or agreements. Following are some questions that must be answered and included in your agreement before you sign and send it off to the client:

♦ How will you be paid? When will you be paid? Where will your payments be directed to?

♦ When is the 50 percent deposit expected? When is the final payment due?

♦ How do you get reimbursed for expenses? What can be included in expense reimbursement?

♦ What's your regular fee? Have you written in the discounted fee showing any savings? Did you indicate that the discounted fee is confidential and that multiple future bookings may not be discounted?

♦ Who is the actual client/billing name? Do you mention the forms of payment you will accept?

♦ Who will book your flight? Will someone pick you up at the airport? Will the client make hotel reservations? Will meals be provided?

♦ Must you provide for the option of taping your message, and if so, what is the extra charge? Have you asked for permission in advance to offer books or other products and services to the audience?

♦ If the client is pre-purchasing materials for each audience member, is that spelled out in the agreement? If you are to customize materials for handouts, do you mention who will pay for what or who will duplicate the materials?

We call these *serving questions*, and the intention behind them is not only to uncover the client's needs, but also to clear up every possible issue before it can become a misunderstanding.

Actually, what can happen as you ask these kinds of questions is that the potential clients who won't be especially profitable for you suddenly back out. The poor fit simply becomes apparent due to the types of questions you ask. At the other extreme, some clients will give you info to help you better strategize how to serve them, amend your agreement, and get paid. In fact, you might turn a one-appearance gig into a contract for one appearance each month due to patiently or in writing providing the above.

def•i•ni•tion

> **Serving questions** are designed to help you understand so you can serve better. There are six serving words to focus on: who, what, where, when, how, and most important, why?

Win Some, Lose Some

It is true that in any kind of business you win some and you lose some, but the most important thing is that you keep going up to bat and never give up. If you have a tendency to quit too easily, say to yourself, "What did Dr. Thom Lisk tell me in that *Complete Idiot's Guide?*"

Success Shortcuts

Professional speakers have to have a thick skin and a sense of optimism. When you lose a possible booking, some great speakers and trainers say to tell yourself simply, "Who is next?!"

No matter how many clients you win and lose over the years, there's no reason for you to lose out financially. By reinvesting your earnings into your business, you ensure that you'll be able to go on and on as a professional speaker, which of course means that you have the potential to score bigger and better.

Reinvesting Profits Wisely

In Chapter 11, I mentioned saving 10 percent of every dollar you take in. Now, I want to talk about reinvesting some of those profits wisely to build your speaking business.

Following you'll find a checklist with ideas about how to reinvest money in your business (after all your debts have been paid, and after you have tithed 10 percent to charity wisely, and after you have invested 10 percent for your future prosperity in an interest-bearing account). Of the 10 percent you invest, some should go into an easy-to-access account for emergencies; a portion can go to retirement; maybe you could have a portion for vacations; maybe you save some cash for your dream auto or a college education for your child, etc., etc., etc.

Then, with the money (not time) you have available to reinvest in your business, these are often the next priorities that terrific speakers wisely have:

- Office technology to help you serve clients best
- Continuing education for yourself that enables you to serve clients better
- Upgrading marketing materials to find more clients
- Better transportation to help you serve clients faster with fuel economy, and maybe with a better image
- Better wardrobe or personal-appearance items
- Better and more nutritional food for energy

- ◆ Fitness club membership, or home exercise equipment

- ◆ A staff person to free you up from administration

- ◆ A staff person to do marketing for your company

Now also realize that time is money, and the way you invest the 168 hours in each week may determine whether you ever have any money to invest beyond the basics. And your attitude toward your time is as important (if not more so) than your attitude toward money. Do you see your time as valuable, nonreplaceable, and limited? If so, you're more likely to do more with those precious workweek hours, whether 40, 50, or 70 of them, hence pulling in more money.

Avoiding Losses

Now, with all of the advice I've given you so far in this chapter, you have more than enough information on how to avoid monetary losses. I truly believe the key to keeping your business in the black is great communication between you and your clients. And because communication is the professional speaker's *forte*, you are adequately equipped to prevent many unfortunate situations.

However, every once in a while, you may end up doing business with someone who isn't on the up-and-up, and you may not find this out until it's too late—when you've already invested a substantial amount of time in working with these folks. The best prevention is research. Check out your prospects with the Better Business Bureau, or with your local Chamber of Commerce, or with other speakers (if appropriate). If you work through a speakers' bureau, you have the protection of their agency on your side. Same thing with agents: they will go to bat for you, so to speak, if something should go awry with a client.

Most speakers (myself included) never have any issues with deadbeat clients or grave misunderstandings. Just make sure to ask all the questions you need (I've listed plenty of them for you in this chapter), and offer and receive all that is needed in writing!

Cutting Losses and Moving On

It is true that in order to have success and happiness, speakers must cut losses, leave the past behind, and move on with the maximum amount of focused energy in order to serve clients. We must cut out any and all negative attitudes. You may have lost money or time on prospective clients or even on established clients. Let it go. Focus on the future and what you can do differently (and better) the next time around. Just as we all have a finite amount of hours in each week, we also have a finite amount of personal energy. Investing it in past negative events only hurts the future and hampers the present.

Cavett Robert, the founder of the National Speakers Association and a man who once called me his protégé, said, "OPE (which stands for "other people's experience") is always the best teacher." Learn from others, especially from great mentors, and cut your losses quickly. More important, learn from your losses, including the loss of precious time, so that you don't have to experience the same losses over and over again.

Here's how I see it: a loss isn't truly a loss if you take something away from it. Everything happens for a reason, I believe, and is part of God's greater plan. All losses end up being to my benefit, not always immediately or even in a financial way, but through the wisdom and understanding I've gained, which help me to serve the client better next time. If you can learn to look at your entire career this way—as one big opportunity to learn and to help yourself and others—then I assure you, no matter what happens, you'll never feel as though you've lost out on anything!

The Least You Need to Know

- Written agreements protect you by outlining how much and when the client is expected to pay you.

- Clients routinely reimburse expenses incurred by the speaker during travel.

- To avoid misunderstandings, ask your client what's acceptable and what isn't, in terms of expenses.

- Learn to see losses of any kind as a potential gain in wisdom and understanding, and ultimately as a way to serve clients better in the future.

Part  5

Career Advancement

When you've got a good thing going, you want to keep it going, right? Speakers build on their successes and use that momentum to go further, do better, and reach more people than they ever dreamed possible. In this part, I'll tell you how to use your positive experiences to boost your career, and I'll also advise you on some sticky situations that could harm your career.

Chapter 19

Momentum Enhancers

In This Chapter

◆ Continuing to move onward and upward!

◆ Learning to serve all clients efficiently and professionally

◆ The truth may hurt, but it also helps

◆ The power of testimonials

One time I spoke to an organization at a themed event. As you now know to do, as the speaker I worked to make my message enhance, reinforce, and further advance the theme of their meeting. Their mantra was all over the place, printed on everything; it was even printed on t-shirts that were given to all participants, and to me, the speaker. The memorable theme was this: KEEP THE MOMENTUM.

So what is momentum, really, and how do you create it (and keep it) in your career? Anytime you do anything to ensure a positive outcome, you're really investing in bettering your career. You're creating momentum. When you go the extra mile to phone several of the leaders in an organization where you are scheduled to speak so as to find out their desired outcomes (even when your contract does not call for this action), you ensure better results.

There are many, many ways to build on your positive interactions and career success; we'll take a look at a few of those ideas in this chapter.

Pre-Program Questionnaires

One of the most important things to do once you secure a paid booking to speak is to administer a pre-program questionnaire to your client. This is a generic form and, of course, one size does not fit each situation. Clients come in small, medium, large, and extra-large sizes (and order of importance); the amount of preparation needed, and the potential ongoing revenue possibilities also differ from client to client. Act accordingly. Customize your questionnaire for each situation if you must.

If you are giving your garden-variety standard, generic speech for the hundredth time (in a low-paying situation, to boot) you may feel as though there's little reason to cover the bases with the client. Guess what? You need to do it anyway. Even though you're comfortable with your presentation and how to tweak it slightly for this par-ticular audience without any input at all from the client, send a questionnaire anyway. It's psychologically satisfying *and* an ethical act of protocol *and* great customer service to assure your client that you've taken the time and effort to learn about her organization and needs. And because pre-program questionnaires tend to increase the comfort level of your meeting planner, this may affect how well she treats you when you arrive and the quality of intro-duction you receive.

Success Shortcuts

In the speaking business, the cause-and-effect principles play out in many ways. One of the most important ways is when you ask the best questions of your clients, thus proving that you understand their needs.

There are some situations where it's impossible to administer a questionnaire. For example, my bureau recently booked Alan K. Mooney to give a teleseminar on fundraising. Because we had no idea who was going to phone in, we couldn't do a pre-program survey. In these cases, you still need to learn something about the people you're offering information to. I was acting as Alan's introducer, so I asked questions of the people who had phoned in, and I passed that info on to Alan, who was able to masterfully tailor his material to those in the audience. The attendees really felt Alan's concern for them as individuals and, as a result, were completely tuned in to his message. At the end of the short program, you could feel the motivation coming through the phone lines!

And that's really the point of the pre-program questionnaire: to reach out and say to each client, "I want to know exactly who you are and what you need from me, and I will provide it for you." Even though your questionnaire may be generic, you never want your client to feel as though *they're* generic! You simply can't make genuine connections that way, and you surely can't create momentum of any sort without a real connection! And the momentum you create is twofold: you want the client to be left feeling as though they're closer to their goals because of your presentation, and you gain momentum in your career by knowing that you're prepared to serve any client. You might also develop an ongoing relationship with the client, and that has a momentum all its own.

> **Words to the Wise**
>
> It's customary to fax or e-mail the pre-program questionnaire to your client, though follow-up phone calls are usually needed in order to work out the particulars of the client's needs.

Scoping Out Niche Markets

To build and maintain your momentum, it's not enough to go after the main leader in any given industry (after all, every speaker wants to land those clients). Set your sights on related fields within a specific industry. For example, if you're an expert on law, don't market yourself only to lawyers' associations. Look for police organizations, victims' rights groups, and media outlets that need an expert opinion or message!

Perhaps you're wondering, "Thom, how exactly do I go about scoping out my A, B, and C niche markets and then reach out to them in the best ways possible?" Glad you asked! A questionnaire—this time administered to yourself—is once again the best tool you can use to check out your niche markets, determine your best prospective clients in those markets, and keep your career moving forward.

- Can you list all markets or industry types that could purchase your kinds of expertise or presentations? (Find 10 or more.)

- Next, which of those markets listed need your expertise most?

- Which markets are most likely to purchase your services?

- Which organizations in these markets have enough funding to afford your programs and ongoing services?

> **Words to the Wise**
>
> If you have not defined your top niche prospects, what are you waiting for? "NO MORE EXCUSES" is the way my speaker friend Randy Snow puts it in his speeches. Confined to his wheelchair, this Para-Olympic athlete is one of the best speakers in America, especially so in his top niche markets.

The last question you need to ask yourself is how to pursue your best clients. You'll find answers to that query throughout this book, but especially in Chapters 5 and 12.

Once you begin establishing these relationships, not only will you feel as though you're truly moving forward in your professional speaking career, but your expertise ranking may also go up a notch or two (anyone who can take a topic and make it accessible to many groups must know everything there is to know about the subject, right?), increasing your visibility and marketability. That's momentum!

When to Strike

Strike when the iron is hot! When you are very enthused and a have deep belief in yourself and the value of what you are offering, that's the perfect time to sell yourself to new clients. One of the best times, I believe, is right after you've given a successful presentation. The accolades you've received, along with the feeling that you've made a difference in the lives of many people are priceless commodities when you're marketing yourself to prospective clients.

Just because this might be the best time for you, it doesn't mean it will be the best time for your client. Sometimes your current client will have meetings continuing and can't spare the time to discuss bringing you on for more work. Sometimes you are in a city far from your home base. Well, use your cell phone. Call your best prospects immediately after you've left the client or presentation location. Leave a voicemail if the client is unavailable. Just let them hear your voice, your enthusiasm, and your ideas for serving them.

Success Shortcuts

Speakers always carry extra brochures, business cards, demo tapes, and so on with them when they travel. Veteran speakers can tell you stories of how they have met people at airports, on airplanes, trains, and so on who ended up being valuable contacts!

If you are out of town, use this time wisely. Schedule your departure for the day after the presentation and walk around the city looking for prospects—they are everywhere in major cities. But don't go in with some shotgun approach. Before you make the trip, do your research and know something about organizations in your top niche markets in the city you are visiting.

And what do you do once you're in a prospective client's lobby? If you can't get in to see the decision-maker, at least make a good first impression on the administrative assistant by saying something like, "I was in your city today as the keynote speaker for XYZ organization at the convention center. May I introduce myself, leave some information, and get your boss's business card?"

Using Realistic Claims

When I was a young speaker, I thought I was Superman after a standing-ovation speech. In other words, I am not sure I was realistic, shortly after my big conquests. The euphoria you feel at times as a speaker is very real, and it can be exhilarating. But before you start believing that you can leap buildings in a single bound (and telling prospective clients as much), take a moment to slow down and differentiate between enthusiasm and reality.

Like a new father who's convinced his child will be the future Miss America or Olympic Gold Medalist, speakers (and sometimes aspiring speakers) are prone to exaggeration, too. This is where, if you are not careful, you can get an unwanted dose of humility. Let me give you an example ….

Recently I was paired with a young man in a golf outing fundraiser for cancer research dollars. In between holes, he told me he worked for a college as a recruiter the past four years. When asked, "What do you like most about the job?" he mentioned several things. When he found out I was a professional speaker and I told him that I run an international professional speakers' bureau, his eyes and enthusiasm picked up.

He said to me, "I love public speaking and have thought about it as a way to make a living." We talked about it, and I was reminded again how few people understand the nature of professional speaking versus public speaking. He said, "I love the euphoric feeling I get when I speak to the classes in the normal course of my job. I can control the audience in the palm of my hand. All eyes are on me." I told him I knew the feeling, but I didn't want to burst his balloon and tell him that in reality, those are not the right reasons to consider speaking full time.

Later during the golf game I chatted with him about the realities of speaking. His target market for his college employer were two-year colleges or trade schools where he could find students who had done well in high school but yet were looking for the right career training or a degree that would open the door to a prosperous future. I gave him a few ideas that could help him. I planted some seeds for his benefit to expand his realities and view of speaking.

That feeling of euphoria is wonderful and, as I said, a great tool for selling yourself to clients. However, that's not *all* it takes to make it in this profession. If you've read through this book and followed the steps I've laid out for you, the realistic possibilities for your career are expanding greatly. That's momentum, too! It's important to have one foot on the ground, so to speak, in order to appeal to (and win) clients with realistic claims.

This young man on the golf course would have had me believe that he is the greatest college recruiter of all time! It's great that he has such confidence, but if I were a potential client, I would want to know what evidence he has to back up those claims. And if he wasn't able to produce any, his belief in himself might take a serious nose-dive, bringing any momentum he had to a screeching halt. Your prospects deserve and expect visual and written evidence of your value, not just claims and stories of your prowess in your current career. Present yourself honestly and realistically, and no matter where you begin your speaking career, you'll move forward with due speed.

Getting Your Foot in the Door

Great speakers, just like salespeople, know how to get their foot in the door of terrific clients; they also know how to keep that door opened, and that's where your momentum with a particular client can take off.

Getting your foot in the door includes respecting the fact that clients are often more open to your offer to speak at certain times of the year. If they have one annual meeting in September every year, they may not consider hiring a speaker until June. So calling them at any other time of the year might be a waste of your time and theirs—and it could do you more harm than good. (You won't have a lot of momentum with this client if that happens!)

So find out who makes the decisions to hire outside speakers and trainers, and ask, "When is the best time to contact you and provide more information about why we may have the perfect program for you for your meeting?" Make a note of an acceptable timeframe in your automatic follow-up system. You might say, "Would it be helpful for us to send material to you for your files, just in case something comes up between now and then?" or "Can you please make a note of our website address and phone number, and save them as favorites so you can find them if and when you need them?" In doing this, you haven't wasted anyone's time, and you've left that door wide open to the possibility of establishing a relationship in the future!

Surveys for Success

Your success can be enhanced and accelerated if you get more answers to more questions from both your great clients and also from prospective clients you never quite land. Let's face it: you can go fishing and some of the big ones may get away from you. You need to know why. Was it the bait you used? Was it where you were fishing? Did you simply not have enough patience? Did they like your competitor's bait better than yours?

Don't be afraid to ask, and don't be afraid to hear negative comments along with the positive. In my years in this business, I have heard comments about my own efforts that felt like bee-stings: they hurt at the time. However, I worked and prayed to learn from each comment and figure out the best ways to improve.

In this section, we'll take a look at some surveys you can send to clients and audiences to get an objective view of your presentation skills and materials. Read through your responses! It's the only way you can fix what needs to be fixed and move forward!

Lost-Speech Survey

Veteran speakers will tell you that even they have lost some speaking opportunities they hotly pursued. Of course, any speaker feels some disappointment over a lost opportunity, especially if something could have prevented the lost booking.

So that you do not make the same mistake twice, have the courage to do a lost-speech survey after every significant lost-speech situation. Here are some questions to ask your lost prospect by phone (the most common approach):

 ◆ "Thank you for the opportunity to be considered. I know you are busy, but so that I can understand how to maybe earn the right to serve you a year from now, or serve others, may I respectfully ask you briefly a couple of questions?"

 ◆ If you prospect says yes, then proceed with the next two questions. If the response is no, it may be that the person simply does not have time at the moment. So you might say, "I so admire you and your company; of course I am disappointed that you did not choose me. Forgive me if it seems overly confident to believe that at some point in the future I can do a great job for you. I simply want to ask your wise insights so I can adjust myself or my materials so as to be more appealing to you in the future. It will only take five minutes to complete a little survey. I really need your help to understand—please? May I call you tomorrow at 4 P.M., or how about 4:30?"

 ◆ If the client has time to talk, go ahead and ask, "May I ask which speaker you chose? What did you like most about this speaker? What did you find in this speaker's presentation that I did not offer?"

 ◆ "What did you like best about what I offered? What did not seem to be right for your organization?"

Now that you have asked these questions, what do you do with the information you have gained? Adjust your approach in the future to increase your closing ratio.

The best time to ask these (and other similar questions) is immediately upon finding out that you were not "the chosen one." This is using negative momentum, of course, but you're using it to your advantage, which means that a lost opportunity is not a complete loss.

Audience Evaluations

You might think, "Why do *I* need to administer an evaluation? My client is taking care of that!" That may be true, but speakers often hand out their own evaluation forms at the end of their presentation. You only need to administer evaluations if you are interested in improving your skills or presentation materials. To do that, you need to see yourself objectively. And to do *that*, you have to get as much feedback as possible, as fast as possible.

You want your audience members to have "Aha!" moments. So you might reflect that in how you structure your evaluation. Many speakers have found that questions with a scale rating system are best. Consider the following:

1. On a scale from 1 to 10 (with 10 being high), how do you rate this speaker in these key areas (circle one):

   A) Professionalism 1-2-3-4-5-6-7-8-9-10

   B) Topic presentation 1-2-3-4-5-6-7-8-9-10

   C) Platform mechanics 1-2-3-4-5-6-7-8-9-10

   D) Presentation performance 1-2-3-4-5-6-7-8-9-10

   E) Opening and closing 1-2-3-4-5-6-7-8-9-10

   F) Relationship with audience 1-2-3-4-5-6-7-8-9-10

2. What "aha!" moments or new ideas did you gain?

3. What did you like most about this program?

4. What could the speaker do to improve?

5. Do you recommend that this speaker return?

There are many other questions that can be answered, but keep it on the brief side. Time is limited and audience members are often anxious to get on to their next assignment or meeting. Remember: KISS—Keep It Simple, Speaker.

Acquiring References

After a meeting is complete, you hope that the attendees have benefited in certain ways. If you helped create some momentum for your clients (by pushing their organization in the direction of their ultimate goal), then you've got lots of momentum going. You have to harvest the happiness your current client is experiencing (because of you) and pass it on to potential clients. You can do this by using your current client as a reference.

Just as in any industry, *references*—clients who can sing your praises—are helpful to the professional speaker's career. Prospective clients will seldom phone many of your references; they simply want to see that you *have* references.

A *reference list* is filled with clients (past and present) who will tell your prospective clients about their positive experiences with you. This list is most effective if you have actually groomed the people on your reference list (this means you know they are only going to say good and positive things about you). The list should have at least three clients, but it's preferable to have seven or more, complete with the name of the organization and the meeting planner's name, e-mail, and phone number.

def•i•ni•tion _____

> **References** are existing or past clients who are willing to tell your prospective clients that you did a great job and they would use you again. A **reference list** contains the names of at least three clients who can attest to your professionalism and skills.

Testimonials

Testimonial letters are one of the best tools, if not the best tool, in a speaker's arsenal to market and close deals with potential clients. These letters are most often written on the client/organization stationery and discuss the fantastic job you did for them. The implied message from the current client to the new client is: "We tried her, we loved her, and so will you!"

Most clients are reputation buyers; they do not want to go out on a limb buying a speaker unless he or she has been a hit elsewhere. It is hard to overcome this for new

def•i•ni•tion _____

> **Testimonial letters** are written by clients on the organization's stationery and mention the great impact the speaker has made on the organization or with their audience.

speakers; that's why you begin, if necessary, speaking for free—but only for organizations who tell you that they will absolutely give you a testimonial letter on their stationery after the event is complete.

If you visit our website, you could read about literally hundreds of speakers (www. terrificspeakers.com). They all look terrific, in my opinion, so how could you tell which one to purchase if you were a meeting planner? Your top-10 finalists will no doubt be those with the best testimonial quotes. Ordinarily nothing can outdo a great group of testimonial letters (or quotes from recognizable or impressive organizations); maybe a top-quality demo tape is the only better tool, and the best of preview tapes sometimes have audience members talking about how great the speaker was.

Words to the Wise

One thing that could help to offset your lack of testimonial letters is the creditability you can gain through other media experiences, like publishing a top-selling book, appearing on TV, or writing a newspaper or magazine column. You must provide clips or copies of these materials.

Consider the quotes some speakers have received, and note how they help sell the speaker:

◆ "You were a great hit with all of our people, as evidenced by the evaluations rating. You're the best speaker we have had. We look forward to working with you again."

◆ "The standing ovation you received was only one demonstration of how well accepted your speech was by all of our people. Thank you for all the extra preparation you did to tailor it."

◆ "My phone has been ringing off the hook with feedback about what a great job you did at our annual conference. As the keynote kickoff speaker, you set the perfect tone and expertly tied your message to our theme and objectives."

Now go to work. If you have given speeches or seminars or workshops and did not receive a testimonial letter or some positive references (at least an e-mail thank-you extolling you) call your past clients and ask for them. If they don't want to take the time to write you a letter on their stationery, ask them for a quote by phone, write it down, and send it to them for their approval before using it.

Reference List How-To's

The most important things I can tell you about how to acquire reference letters or how to build your list of quotes is as follows:

◆ Expect them and ask for them.

◆ Ask for them immediately after your great presentation.

◆ Ask for them when you're sealing the deal, as something that *must* be received after your program is complete.

If the client is the type who is so busy and will procrastinate, then ask, "May I write a suggested letter and send it to you for you to sign and place on your stationery?"

Place your references and testimonial expert quotes on your one-sheet brochure, on your website, and so on. Use copies of complete testimonial letters (with the client logo on it) in a full-size, color version in your press kit, or when sending out demo tapes.

And because testimonials and references are all about building momentum, don't use them if you are not 100 percent sure they will support your efforts to further your speaking career! It's better to have just a few glowing reviews than a bunch that are iffy (at best).

Organizational Systems for Serving Clients

The last topic we'll cover in this chapter is your organizational efforts and system for serving your existing clients. After all, without organization, you're bound to make errors ... and errors are *not* momentum builders!

You need a system for serving clients that helps to ensure they are satisfied with you now and, ideally, for months to come. Here are some guidelines and good options:

For starters, every client has a paper file, divided into these categories:

◆ Files or leads containing prospects who are not yet clients but are hot for constant follow-up.

◆ Files of current clients with upcoming dates scheduled.

◆ Files of past clients who also are recontacted at appropriate times each year.

◆ Lost-sale client files. These are also recontacted at a pre-agreed date.

Although you have actual file folders on each client, you should also have an electronic file or correspondence with each client for easy access to their account. It is also wise to add each client you've worked with to a master electronic list so that they can be included in your e-mailed newsletters. (This list could be labeled in your Word address book: clients served 2007, 2008, 2009, ... a different file for each year.)

Have a list of your best target niche prospects in electronic files (labeled Prospects A for your top prospects, B for your second-tier prospects, and so on). Send them an e-mail newsletter monthly. The idea is to keep proving your value and expertise. And remember: lost-sale clients are still some of your best prospects. You may have come in second place in a pool of 25 speakers they considered this year, so next year you might be the right choice … as long as you have a system that keeps in touch and keeps your name before the decision-maker.

You get the idea. Organizational systems can take all shapes and sizes. You undoubtedly have been in a doctor's or dentist's office and seen the files that are all color-coded with extremely well-documented details on each client (in this case, patient) file. You may not need to go to the extent that my dentist brother Greg Lisk, DDS, goes to with so much detail. However, the more detailed you are with placing notes about all client or prospective client contacts in their individual files, the more likely you are to A) discover the solution for how to sell a new client, B) serve an existing client better, C) re-activate an old client, D) acquire more business from the same client (through different divisions or departments), and E) win a lost client the next time around.

There can be more purposes for effective organizational systems, just as each file can be full of important details that enable you to maximize your client service. Please, always remember "He who serves best, profits most."

You want nothing to slow you down as you create and maintain, and then accelerate momentum toward your great successes that are just ahead and may soon be realized.

The Least You Need to Know

- To better yourself and your career, you need to tap into your positive experiences and use them to keep moving forward.

- Using a pre-program questionnaire for each and every client helps to assure the client that you've taken the time to prepare your presentation specifically for them.

- You can make a lot of contacts in niche markets, thus building your career and increasing your momentum.

- Administering a lost-speech survey is a way to find out how to serve a client in the future, and also a way to turn a negative to a positive.

- References and testimonials are must-haves for the speaker who wants to acquire new, bigger, and better clients.

Chapter 20

Sticky Speaker Situations

In This Chapter

- Ethics for the professional speaker
- Where to find a code of ethics
- What to do when the audience wants to "shoot the messenger"
- Don't "borrow" material without acknowledgment!

This is a sticky chapter to write and read, but I hope that you will take the lessons taught here to heart so you don't regret it later. This information will help you succeed by enabling you to make better decisions, eliminating trial and error, and avoiding possible potholes in your wonderful journey ahead. Believe me, I have had some sticky situations over the years, and I also know famous speakers who have felt stuck in some hairy situations, not knowing what to do.

Many speakers have wisely turned to other veteran speakers and asked for help, "How would you, confidentially, handle this situation?" Yes, many times these situations are confidential, so the situations we talk about in this chapter do not find specific speakers mentioned. This has been the case in other parts of the book as well, as the specific speaker or client or situation did not need names with it to make the point, or at least I have hoped that is the case for you.

Although I am an expert, granted, this book is not the Gospel of Professional Speaking according to your author, Thom Lisk. That would be a mistake to assert. We must not present as if there is only one way. You and I are not trying to set ourselves up as gods, but rather as experts. You are an expert, too, I hope, whether now or soon to be.

Sticky mistake number one comes as a result of not realizing there may be more ways, better ways, and that you don't know it all. Even the best of speaker experts are very prudent if they help people to realize something like, "I am a speaker on the journey of life, just like you. I am still learning, just like you. I have dedicated a great deal of time and interest to the area of my expertise, and I have many ideas and solutions that may work for you as they have worked for others."

Research has shown, as an example, that a medical doctor who comes across as so absolutely certain that his diagnoses are always 100 percent correct is not only sure to be wrong (sometimes), but this person will be wrong more often than the person who presents some uncertainty when discussing a health issue with a patient. A second doctor, the one who empathizes fully while providing information for the patient to make the most informed decision possible, is the doctor who is the most respected and who most likely has the fewest malpractice law suits.

Code of Ethics for Speakers

Every speaker needs to be committed to a personal code of *ethics*. After all, you are in the public eye. You will be scrutinized as a professional speaker, and the higher you are privileged to go in this business, the more your ethics may be evaluated.

def•i•ni•tion

Ethics refer to codes of conduct that professionals are expected to uphold and encourage in their peers.

Throughout this book, I've worked to help you lay a proper foundation in your life and business so that you do not violate codes of ethics even if you are not aware that they do exist. Ethics are a set of standards that certain professions adhere to. For a speaker, ethics may start and end with the golden rule, "Do unto others as you would have them do unto you."

It is right thinking and right action; it is taking the high road of honesty in all your relationships … and more, maybe much more.

Several organizations influence the speaking and meeting professions. Even if you are not a member or never desire to become a member of the following associations, it is a good idea to go to their websites and review each code of ethics. The association from your prior work background may have a code to which you have agreed.

- Meeting Professions International (MPI)

- National Speakers Association (NSA)

- American Society of Training & Development (ASTD)

- Toastmasters International

I believe it's wise to belong to one or more of the above groups (there are also others listed in Appendix B) in order to sign off on their code of ethics, for starters. Doing so represents your commitment to being as ethical as possible as a professional speaker.

No one is perfect. That's not what I'm asking of you. But by subscribing to a set of "ethical codes" in any profession, you're holding yourself to a very high standard. I've included the code of ethics from the Professional Speakers Bureau Int'l Association (PSBIA) so that you have a better idea of the expectations of professional speakers—just keep in mind that these are the expectations of one organization. Ethics may vary from association to association.

PSBIA's Code of Ethics:

The success of professional speaking, like any profession, is based on individual speakers solemnly acknowledging the need for total integrity in all their actions and words; the members of this association are committed to the best wisdom and understanding, leading to an ethical life.

Toward this desired highly ethical life from which we can best walk the best talk, we do more than subscribe to this code of ethics; we pledge to be ethical in all of our professional relationships and services. In America we say "we are one nation under God," so we invoke God's standards, which are higher than those that any person or group of persons can create.

With this in mind, we are not the judge of other members, but rather noble servant leaders who point out better ways (more through action than through words) to upgrade the profession of speaking. This is done regardless of any prior or current affiliation our members may have with other organizations. We are not police who point out violations of the following code of ethics, but rather sojourners who are always striving toward perfection ourselves.

The following is submitted humbly and prayerfully as a code to point to, as part of your highest purpose as a speaker.

- Part One: The PSBIA terrific speaker accurately represents prior experiences and qualifications at all times.

- Part Two: The PSBIA speaker shall do all possible without constraints of time and money to operate her or his speaking business uprightly to bring respect to pro speaking.

- Part Three: The PSBIA speaker must do all possible within constraints of time and money to wisely understand clients so as to prepare and ethically serve their objectives.

- Part Four: The PSBIA speaker does all possible to never present material as his or her own when indeed it originated with someone else; we give credit where credit is due.

- Part Five: The PSBIA speaker shall treat other speakers, and for that matter all people, with respect, dignity, and courtesy, never projecting ourselves as better than others, but rather humbly realizing our expertise is unique.

- Part Six: The PSBIA speaker understands that people make mistakes, so we always grant opportunities for others to be right and to do right while never bringing hurt to any person. Our goal is to be a blessing to others.

- Part Seven: The PSBIA member does not condone any illegal action of any type by any person for any reason. We do everything possible to self-examine and eliminate faults, errors, mistakes, misperceptions, and so on from our own lives.

- Part Eight: The PSBIA member agrees to uphold all laws and acts of fair and ethical treatment of all people where we serve, never discriminating in any way for any reason.

Members of PSBIA are deeply concerned about the profession of speaking and how we impact people and groups of people. We work hard so that all people who we come into contact with will be enriched and/or benefited by our lives. Toward this end, we administer this pledge of ethics to each speaker:

"I pledge myself to comply with this Code of Professional Ethics.

I pledge myself to integrity and honesty, compassion and loving service, and forgiveness, as I would want to be forgiven when I am wrong or wronged, but I strive for perfection in all that I do and say.

I pledge to respect all persons in the membership of PSBIA and other speakers and related associations, and to honor them all, competing fairly and most ethically so that clients I am privileged to serve are the biggest beneficiaries.

If you see the value in this code, place your initials here and now _____."

Members of an association like PSBIA or NSA are not always the best judges of our members' ethics; the best judges are usually the clients who are served by the speakers.

In many ways this section is the *most* important section in this entire book. After all, what good is it to build any business if it all collapses due to unethical behavior—either your own behavior or the actions of those you've hired in your organization? Think about the downfall of businesses like Enron, WorldCom, Arthur Anderson, and even the sexual scandals in religious organizations. What do these unfortunate events all have in common? Someone (and in most cases, many people) acted unethically.

> **Words to the Wise**
>
> If you currently work for an unethical manager or owner, don't go with the flow! Hold yourself to a high standard, correcting your own work and personal issues quickly so that no one can point out your lapses or mistakes.

Bad ethics can lead to litigation and even time in jail. Financial loss is always a real threat when unethical actions come into play, but the loss to your reputation can be even more damaging, because that's something that's often more difficult to restore than money.

So how can you avoid falling into a bad ethics situation? Dot your i's and cross your t's. Building your speaking business and career at a slow pace is a good idea. If you move too fast, you're in more danger of taking shortcuts that could be viewed as bordering on unethical behavior.

Most of us prefer to believe that a person's conscience—if given the right kind of complete ethical or morally sound upbringing and education—is shaped so that they always make ethically correct choices. But let's face it … even the best people with the best ethical training are presented with temptations and may eventually break in a weak state of mind.

It is true that sometimes people do things that are wrong—they make mistakes. In other words, there was no intention to do anything unethical, or they just slipped up in a particular situation. Part of being ethical is forgiving those who have done something wrong by accident. Furthermore, we need to give these folks the opportunity to make things right. The most important thing, however, is that we shouldn't rush to judgment and label someone who's made an honest error as an unethical person. If a colleague's actions are questionable, correct him. Give this person the information he seems to be lacking and a third chance to get it right.

Let me give you an example of an ethical man who believes in holding others to a high standard, but also believes in second chances. At Ohio State University, there is a famous football team with a well-respected and famous coach, Jim Tressel. Mr. Tressel is truly a values-driven coach, a deeply religious man who does not wear his religion on his sleeve but one who plays it out in the decisions he makes to shape champions. Not all college boys who earn the right to be on the team have the same values of Coach Tressel, but to excel on his team you have to buy into his system, and that includes working with his ethics and his values.

I recently read about a quarterback on the OSU team who was caught soliciting an undercover police officer for sexual favors. Needless to say, the young man found himself in serious trouble, facing a possible jail sentence, fines, and at least a temporary suspension from the team. Whether or not he redeems himself and later rejoins the team remains to be seen at this writing. I do know Tressel is the kind of ethical leader who will give people a second and third chance, if at all possible, and the benefit of the doubt, too.

While I advise you to strive to emulate Tressel in your business dealings, I also urge you to be a person of integrity at all times. Unfortunately in business, a single act of misconduct may get you two orders: "Get out and stay out."

Hostile Audiences

What do you do on an ethical basis to deal with a hostile audience? Most of the time audiences will be accepting of your message. That is, unless you are one of those extremely brave souls who dares go into hostile situations in an effort to make things right—to bring some badly needed light and salt to season the situation for good, to offset some evil.

Words to the Wise

Clients sometimes need outside experts to address topics that they may be uneasy about presenting themselves. So don't be surprised if it feels like the audience is ready to shoot the messenger (you) before you begin a message they don't want to hear. That's just human nature!

Speakers do get hired, sometimes unknowingly on their part, to come in and right a wrong, to say something the boss cannot say or even if he or she does it can't be heard, understood, and acted upon. The outside expert has long been used to shake things up in organizations, and to affect change.

You might shake someone up in an audience so much that he or she stands up and shouts out right in the middle of one of your best stories. What do you do?

You might shake up a group of people so much that they get up and walk out, in a clanging loud way, right in the middle of your high point. What do you do?

You might shake up an audience even before you show up, simply because people read that you will be appearing and they object. What do you do then?

Seldom will you have an entire audience who is hostile, unless you are a politician attempting to speak to the opposing party, as one example, or are speaking about some issue or cause that raises extreme emotions in people, as another example. In all of my years of professional speaking in situations of all sorts, personally, hostile audiences have not been a big ongoing issue for me (or for most of my colleagues, for that matter). Consultants, however, tend to deal with this matter more often.

Think about a business that needs a turn-around expert or they will soon go out of business. Immediately after the consultant is hired, she is required to speak to groups of people and tell them that if things don't turn around in 30 days, people will begin to lose their jobs. No matter how diplomatic one might be, this kind of news isn't going to win the consultant a lot of friends. And because the consultant isn't just the bearer of bad tidings but the person responsible for turning things around in the company, she's often seen as a (for lack of a better word) weasel.

Many relationships (both personal and business) fail because people position themselves in an adversarial way or role. Speakers must try to avoid that. First, focus on friendship and caring for all people before you present the problem and possible solutions. Tell people you are merely the problem-solver, and you hope and pray that everyone is ready to be a part of the solution. But even with this kind of wording, there are problem people everywhere. That is why speakers who deliver skilled messages about conflict-reduction or dealing with difficult people and difficult personality styles are in such demand!

So how does a speaker or consultant deal with negativity and move on in a positive manner? One time I gave a keynote speech along with a university president to a prestigious group of managers from all kinds of businesses in a big city. After I received a standing ovation, a great many people came up to congratulate me for "an outstanding job." I grew from my normal nearly 5'10" height to about 9 feet tall due to the positive feedback.

Quickly, though, I was deflated by the last two people in the line of well-wishers. These two blasted me with some negative comments and I shrank to about 3 inches tall before I slumped and slinked my way out of the auditorium. This kind of negative feedback from one or two people (even when 150 people stand and applaud and rate you as an A+) can be devastating to a speaker who is not prepared.

That same day, I was giving a three-hour seminar for another client. As I drove away from the site of this first speech, I found myself mumbling to myself and questioning my right to be a speaker—my self-confidence was nearly destroyed by these two "trailers." Fortunately at the time, even though I was young in the business, I knew that I needed a quick prescription of positive thought to offset that recent, very negative assault.

I was not far from the state capital building at Broad and High Street in downtown Columbus, Ohio. I remembered and affirmed the Ohio motto, which is etched in granite and in concrete at the center of Ohio, "With God all things are possible." I found myself bounding back from this adversity as I began to think right again about myself, my God, and serving other people.

If you think you will have hostile people in your next audience, you probably will find a few. But on the other hand, if you really love everyone in your next audience and you have every person's best interest at heart, then they are more likely to respond to you in like manner. Some people call this the Law of Attraction, some call it a positive mindset, and some cynical folks might call it selective attention, but I think this is the best way to prepare for and then control any hostile audience.

Plagiarism

Doesn't everyone already know that *plagiarism* is very wrong, I ask myself? Apparently not, because my bureau continues to see signs of it from speakers—whether this is done purposefully or by accident, I can't say, but it does happen. Copying the work of another speaker verbatim is wrong. Here is how it appears in the speaking world sometimes.

def•i•ni•tion

> Plagiarism refers to presenting someone else's original thoughts and materials as your own.

Speakers realize that most audience members attend few speeches and seminars. So if a speaker borrows a story from someone else and does not give the originator credit, the speaker rationalizes that no one will know. After all, a speaker could be thinking to him- or herself, "I heard this from a not-so-well-known expert in California and I am now speaking in New York … and besides, who knows if it is original with that California speaker expert anyway?" So no credit is given, even though the story clearly did not originate with the speaker who is currently using it.

Some speakers get away with sharing material that originated with other people for years and years until they think the material is actually theirs! But there's a difference when you're talking about universal principles, which are the domain of everyone, so credit may not need to be given. If you're sharing a folktale to make a point, for example, or if you are sharing truths that have come from a religious philosophy, you don't have to say, "I found this passage in my King James Version Bible" (although you usually can if you want to).

Just be careful and give credit when you can; doing so does not really take away from the validity of your message. Actually, when you share information that you've heard along the way, your audience might think, "Wow, this guy is really well read and well traveled. What a great expert!"

And here's what can happen when you don't give credit where credit is due: one time I heard a well-known woman speak in my hometown. She actually called our office and invited me to come and preview her presentation. She said, "This way you can better determine which of your clients can book me." Well, rather than rise in my estimation, she slid to the pits in my opinion of her. Yes, her overall speech was excellent that day, but to me she flunked when she claimed a story as her own that I knew belonged to someone else.

Don't get me wrong, I wish this speaker good tidings, but I will not book her from our speakers' bureau unless she redeems herself with me somehow.

We all need innovation and to be innovators. It is okay to take ideas and work them around for your use. This book is certainly an example of that, as ideas are not copyrightable.

And not one word of what I share in this book is copied from any other book or any other speaker. Again, some of it may be similar to what you will find elsewhere, but it won't be organized as we have organized it, for your success in one source book. And if something is similar, then it is in a totally different format and sentence structure; anything different from what I just described would be totally coincidental.

Coincidence is one thing; plagiarism is something totally different. Know the difference and work hard to be better, unique, and different in all you present.

The Least You Need to Know

◆ Professional speakers strive to act mature, in control, and ethical in all situations.

◆ Every speaker needs a code of ethics to help guide him or her through sticky situations.

◆ Codes of ethics may be interpreted differently by different speakers and organizations.

◆ Presenting someone else's stories as your own can irreparably harm your reputation.

Chapter 21

Ongoing Success

In This Chapter

- ◆ Behaving as though you've already achieved success
- ◆ Finding a workspace that inspires you
- ◆ Always seeking to serve more
- ◆ Motivating others to be their best—and reaping the rewards
- ◆ Putting your goals in writing

Based on the definition of success given to you earlier in this book, it is fairly easy to know if you are setting and reaching your predetermined personal goals. Of course, speakers are just like all other members of the human race: though we are sometimes perceived to be a cut above, we sometimes fail to stay focused on the thoughts, actions, and habits that brought us success in the first place.

Before this book is complete, let's consider how to have more, ongoing success in all areas of your life, but especially in your speaking career. Many speakers have learned that a memorable poem is a great way to summarize what has been presented in the speech, so to set the tone, let's consider the poem "Success" by Ralph Waldo Emerson:

Success is to … Laugh often and much; to win the respect of intelligent people and affection of children; to earn the appreciation of honest critics and endure the betrayal of false friends; to appreciate beauty, to find the best in others; to leave the world a bit better, whether by a healthy child, a garden patch, or a redeemed social condition; to know even one life has breathed easier because you have lived. This is to have succeeded.

In each section of this last chapter, I intend to ask you to take make some significant decision and then take significant action. As with earlier chapters in this book, each piece of information is a building block for your ongoing success as a speaker. In this chapter, I give calls for action. Knowledge is power, but action is omnipotent!

Holding Yourself to the Highest Standard

A few years ago, a new freeway bypass was built around the relatively small city of Wheeling, West Virginia. Truck traffic, especially, was instructed to take this route through a tunnel, leading away from the main route that ran right through the heart of the city. The new freeway made you climb a sharp incline to take a much higher road a few miles out of the way to ultimately reach the same destination.

The first time I drove this new freeway, I found a three-lane highway with less traffic and higher speed limits. When I arrived at the other side of the river, I was sure this new route had taken about the same time as the old one. In addition, the air was clearer and the sky seemed brighter on this higher, longer route. My stress level was also reduced, as the traffic was much less congested and moving much more smoothly.

Life lessons for all of us are hidden in the simple activities of every day, and as we forge ahead we learn these lessons (hopefully sooner than later). Going out of your way a bit can save you time and give you better health. When you take the high road, you have less competition on the road to your destination and success.

You Take the High Road; Leave Others on the Low Road

In Chapter 20, you were asked to consider ethics from a variety of perspectives, but mostly from a business standpoint. Signing off on a code of ethics and giving it intellectual acquiescence is necessary if your commitment to professional speaking is genuine. I honestly believe that those entrusted with the platform for speaking (and maybe writing, too) should hold themselves not only to high standards, but to the highest possible standards. If you do not, guess what? You will find audience members and clients who will do this *for* you and call you on the carpet for your behavior and words. High standards prevent potential problems, although I will grant you the following ….

People view and interpret each situation, including the words you share, from their own frame of reference. And they draw conclusions that might be totally different from the conclusion you would draw from the same situation and information. That's okay; but if you feel you're entering into a situation where you're going to have to compromise your high standards, stay out of that situation! In that case, the only perspective that matters is your own. Trust your gut and know that you might be much better off without certain clients or people who pull you down toward their lower standards.

Work Habits

Part of holding yourself to a high standard is meeting your deadlines, and you can't do that until you've established effective work habits. Put simply, you need to find out what works best for you—and that may be very different from what works for your speaker colleagues.

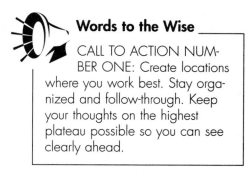

Words to the Wise

CALL TO ACTION NUMBER ONE: Create locations where you work best. Stay organized and follow-through. Keep your thoughts on the highest plateau possible so you can see clearly ahead.

When I first wrote the manuscript for my book *Become #1 in Selling!*, I was living in San Diego on a one-year partial sabbatical. Every Sunday afternoon after church, I would go to a mountaintop to work on the book (and actually, also to work on another book that served as my dissertation for my doctorate degree). In this rarified air I could see straight to the Pacific Ocean about 15 miles away and consider the vastness of Earth and all of the creatures it contains, including people like you and me. I would find myself inspired, calm, and ready to get to work.

That worked for me then, but now, 17 years later, I know I write better in the second story of our home in my upstairs office than I do elsewhere. As time goes on, you'll change and grow, too. Pay attention to whether you need a different workspace. If you find yourself lacking passion, becoming impatient with clients, and forcing yourself to work day after day, then you're not serving anyone, including yourself. Change your surroundings and see if that helps your attitude to make an about-face.

Follow Up with Clients

Not long ago, I was giving a seminar for a group of realtors, and I likened their work to that of politicians—just like political glad-handers, realtors must work at being visible and be seen as friendly meeters and greeters. Realtors, just like retailers, are taught that success can be determined by location, location, and location. I had to tell them that there's something even more important to their success: follow-up, follow-up, and follow-up. And the same is true for you, the professional speaker.

Words to the Wise

CALL TO ACTION NUM-
BER TWO: Follow up before, during, and after your presentations in such a way to so ingratiate yourself to your client's key people that they are always very happy to be interacting with you. Always be giving something of value to them, starting with a smile and a warm personality.

As I reflect on the many clients I have served, either as a speaker myself or by booking a speaker for them, I must admit one of my biggest failings is a lack of appropriate, effective, and timely follow-up. At times, I simply failed to create more business once a speech or seminar was complete. Obviously, I may have missed out on a lot of business, but even more than that, I didn't seek to serve my clients as completely and as thoroughly as I could have. And who knows what kind of positive impact I could have had on their business had I kept in touch?

Here are the major reasons why a lack of follow-up has happened with my bureau and why it happens with other speakers as well:

♦ A wrong attitude that the client will not spend more money for speakers, trainers, or consultants. Sometimes this idea comes from something the client has said, but even when that is the case, a speaker needs to stay positive and try, try again.

♦ An unnecessary preoccupation with a calendar that demands you pay attention to what is next and who is next, almost as if clients are conquests rather than new relationships that must be cultivated and nurtured. Sending one thank-you note is not enough. Keeping in touch via newsletters, e-mails, and phone calls is vital!

♦ A lack of appropriate and timely follow-up with clients at regular intervals while sharing something of value to the client each time. It's not enough to keep in touch; you have to have something to offer each and every time you touch base with a client.

◆ Not cultivating eye-to-eye communication and relationships with the client at the time of the presentation. Certainly you have to prepare for your program, but arriving early enough to connect better with clients and audience members is also key.

Carl Stevens, CPAE, the mentor who originally recruited me into speaking full time in 1977, always told his audiences, "Smile! People might wonder what you have been up to!" Smiling, like with your attitude, is contagious.

Public Relations Efforts

My father was a very successful journalist. During his career and after his retirement, he helped me to understand the important need for public relations skills and the important tone to set while approaching others: show others that you care about them, and they'll take an interest in you.

I realize this is often easier said than done. Let's face it: some people can be hard to stomach, especially when those people are your clients (reread Chapter 15 to get a good idea of how you should be treating your clients—both the easy-to-please type and the *other* kind). Regardless of your personal feelings for a client, it's wise to do what you can to create an air of friendliness and respect between the two of you.

It takes a big person—one who is taking the high road—to see the best in every person and every situation. Maybe a client dislikes your presentation and lets you know this, using colorful language. Maybe an audience member heckles you or derides your book or marketing materials. Perhaps another speaker takes your material and uses it as his or her own. No matter what the offense, you don't have the right to sink to a lowly level. Doing so makes you look unprofessional, overly defensive, and downright amateurish—and you can forget about receiving positive word-of-mouth references if this happens in front of a client! If you hope to inspire others to become their best, you have to show them that you strive to be at your best, no matter what challenges you're facing.

There is a group called the Public Relations Society of America (PRSA) with chapters in major cities; you can really learn a thing or two from these folks that will help to improve your professional speaking career. Go to an association meeting and network with these professionals and you'll learn what's most important in dealing with clients.

One PR man I remember well from my years as a speaker is Mr. Gene King, a man who became *my* king because he hired me as a speaker at a time when he simultaneously ran several associations. He was a lobbyist as well as the life of every gathering, but not in a way that drew attention to himself—rather, he drew attention to others, especially the leaders of the associations he managed.

Mr. King opened my eyes to a simple fact: speakers too often want to be the center of attention all the time. Obviously, when a speaker holds the floor during a presentation, that is her moment and all eyes are on her—that's to be expected. But it's important for speakers to realize that the audience is truly the *other* focal point of the presentation, and that the client needs to be the center of attention once the presentation is through. Reread Chapter 15 for ideas on how to make your clients feel as though they're the most important people in the world.

Mr. King was also great at identifying and building leaders for his many association clients. Those who were initially unsure of themselves or their ability to become president of a local, state, or a national association became experts after "the King" was finished with them. Mr. King was so humble he would seldom take any credit to himself, but, rather, he always gave it away to others. (No wonder everyone loved him!) This is what a great speaker should strive for—to be the impetus for someone else's success (while achieving your own goals as well).

You can bring the spotlight to other people because you have the microphone. You can help those in the audience believe in the management team of an organization and, as a result, you are much more likely to get invited back.

The Least You Need to Know

♦ In all situations, hold yourself accountable for your actions and responses to others.

♦ Find a workspace that inspires you.

♦ Work to change the lives of others and to inspire them to greatness.

♦ Don't put your career above your family.

Chapter 22

Your Message Creation, Perfection, and Delivery

In This Chapter

- ◆ Dedicate yourself to perfecting your presentation
- ◆ Using pauses, emphasis, and timing in your message
- ◆ Ways to make yourself memorable
- ◆ Find a spot to let your creative juices flow!
- ◆ Critique and adapt your message to make it its best

You may have been to performances of the opera, for example, where the standing ovation was so sustained that the performer had to come out for a second and maybe third curtain call for more appreciative applause. Can you see that happening after one of your programs?

You may not have those kinds of lofty goals; you might be satisfied with a bronze or silver medal, not the gold.

Well, I work with Olympic athletes sometimes in our effort to market and book speakers, and I can tell you anyone who earns a silver or bronze (second or third place) is the kind of person that is dedicated to winning and going for the gold. This is the type of speaker you must aspire to be!

For longevity in this business, you need 100 percent of the audience to consider your message an A+ magnificent success, not to simply applaud politely at the conclusion of your program. This kind of response is possible.

More Than an Outline: Creating a Masterpiece

In Chapter 6, you were given ideas on how to outline your speech or seminar (or any kind of message) using the tried-and-true vignette method. That is only one part of creating a masterpiece message—before the outline, before fleshing out the vignettes. The first step really is a dedication to creating the perfect message, then learning how to present it with all the verbal and nonverbal cues possible.

Researching your audience demographics and the purpose of the meeting planner and having a great outline are all required elements for delivering an unforgettable, life-changing message. But let's again think of the operatic singer, or the ballet dancer, or the comedian who has perfect timing (or other entertainers who excite and thrill audiences). Their perfected deliveries are what sell these people to their audiences! In other words, these entertainers are so good at what they do, they might appeal to folks *outside* of their targeted demographics (and gain new fans in the process)!

Words to the Wise

> When you purchase any product or service, what is the deciding factor for you? Is it top quality? Is it price? Is it something that makes a positive impression on you so you make a purchase? Is it something different in each new and different situation? Don't ever forget that you are the product you are selling and are subject to buyer scrutiny!

I recently delivered the following dramatic opening for a speech to several groups. The material in quotes indicates me speaking to the group; this is interspersed with my running commentary of their reactions.

E-mail Confusion by Dr. Thom A. Lisk

"How many of you use the Internet for communication? Since this is a speech largely titled *Effective Communications for Increased Success*, please consider the following. Did you see this in your local newspaper?"

Everyone seemed to nonverbally reply, *No, tell me more.*

"This is a lesson learned from typing the wrong e-mail address and not critiquing what you type, as well as say. A Minneapolis couple decided to go to Florida to thaw out during a particularly icy and cold winter. They planned to stay at the same hotel where they spent their honeymoon 20 years earlier. Because of hectic schedules, it was difficult to coordinate their travel schedules. So the husband left Minneapolis and flew to Florida on a Thursday, with his wife flying down the following day."

I looked to see if the audience was listening attentively, and indeed they were, so I continued.

"The husband checked into the hotel. There was a computer in his room, unlike 20 years earlier, so he decided to send an e-mail to his wife back in the cold north. However, he accidentally left out one letter in her e-mail address, and without realizing his error, sent the e-mail into cyberspace. Meanwhile somewhere in Houston, a widow had just returned from her husband's funeral. He was a minister who was called home to glory or his reward, as the widow put it, following a heart attack.

"The widow decided to check her e-mail expecting, apparently, messages of condolences from relatives and friends. After reading her first message, she screamed loudly and fainted. The widow's son rushed into the room, found his mother on the floor, and he saw the computer screen on which he read. It said:"

(Now I read the following with appropriate pauses, emphasis on certain words, and more …)

"To: My Loving Wife

Subject: I have arrived!

Date: Today

Message: I know you are surprised to hear from me! They have computers here now and you are allowed to send e-mails to your loved ones—you. I've just arrived, and when I checked in I made sure they have <u>everything</u> prepared for your arrival … <u>tomorrow</u>. I am looking forward to seeing you again soon! Hope your trip is as uneventful as mine was. Love you, your devoted husband.

P.S. It sure is HOT down here!"

This *created* story always gets lots of laughter if *delivered perfectly!* And it helps to emphasize several points, which I'll go over in the following section.

Delivery: What Is Most Important?

Let's focus here on the actual delivery of your material. All of the following are important to an A+ delivery of any speech:

- Keeping attention

- Positive nonverbal communications

- Eye contact

- Quality of the spoken word

- Use of understandable words

- Use and quality of visual aids

- Tone of your voice

- Questions asked to involve audience

- Energy level of speaker (helps lift audience)

- Stories—effectiveness and delivery

- No notes used by speaker

- Transition effectiveness between each point

- Great opening

- Great closing

After your next 10 presentations, rate yourself on these aspects of delivery, using a scale from 1 to 10 (with 10 being high), comparing yourself to the very best speakers you can find. Ask some objective or expert people to do the same for you as well.

You can prioritize this list, of course, according to your specific presentation. Add to the list if you can think of other items that are important to your creating, perfecting, and delivering. I'll expand on some of these points now.

Pauses, Nonverbals, Cues, and Clues

Using dramatic pauses, as I do when I tell the story of the e-mail mix-up, effectively takes time and practice. Have you ever spoken to someone on the phone who really knows how to use her voice with dramatic pauses, inflections, emotion, and various pitches to get your attention? If this person is in sales, I assure you she sells much more than the average person who doesn't account for the quality of the voice (along with cues planted) for desired responses.

Silence can be truly golden in speaking if used properly. A spouse who gives her partner the silent treatment can change behavior faster than with a lot of criticism, that's for sure! Likewise, a speaker who allows space for people to think about the questions, the message, the visuals, and the nonverbal expressions may often get a better response than others.

Listening Leadership is one of the seminars I give that helps people develop the use of silence and my golden rules for listening so as to lead and succeed more.

Speed Is Not Everything

Your audience demographic may run the gamut from 20-year-olds to 98-year-olds, as happened to me recently. Some of these folks will be fast thinkers; others will be slower in thought and action. Understanding the generational differences and, yes, all the demographics of your audience is a secret to success. Strike a happy balance between the young, fast, aggressive learner and the old, tired, set-in-his-ways listener. Find a speed somewhere in the middle and you won't lose anyone!

Not long ago in my company offices, we hired a wonderful young lady, Taylor. She is efficient, friendly, and will do anything asked of her in a really effective way. But she is young and inexperienced, and knows it, so she needs some coaching advice. Taylor responds well to that, as she has been a noted athlete in track and soccer. But this speed didn't translate well to working on the phone: she had to be coached to slow down so her message would be received, heard, and responded to.

In order to get your message across in the most effective way, people must *hear* you, not just listen to you. Is that happening in your group presentations, or for that matter one-on-one? Asking questions is one of the best ways to have better-received messages … even if you answer your own questions!

If you find that you speak quickly, try using those words for another purpose: visualization. One famous speaker, Zig Ziglar, used to say something like, "The average person speaks at 150 words per minute. I speak at 210 words per minute, with gusts to 450. But don't worry, you can keep up. How? Well, the human mind thinks at 1,500 to 2,000 words per minute. And you see in pictures."

The words you use and choose paint pictures on the canvas of the human minds in your audience. Take time with your words—they will determine the image creation for the picture you want to be captured by each audience member. This is one reason why visual aids can be helpful. Remember what a picture is worth ….

Use Prompts Sparingly

Speaking of making a personal connection with the audience … I hate it (how about you?) when I see someone flipping pages when they give a speech. That is not a sign of a practiced professional speaker. Forgive me for being so blunt, because your ministers, as one example, may do this in your house of worship, as they do mine. I much prefer to follow this example through, a minister who seems to speak extemporaneously from the heart, don't you? One who also steps away from behind the ambo or podium seems to connect better with his flock—what do you think?

If a speaker is not shuffling notes, this does not mean that she is not speaking from an outline or script, but somehow she has developed a system for remembering the main points of the message. Or if she's confident enough like some I know, the speaker is "led by the spirit," trusting that the right words will come through at the right time.

Success Shortcuts

Personally, this is how I speak most of the time. It was not always so. Some speakers use prompts like an acronym as an example upon which to hang their message and help them remember. Or they can use 3×5 cards with key points outlined. Acrostics can help the audience remember, too. T in Thom stands for … H for … O for … M for ….

If you want to become a distinctive, paid speaker on an ongoing basis, never simply read your message to the audience. This is very amateur. Audiences want a lot from a paid speaker, and looking at them—and connecting with them—is a must.

Obviously, knowing your presentation inside and out requires a lot of practice. The legendary football coach Vince Lombardi was once quoted as saying, "Practice does not make perfect! Perfect practice makes perfect!" This held true for his winning team, and it holds true for professional speakers as well: you must practice your presentation perfectly in order to deliver it perfectly.

Make Yourself Memorable

Within 24 hours, people have forgotten at least 25 percent of what they hear. They forget 60 percent in 7 days, and 95 percent in 16 days. Obviously, making yourself as memorable as possible is important in this business! Learning the finer points of this skill may include selling points, but can also be a part of perfecting and delivering your message. How to do this?

Staying Connected

You can pass out material that helps people remember your message, as sort of a friendly reminder. But also consider sending a questionnaire to all audience members in advance. Then incorporate the answers the audience gives you in your presentation, along with your own, also tabulated in a handout. If someone sees or hears their name mentioned, they are going to listen better.

Try to collect the e-mails of all the people in your audience and tell them you will send them the outline or script of your message, or the PowerPoint slides. In this way, you benefit them more and get valuable e-mails while also gaining insight so you can perfect your message further.

Words to the Wise _____

Do not automatically send the entire audience an e-mail without their permission! Of course, if the boss gives you the e-mail addresses of all who will be attending and agrees to allow you to use that list to survey people before the event (or afterward), that is great. But first ask the boss to send an e-mail alert asking the attendees to pay attention to and, if appropriate, respond to your e-mail.

Crafting a Customized Connection

Nearly every day, I talk with speakers who have wonderful messages (or so they tell me), but not enough audiences. Sometimes a speaker is so strongly entrenched in his particular niche, both industry and/or topic, that he does not know what the other possibilities are for the same message.

Often, the same message that has been well accepted in one industry can be adapted and sold to other markets. In other chapters, you were given some ideas about how to market and make that possible—now consider how to adapt your particular message so that you can deliver it perfectly to each group you speak to. First, you may want to turn it into a generic message (complete with an outline) and then record it so you can critique it, before attempting to customize it for a new industry.

Success Shortcuts _____

Every great performer practices and looks for coaching assistance! Taping your message can help you improve, especially if you listen with an open mind and a critical ear to improve the message. Follow up by asking others who are in the know to offer feedback, too.

I know a nearly retired speaker very well who only had one message … but he made a small fortune in the speaking industry! He used the vignette approach (as shown in Chapter 6). About every seven vignettes out of his 50-vignette keynote message, he would insert one or two lines focused on information pertaining to the people in front of him, and suddenly (as they were disarmed laughing at the stories or jokes), they thought he was an expert on their problems, their industry, and their challenges!

Have you heard the expression, "It is all in the mind"? Well, it is usually true, at least with speaking; that is, if your audience perceives and concludes that you have the right prescriptive message, then your background (and/or your original message) actually may have little to do with your success. Your success will depend more on what you can do today: can you deliver the best information for the best clients in the best and most memorable way possible (using the tips you've gleaned from this book)? If so, you will do well in this business!

Winning Openings and Closings

Your opening and closing are two of the most memorable parts of your presentation—use them to your advantage to hook your audience and make yourself memorable!

Personally, my favorite opening line after "Thank you for that kind introduction!" is "How many of you have heard of Thom Lisk before?" I pause briefly to see if hands go up as I have raised mine to prompt the audience. "Now, how many of you don't care that you have never heard of Thom Lisk before?" This never ceases to get a laugh, and after the high, lofty—but important—introduction of myself with all my credentials presented in a way that might cause one to think I can walk on water, I find it wise to humble myself, and use a little self-depreciating humor (the best kind).

Another similar comment I heard a speaker use one time was, "That was a great Burger King introduction! One whopper after another whopper! I am really just like you," he said to the audience in an effort to connect at the opening, "I care about the problems you are facing and am here to present some proven solutions." See the value in that kind of approach?

Closings are just as important as openings, maybe more so. You want to leave the audience on a high note, feeling and thinking things like, "Yes, I can do it!" Of course near the close, you summarize your main point or points of your message, but an uplifting last sentence or a three-stanza poem can set the right tone.

The Guy or Gal in the Mirror©, by Thom A. Lisk

(Notes help to demonstrate nonverbal communication)

"**When you get what <u>you</u>** (point at people all over the audience) **want in your struggle for self,**

And then the world (make a dramatic circle motion with both arms) **finally crowns <u>you</u>** king or queen for a day,

Go to the mirror and see (place hand over your brow, look far and wide, right/left) **what that guy or gal has to say.**

You see, it is not others—your boss, your customers, your spouse, etc.—upon whose judgment you must pass, (pause). **The one who must count <u>most</u> in your life, at least in mine, is almighty God,** (point up) **and then that guy looking back in the glass—the mirror** (hold up open hand as if looking in a mirror—pause so all can understand what you are doing).

Never mind all the rest because he or she (look in the mirror, whether a real mirror of your hand as a mirror)**, is the most important one to please ... never mind all the rest—yes, serve others as best you can ...** (sweeping motion of one arm outstretched moving over the audience), **for he or she** (looking in the pretend or real mirror) **is the one to please** (look at the audience intently) **for <u>you</u> are with yourself clear to <u>the end</u>** (dramatic pause now).

You can be like Jack Horner and go out and chisel a plumb (raise one hand so all can see with an outstretched upward pointing thumb) **and think you are a wonderful guy or gal. But ... please remember** (looking intently at the audience) **your final reward may be heartache and tears** (point to your eye with your finger nearly on your face, then drag the pointing finger down as if you are following a tear down your face) **... if you cheat the guy or gal** (hold up pretend or real mirror again in front of your face) **in the mirror.**

Ladies and gentlemen ... whatever you do ... please do not cheat yourselves ... use all the ideas in my program today to be and do your best. Remember ... YOU ARE TERRIFIC! God bless you!"

Most of us respect the President of the United States when he (all have been men so far as the first edition of this book is completed) closes a speech with a "God bless you" (or "God bless America"), so if it is good enough for a U.S. President, it might be good for you, too. And don't worry about being so politically correct! I have done this in over a thousand speeches or seminars and never had anyone object. Instead I have had people very appreciative and want to do more business as a result!

It's Not Over Yet ...

Knowing and controlling the environment, if possible, where you will deliver your message is another important issue to consider. It does not make sense to invest gobs of time and money creating your message and then have some jerk give you a lousy introduction and/or wrap-up. Amateurs are everywhere, and too often they think they know better than the pro speaker, so they just wing it. You need to write your own introduction and *insist* that it is read the way you wrote it!

In many speech situations, you have a Masters of Ceremonies who will get up (after your message) and make some kind of wrap-up comment about your message. Controlling those words can make or break whether you are remembered the way you would like and whether you get invited back or whether you sell books at the back of the room, too, if that is an objective. So what do you do? Do all you can to control the everything ... expect the best but plan for the worst-case scenario and prevent anything bad from happening to you if at all possible.

Success Shortcuts

Writing your own introduction and then presenting it to your Master of Ceremonies in large type—at least 18-pt.—is important. Write it with a touch of humor, if possible, and do so in a way that connects to the audience you are addressing that day. At the end, the introducer says something like, "Now ... please help me welcome with hearty applause our super great speaker (your name inserted), whose message today is (title of message) ...."

Creating/Writing/Perfecting

This *Complete Idiot's Guide* book is about the business of professional speaking. Now consider, briefly, the importance of having a creative environment where you can do your best message creation. For some people, it might be the same business office environment where you are exercising the left side of your brain. But for most people, it is wise to have another, separate area in the same home where you can exercise your right brain, the creative part, for crafting an articulate and unique message.

Keep Business in the Business Office

For the artistic masters, a business office is always different than the place where their craft is perfected. Two of my favorite mentor speaker-authors were Dr. Norman

Vincent Peale, author of 56 books, and the late great Pope John Paul II, author of at least as many books and other documents. Each had a special way in which they looked for and captured inspiration to create, and used that inspiration to write their messages before delivering them in person or word. If the best and most prolific do this, who are we to do less?

The object is to keep the business side of things—invoices, telephones, computers, and so on—in a completely separate room. In this separate creative space, you may have things only for preparing your presentations, not for the business of speaking. For example, you might have inspirational books or music, comfortable seating, beautiful artwork in your creative space, or anything that sets your creative side free. Give this a try!

Your Personal Library

In my own home, I have three desks and two significant office spaces, both with different kinds of libraries close at hand for reference and research. What does a speaker need in his personal library (in addition to *this* book of course)? Some of the books I would recommend keeping on hand are listed in Appendix C in the back of the book.

You can, of course, get much of what you need via web searches, including access to some of the best libraries of materials worldwide. However, nothing replaces the need for a personal library for the expert professional speaker, as well as for speakers who want to speak more professionally. Set aside a financial budget each month for building your library during the first five years of your speaking career, and budget your time so that you'll be able to read appropriate resources. Look for anything that inspires you to be the best person (and therefore the best speaker) that you can be: inspirational/motivational books, advice from experts in your field or in the speaking arena, biographies, theological works … whatever makes your spirit soar!

Using Google and the Library and Connecting the Dots

Years ago, I heard this expression, and it still pops up today: "Fake it until you make it." I discussed this term with a veteran research-based speaker and she was appalled that people actually believe this statement. Her take on it (and mine, too) is that you had better *not* be faking it, because audiences can see right through you in many cases! They are looking for reliable speakers they can trust—is that you? What happens if you are forced to answer audience questions at the end of a speech or seminar you simply have memorized or scripted (and not invested much of your own time and learning in)? To deliver a message with perfection means with all the skill and technique possible—the least of which is knowing your topic inside and out.

Google is a God-send for speakers who want (or need to be) experts; in addition to finding information on your topic, there are plenty of expert speakers out there in cyberspace sharing their knowledge!

To find the best professional speaker-leaders, do a Google search like I did recently, entering Leadership Research and see what you get. (You can use other terms in your search, like "speech research" or "U.S. Presidents research," but do use the word "research" or something that designates you want the latest researched material.) In my search, the main search column produced a website for a university, then "History of Leadership Research," having to do with school change and so on. On the right-hand side where you find—please realize this—the *paid* sponsored links, I found some groups trying to sell leadership training. Which is the reliable information? Your answer might be as good as mine, but as a CEO who has paid to attempt to get to the top of these lists for Google searches, I know you have to sort through a lot of advertising to get to the meat and potatoes.

Words to the Wise

My friend, Dick Stoner, a comedy magician who once was on the Johnny Carson show, has been at it for many years. Dick is in his 70s, owns magic and comedy retail stores, and *still* must do research to stay current and competitive! He knows how to get you rollicking with laughter by connecting the dots with current humor.

Research Resources

In the regular library, you will not be subjected to (or have to sort through) advertisements from someone trying to sell you something. In fact, the library also offers you something the Internet cannot: human help! You can get a research assistant like my friend Tom Atzberger's wife Chris, who has worked at the Bexley Library for more years than she may admit. Chris can help you quickly find current details about any topic. My precious daughter-in-law Carrie, married to my step-son Andrew Narcelles, M.D., graduated Summa Cum Laude undergraduate and has her Master's with the same high honors in library science. These are the kinds of *professionals* who can save you time and money and help you become the expert you desire to be. Ask for help!

Critique, Practice, and Perfect Your Message

Now that you've read all of the work that goes into designing a winning presentation, ask yourself, "In my experience, how do I best perfect things in my life?"

It probably is not by trial-and-error—that is, unless you have someone to critique you. A good example is the process of writing a book like this one with a huge NYC-based publisher. Before the book is complete, even though I write the manuscript, every sentence may have, in this case, several sets of eyes look at it before it goes to print. Since a speech is designed to reach many, many people (like a book), shouldn't it also go through the same rigorous examination?

No matter how hard you work on your material and/or how much time you put into preparing yourself for its delivery, you are doing yourself, and therefore, your audiences, a disservice if you do not ask, at minimum, two or three trusted allies for their opinions on what you are planning to present. I do not necessarily mean that you need feedback on every word you will present, but certainly on the primary outline and the main points. Practicing in front of a mirror is always a good idea. And you could set up your video camera at home to tape yourself, and then watch it while taking notes as you go about how to improve.

Caring about what each audience member thinks or will think or feel as a result of your message is the master key to connecting—and succeeding—in this business. If you care, then you take time to look into the eyes of people in the audience, nod your head in the affirmative so they will do the same, smile because you know it is contagious, and the like. Work at connecting with your audience—practicing on family members is always a good idea; after all, they are your most important VIP's.

You will not become your best by comparing yourself to amateurs or average speakers—someone you heard at some college class, or church service, or at some conference with nonpaid speakers. Remember a public speaker is not the same as a truly professional speaker; the latter has a perfected message delivered so flawlessly it may seem easy—but by now, you know it is not!

The enterprise of the future in the twenty-first century must transform itself to be cutting-edge competitive. Sometimes change—a 180-degree change—is necessary on short notice to not just succeed, but also survive. Therefore, practicing new methods are not always thought about; organizations need people who can get things nearly perfect from day one.

Words to the Wise

I like to watch other master speakers—those who have perfected their messages—on DVD on our big-screen TV. These men and women inspire me to improve my own skills! If you have not listened to other speakers with near-perfect and flawless messages both in person and on DVD, what kind of basis of comparison do you have, really?

Is that you? You can be the perfect change agent that makes things better for entire organizations, but to do so you need to embody or live the message you are prescribing—at least when practical and possible.

The Least You Need to Know

- Even the best-researched presentation can flop if the delivery of the material is poor. Put time into word choice, word emphasis, pauses, and non-verbal cues.

- Regularly critique yourself and your material—better yet, find a knowledgeable friend or colleague to do it for you!

- Never read your speech from notes or a script—you will lose (and bore) your audience.

- Write your own introduction and/or wrap-up when you know a Master of Ceremonies will be speaking before or after your speech.

- The business side of speaking is important, but so is the creative side. Develop a good balance between the two in order to do your best work!

Glossary

agreement   Similar to a contract between a speaker and a client; it spells out the date of the event, your payment, cancellation fees, and the like.

all-inclusive fee   Speaker payment structured to anticipate travel and lodging expenses and build them into the speaker fee.

base fee   The minimum fee a speaker is willing to accept.

boiler plate agreement   Indicates that the terms are fairly simple and standard.

booking   The act of scheduling a speaking engagement.

bureau-friendly   The act of removing any hint of a speaker's contact information on material used by the speakers' bureaus to present to clients.

certifications   Verification that one has arrived at a certain level of competency in her field.

coach   Holds a team of people or individuals accountable to their goals while helping them to come up with solutions.

consultant   An expert with very specialized knowledge who works with organizations or corporations; a professional problem-solver who sometimes works on retainer.

elevator speech   A short summary of 25 words or less that captures who the speaker is and what he offers; this can be offered to any prospective client or person, anywhere, at any time.

ethics   Codes of conduct that professionals are expected to uphold and encourage in their peers.

expert speaker   Has greater expertise in specific topic areas than nearly all other people.

facilitator   Gives either seminars or workshops; this person helps a team of people work toward a desired goal.

fee basis   Reflects what clients may be willing to pay.

for-profit   Companies that may be answerable to stockholders and must earn a certain amount of money each year.

holds   Dates that are potentially sold to clients but not yet officially contracted.

industry speakers   Experts who often have worked in a particular industry for many years and share their knowledge with audiences in that specific industry.

intellectual property   Your original ideas and opinions and the way in which you present them.

keynote speaker   An expert who addresses an audience and covers the issues of the topic or conference theme. Her goals may include informing and creating motivation.

markets   Groups or organizations broken down by industry type or niche.

mission statement   A series of short "to" sentences highlighting your intentions as a professional speaker.

nonprofit   An organization whose main focus is serving their specific community, not making excess profits. They have a special tax status.

one-sheet   A brochure or sheet of paper listing pertinent details about the speaker and the speaker's offerings and experiences.

patron   Someone who's willing to support and help a speaker professionally or financially; a loyal person.

per diem fee   The amount of money the speaker figures he will spend on food and travel each day he is working for a client; this is paid by the client in one lump sum.

plagiarism   Presenting someone else's original thoughts and materials as your own.

press kit   Contains information about the speaker and her products and services.

press release   Statement written in third person, used to alert media outlets about a speaker's books, appearances, and the like.

preview (or demo tape)   A short 5- to 15-minute video brochure that contains the best clips of the speaker's services, and may present credentials and testimonials.

professional speakers   Experts or others from a given field, topic, or expertise area who are paid to speak to groups.

realized value   The fee that a speaker expects and can reasonably earn and receive from a client.

reference list   Contains the names and contact information of at least three clients who can attest to your professionalism and skills.

references   Existing or past clients who are willing to tell prospective clients that the speaker did a great job and is welcome to serve them again.

seminar   An interactive session led by a trainer or expert speaker that is longer in duration than a workshop.

serving questions   Designed to help the speaker understand the client's needs: who, what, where, when, how, and why?

showcase   An event hosted by a speakers' bureau, where speakers are able to present their material to decision-makers in the hopes of creating a booking or where they have some other important benefits.

speakers' agent   Represents the interests of the speakers—and may book engagements for the speakers, and take a cut of a speaker's earnings. They may also only help speakers create marketing materials or do marketing.

speakers' bureau   Agency representing the interests of the client. Bureaus help clients find speakers for their individual and organizational needs. They also proactively market speakers and want the best interests of speakers.

teleseminar   A seminar delivered by a professional speaker via the phone. Clients sign up and phone into the event.

test market   A relatively small region or market where a product makes its debut.

testimonial letters   Written evidence of the great impact the speaker has made on an organization or an audience.

Toastmasters International   A collection of small, local groups who focus on refining their speaking skills.

trainer   A speaker who specializes in interactive programs.

webinar   A seminar offered via the World Wide Web and led by a professional speaker.

workshop   A trainer-led session meant to help a group of people work through problems and issues and develop workable solutions.

Important Organizations for Professional Speakers

Following I've compiled an alphabetical listing of organizations and agencies that may be helpful for the aspiring speaker. Please note that I've included my own bureau (Professional Speakers' Bureau Int'l). If I can be of assistance, please let me know!

American Society of Association Executives
1575 I Street, NW
Washington, D.C. 20005-1168
Phone: 202-626-2803
www.asaecenter.org

Many people who work full time for associations all over America and other parts of the world belong to this association for association executives. Associations hire speakers; a speaker can become a member just to network with decision-makers in various associations. It's best to join a state branch of this organization first.

American Society for Training and Development
1640 King Street, Box 1443
Alexandria, VA 22313
Phone: 1-800-628-2783
www.astd.org

This association has a membership of trainers who work full time for organizations as well as trainers who are self-employed, independent people. Members usually do more training than keynote speaking. You can learn a lot about how to be a better trainer by attending meetings. They have chapters in many major cities.

U.S. Chamber of Commerce
1618 H. Street NW
Washington, D.C. 20062-2000
Phone: 202-659-6000
www.uschamber.com

Big businesses mostly belong to national and state chambers of commerce. Every city in America has a local chamber of membership that is comprised of small businesses. A speaker can benefit in many ways from developing a relationship with the locals.

Chamber of Commerce Executives Organizations
(Check with your state chamber)

Each state may have its own organization for those who are the staff people of all chambers in that state. You can do a search for the CCEO in your state.

Convention & Visitors Bureaus
(Check your city and state organization)

Every large city and every state has a convention and visitors' bureau. These groups work to bring conventions to the area. You can benefit from membership by getting lists of upcoming conferences that may need a skilled speaker.

Institute of Management Consultants
2025 M. Street NW, Suite 800
Washington, D.C. 20036-3309
Phone: 1-800-221-2557   Fax: 202-367-2134
www.imcusa.org

This organization is for speakers who want to expand their consulting businesses.

International Association of Speakers' Bureaus
7150 Winton Drive, Suite 300
Indianapolis, IN 46268
Phone: 317-328-7790   Fax: 317-280-8527
www.igab.org

Many speakers' bureau owners are members of this organization, but not all. A speaker could benefit most by showcasing at one of their annual meetings in order to be discovered by many bureaus.

International Platform Association (IPA)

This association was co-founded by Daniel Webster in 1830. It was originally an association of town-hall meeting organizers who brought in lecturers and speakers to help educate and/or entertain the community leaders. It was mismanaged and fell into hibernation in 2003, but it may be reactivated at some time. Because it has been such a great positive force for speakers, I have listed it here.

Meeting Professionals International (MPI)
3030 LBJ Freeway, Suite 1700
Dallas, TX 75234-2759
Phone: 972-702-3000   Fax: 972-702-3070
www.mpiweb.org

Speakers can join this organization as a "supplier member." MPI membership consists of planners who purchase (or influence the purchase of) speakers.

National Coalition of Black Meeting Planners
8630 Fenton Street, Suite 126
Silver Spring, MD 20910
Phone: 202-628-3952
www.ncbmp.com

An association of black meeting planners with a membership consisting mostly of black meeting planners and those who serve them.

National Speakers Association (NSA)
1500 South Priest Drive
Tempe, AZ 85281
Phone: 480-968-2552   Fax: 480-968-0911
www.nsaspeaker.org

This association officially founded and provided sales/marketing ideas and leads. Now it is an association with qualifications for membership and chapters in many states.

Professional Convention Management Association
McCormick Place
2301 South Lake Shore Drive, Suite 1001
Chicago, IL 60616
Phone: 312-423-7262   Fax: 312-423-7222
www.pcma.org

PCMA has several categories of membership, including professional, supplier partner, associate professional, associate supplier, faculty member, and student member.

Professional Speakers Bureau Int'l Association
1112 Firth Avenue #101
Worthington, OH 43085
Phone: 614-841-1776   Fax: 614-846-1377

This organization is an association of speakers that also operates as a speakers' bureau, which proactively markets and books speakers. They have categories of membership for aspiring speakers, new speakers, trainers, and veterans.

Religious Conference Management Association
1 RCA Dome, Suite 120
Indianapolis, IN 46225
Phone: 317-632-1888   Fax: 317-632-7909
www.rcmaweb.org

This association has membership represented only by religious organizations' meeting planners and suppliers.

Sales & Marketing Executives International (SMEI)
PO Box 1390
Sumas, WA 98295-1390
Phone: 312-893-0751   Fax: 604-855-0165
       1-800-999-1444
www.smei.org

This association founded in the 1930s and became the "voice for sales and marketing executives," with chapters and annual national or international meetings, as well as local chapter meetings in a few cities. They need speakers.

Society of Government Meeting Professionals
908 King Street, Lower Level
Alexandria, VA 22314
Phone: 703-549-0892

This association has primary members who work for the government as meeting planners; supplier members are also welcome to join. They have a few chapters in major cities, usually in state capitals.

Society of Human Resource Professionals (SHRM)
1800 Duke St
Alexandria, VA 22314
Phone: 1-800-283-7476   Fax: 703-535-6490
www.shrm.org

Human Resource professionals and those wanting to serve HR are members of this national association. SHRM has chapters in many major cities. Earned certifications are among the membership benefits. They need speakers.

Toastmasters International
www.toastmasters.org

Toastmasters is an organization comprised of thousands of small, local groups. Members have the opportunity to sharpen their own communications and group-speaking skills and offer constructive criticism to their member peers.

Travel Industry Association of America
1100 New York Avenue NW, Suite 450
Washington, D.C. 20005-3934
Phone: 202-408-8422   Fax: 202-408-1255
www.tia.org

Membership consists of several categories: accommodations and food service, attractions, transportation companies, travel agencies, and allied organizations.

Travel Show Exhibitors Association
McCormick Place
2301 South Lake Shore Drive, Suite 1005
Chicago, IL 60616
Phone: 312-842-8732   Fax: 312-842-8744
www.tsea.org

Membership includes anyone who is involved in planning or putting on a trade show. They have active and allied members.

Further Reading

If you want more reading in a particular subject area and further rec-
ommendations, please e-mail me at speak@terrificspeakers.com. I have
literally hundreds of useful books in my personal and business libraries;
I only regret that I can't list all of them! For info on seminars, please call
614-841-1776.

Aubuchon, Norbert. *The Anatomy of Persuasion, How to Persuade
Others to Accept Your Proposals.* New York: American Management
Association.
This book gives ideas to assist speakers and trainers, starting with
getting your proposal accepted by the client!

Bartlett, John. *Familiar Quotations.* Canada: Little Brown Publishing,
1968.
Using quotes from history can support the current-day solutions that
you offer in your presentations. This book is filled with them!

Bloch, Ann. *Business Writing. Get the Action You Want in Only One
Draft.* Lenox Dale, MA: Swiss Alp Publishing, 2001.
Speakers must be skilled in business writing; this book gives you the
basics on how to write a successful proposal, how to outline your
expectations of clients, and how to make sure your requests are met.

Dychtwald, Ken. *The Power Years. A User's Guide to the Rest of Your Life.* New York: John Wiley & Sons, 2005.
Dychtwald is an expert speaker in generational differences, especially for baby boomers.

Foreman, Ed. *The Successful Life Course.* Dallas: Executive Learning Systems, 1998.
Foreman is one of the top speakers in America. He presents workable ideas for all kinds of success, health, and prosperity for your personal, family, and business life.

Freedman, Anne. *Unforgettable Speeches and Sales Presentations in 8 Easy Steps.* Coral Gables, FL: Speak Out Inc., 1998.
A speaker who trains and who also publishes her own books to serve her clients teaches presentations ideas and skills in this book.

Hayakawa, S. I. *Use the Right Word: Modern Guide to Synonyms and Related Words.* New York: Readers Digest.
This 700-page book can help you broaden your word usage.

Gross, T. Scott. *Positively Outrageous Service. New & Easy Ways to Win Customers for Life.* New York: MasterMedia Limited, 1991.
He outlines plenty of ideas for offering outstanding service designed to keep clients.

Hughes, Elaine Farris. *Writing from the Inner Self.* New York: Harper Collins Publishers, 1991.
Speakers need to become published authors, to speak and write from their inner self, and share from the heart. Anyone with writer's block will benefit from reading this book.

Jaffee, Aziela. *Honey, I Want to Start My Own Business.* New York: Harper Business, 1996.
This planning guide for couples can help a speaker gain and keep support from his or her spouse, an essential building block of speaker success!

Jeary, Tony. *Inspire Any Audience. Proven Secrets of the Pros for Powerful Presentations.* Tulsa, OK: Trade Life Books, 1997.
The title of this one really says it all—learn to reach and motivate an audience on a deeply personal level.

Leech, Thomas. *How to Prepare, Stage, and Deliver Winning Presentations*. New York: American Management Association, 2004.
This book, written by a speaker-author, gives plenty of ideas for using props, visual aids, and so on.

Lisk, Thom. *Become #1 in Selling! Beyond Success to Significance*. Lima, OH: Fairway Press, 2001
The author of the *Complete Idiot's Guide* you're reading shares secrets for success in personal development, selling, and marketing to motivate you to action. It contains 365 pages with worksheets, stories, etc.

———. *Noble Leadership. Powerful Lessons for Business or Any Institution. For improving Personal Life*. Lima, OH: Fairway Press, 2002.
The author of the *Complete Idiot's Guide* you're reading shares how to be an ethical leader and avoid potential issues and problems.

Littauer, Florence, and Marita Littauer. *Personality Puzzle. Piecing Together the Personalities in Your Workplace*. Grand Rapids, MI: Fleming H. Revell, 1993.
The authors of this book help you understand all kinds of people, a necessary skill in the world of professional speaking.

Mackay, Harvey. *Dig Your Well Before You're Thirsty*. New York: Doubleday, 1997.
The only networking book a speaker might need. McKay is the author of other helpful business books, too.

McCarthy, Kevin. *The On-Purpose Business. Doing More of What You Do Best More Profitably*. Colorado Springs: Pinion Press, 1998.
Provides a modern parable to help us be on-purpose all the time: a speaker who stays focused on his or her purpose, mission, and vision has more success.

Meiers, Mildred, and Jack Knapp. *5600 Jokes for All Occasions*. New York: Wings Books, 1980.
Whatever kind of humor you love best is contained in this kind of book (although speakers are wise to develop original humor, too).

Millbower, Lenn. *Show Biz Training. Fun and Effective Business Training Techniques from the Worlds of Stage, Screen, and Song*. New York: American Management Association, 2003.
Speakers can learn a great deal from actors and other performers about reaching audiences.

Pagano, Barbara, and Elizabeth Pagano. *The Transparency Edge. How Creditability Can Make or Break You in Business*. New York: McGraw-Hill, 2004.
From the title of this book, you can see what speakers need to focus on! Voted Fast Companies book of month.

Peale, Norman Vincent. *The Power of Positive Thinking*. Prentice Hall, Englewood, NJ, U.S., 1952, 1978.
This book is an all-time worldwide best-seller, with more than 20 million copies sold. Peale was voted one of the top speakers of the twentieth century.

Schuller, Robert H. *Believe in the God Who Believes in You*. Nashville: Thomas Nelson Publishers, 1989.
Schuller, a Protestant minister, has been a prolific author. He has been a popular paid speaker and offers materials that can keep the speaker inspired and dreaming big.

Spinrad, Leonard, and Thelma Spinrad. *Speaker's Lifetime Library*. New York: Parker Publishing, 1980.
This huge book gives definitions and details about topics that give a better and deeper understanding of areas affecting audience members. Includes quotes from history.

Steil, Lyman, and Richard Bommelje. Listening Leaders. *The Ten Golden Rules to Listen, Lead, & Succeed*. Edina, MN: Beavers Pond Press, 2004.
Speakers must first and always be great listeners; this book gives you great tips for becoming an active listener.

Sue, Marsha Petrie. *The CEO of You: Your Own Uniqueness*. Scottsdale, AZ: Communication Results Press, 2002.
The terrific speaker in this book helps you "discover the emotional reality of success." CEO stands for Chief Energizing Officer. Speakers need to be energizing and therefore need to be energized on an ongoing basis.

The New American Bible, St. Joseph Edition. *Translated from the Original Languages with Critical Use of All the Ancient Sources*. New York: Catholic Book Publishing, 1986.
The Bible can provide great inspiration and timeless truths for a speaker of any faith, so it can be a resource for further reading. I read it daily.

Theiderman, Sondra. *Bridging Cultural Barriers for Corporate Success. How to Manage the Multicultural Work Force.* New York: Lexington Books, 1991.
A speaker who is an expert in cultural barriers helps the reader understand—and approach—audiences in better and more effective ways.

Wacker, Mary, and Lori Silverman. *Stories Trainers Tell: 55 Ready-to-Use Stories to Make Training Stick.* San Francisco: Jossey-Bass Pfeiffer Publishing, 2003.
Speakers often do training, too, and this book gives lots of thoughtful tips to use when working with groups.

Walters, Dottie. *Sharing Ideas: The International News Magazine for Speakers, Meeting Planners, Agents, Bureaus, Trainers, Seminar Leaders.* Glendora, CA: Royal Publishing.
This is a helpful magazine complete with articles, advertisements, tips, and so on. Published four to five times yearly. Phone: 626-335-8069.

Warum, Roger. *How to Succeed in Family Business.* Hudson, OH: National Center for Family Business, 2003.
This book is written by a speaker who self-publishes, as many speakers do.

Weinstein, Matt, and Luke Barber. *Work Like Your Dog: Fifty Ways to Work Less, Play More, and Earn More.* New York: Villard, 1999.
Weinstein is an accomplished speaker as seen on www.terrificspeaekers.com. In his book, he shows us that it is okay to mix business with pleasure.

Wieder, Marcia. *Making Your Dreams Come True.* New York: Harmony Books, 1999.
The author of this book is a speaker who has appeared on the *Oprah Winfrey Show*. Any speaker would benefit from that kind of media exposure, which creates bookings, increased fees, books sales, and so on.

Williams, Pat. *The Paradox of Power. A Transforming View of Leadership.* Atlanta: Warner Books, 2002.
Mr. Williams is a great speaker, the author of many other books, and senior vice president of the Orlando Magic basketball franchise.

Yager, Jan. *Business Protocol: How to Survive & Succeed in Business.* New York: John Wiley & Sons, 1991.
This speaker provides ideas about how to avoid putting your foot in your mouth, gift-giving strategies to get to the top, male-female relationships, party etiquette, and how to make a positive lasting impression.

Professional Speaker Case Studies

Last but certainly not least, I have gathered the advice of 22 professional speakers and present their collective insight to you here in this appendix. Please note how different each of their backgrounds are—this should be living proof to you that the desire to become a professional speaker is the all-important first step in the process of fulfilling your dream.

In addition to sharing their greatest triumphs, the speakers featured here also let you in on their biggest mistakes. That's right—even professionals have career regrets, but instead of letting those errors drag them down, they view them as lessons learned. Please learn from what these speakers share with you and use their advice to advance your own speaking career.

Most of what follows supports the various points in the book and gives you real live recent examples. These should inspire you, I hope. Also read more about each speaker on the website link. And please help introduce these speakers to anyone who can benefit from their work. I hope you have a great speaking career, too!

Charles (Chic) F. Dambach, MBA

President and CEO, Alliance for Peacebuilding

Background: My first speech of any consequence was in the basic introduction to public speaking course at Oklahoma State University. Like most students, the prospect of facing an audience, not to mention the professor, was terrifying. To my amazement, however, I actually enjoyed the experience; I received an A, and I became a speech major. After an injury knocked me off the football team, I joined the debate and competitive oratory team. Even though I entered school on an athletic scholarship, I helped produce championships with my voice rather than my body. I have been giving speeches to audiences from a few dozen to a few thousand ever since.

Mentor: Dale Stockton, the debate and oratory coach at Oklahoma State in the late 1960s, was one of the greatest men in the entire field of speech and communications. His own speeches (and the sermons he gave whenever he substituted for local preachers) were memorable, but his ability to teach and inspire others was beyond compare. His "Introduction to Public Speaking" became the most popular course on the entire campus. His debate teams became national powerhouses. Only in his early 30s, Dale was emerging as a major figure in the field of social ethics as well as communications. He took special interest in a few of us, and he spent countless hours with us outside the classroom applying the Socratic method. It was exhausting and exhilarating. We learned to listen to and understand others, to think deeply and critically, and then to express ourselves honestly and clearly. I moved into his garage just to be able to learn as much as possible. After graduation and two years in the Peace Corps, I returned to Stillwater to continue my studies with him. Tragically, the following spring he was murdered in a random robbery in Dallas. The great challenge of my life has been to live up to his standards.

Greatest Success as a Speaker (So Far): All of my previous points tie in together. I have given hundreds of speeches all over the world, but the greatest success for me was addressing the honors graduates at Oklahoma State University in 2004. I had been named a "Distinguished Alumnus," and I was asked to share my perspective and provide advice to these remarkable graduating students. Because the school had done so much for me, I worked harder in preparation than I had ever done before. I feared some of my points might be controversial in that environment, so I tested them on friends in advance, and I chose my words carefully. I spoke from the heart with all my soul, and I received a long standing ovation—and an invitation to return and lecture for the student body next year. When it was over, a professor who had been a friend and colleague of Dale Stockton approached me and said, "Dale lives." It was the reward of a lifetime.

Biggest Career Mistake: I once spoke at a large international education convention in Nice, France. It was a great place to be, but I missed the mark completely. I told them what was on my mind, but it had nothing to do with their needs and interests. Every time I fail, it is for the same reason—not knowing in advance what the audience wants and needs.

Niche Topics and Markets: My areas of expertise are organization leadership, conflict resolution, and intercultural relations. Therefore, my primary market includes students and educators, government officials, and community leaders.

One Suggestion for Speakers' Success: Know your subject better than anyone else, and know your audience as though they were your own family.

Goals for the Future: My mission is to help build respect among people and cultures and promote peace among nations. Therefore, my goal is to be effective—to help audiences embrace the concept that we can share this planet with people who may be different, and that we all benefit from positive interaction.

Check out Chic online at www.terrificspeakers.com/html/chic_dambach.html.

Karen Wolfe, M.B.B.S., MA

Australian Physician Who Brings Mind and Spirit Back to Medicine via Speeches and Seminars

Background: As a physician, I felt frustrated that I was treating illness and I wanted to be part of the solution to keep people well. What I found when I spoke to audiences was that the combination of education, inspiration, and motivation can change lives. Now my speaking career is a way to reach so many people with an inspirational and educational message, and I love the work I do. My presentations and music deliver a sense of vibrant health and energy and provide new tools to create the healthy body and mind we all want.

Mentor: My first mentor was the late professional speaker, Dottie Walters. She took me from being a casual speaker to a professional speaker.

Greatest Success as a Speaker (So Far): My greatest success has been to publish (and sell out!) the first edition of my book, *Create the Body Your Soul Desires* (co-authored with Deborah Kern, Southern Century Press, 2003) and have the method in the book replace weight management programs in many hospitals. My tour as the keynote speaker for an organization called "Speaking of Women's Health" has also been a highlight. I spoke in over 10 cities and reached a total of over 5,000 women with my presentation called "Trusting Your Gut."

Biggest Career Mistake: There are always ups and downs as a speaker. I remember sleeping in the baggage claim section of the Chicago airport one night because I missed my connecting flight for a speaking engagement city. I now book early morning flights so I have plenty of time for connecting flight choices. I also remember when I had a tornado alert in the middle of a keynote I was giving and I learned how important it was for me to go with the flow.

Niche Topics and Markets: My passion in my speaking is to empower individuals to take charge of their lives and to live their life on purpose. My number-one niche market is women 30 and over who are looking for "something more" and want to create the life their soul desires.

One Suggestion for Speakers' Success: My biggest advice to other speakers is to be true to yourself. Find what you are passionate about and share it with your audience. Remember in communicating your message that the actual words you use are a small part of communication. Effective nonverbal language plays a huge part in the success of you as a speaker.

Goals for the Future: My goals for the future as a speaker are to expand my message of health to include the importance of financial health and link this with the Laws of Prosperity and the Laws of Abundance.

Check out Karen online at www.terrificspeakers.com/html/karen_wolfe.html.

Dr. Andy Edelman

Speaker for Leadership Development, Conflict Management and Systems Design, Mentoring, and More

Background: As a very fearful public speaker early on, it was not until I became a teacher of high-risk juveniles with behavioral and learning disabilities that I realized that I had a unique gift for reaching and holding the attention of difficult audiences. I learned that the most powerful way to keep the attention of my audience was to entertain, inform, and involve them in a meaningful and memorable way. So I decided to transition and become a pro speaker.

Mentors: Retired Baltimore, Maryland, area police officer and security consultant Paul W. Tolle and internationally renowned martial arts expert Sensei Brian Sutherland were the first people to introduce me to the world of public speaking in the mid-1990s. They presented large-scale law enforcement and personal protection training projects for audiences throughout the northeastern United States.

Greatest Success as a Speaker (So Far): In 2002, I was asked to present to what I thought would be a breakout session round-table audience of 50 teachers at a national conference in Ft. Lauderdale, Florida. To my surprise and shock, my audience turned out to be 1,200+ school district administrators from all over the world. I decided to make the most of it, taking a risk by modeling the style and delivery of talk show hosts, and engaged members from the audience in a variety of ways. My decision paid off and gave me the confidence to continue on in my career development to become a professional speaker.

Biggest Career Mistake: My greatest failure was early on in my career not preparing for technological failures such as burnt-out bulbs or corrupted PowerPoint files. I now prepare presentations with the mindset that everything that could possibly go wrong will happen all at once. I have backup plans for my backup plans and can move from projector to flipchart or whiteboard in a second's notice.

Niche Topics and Markets: My niche topics include Leadership Development, Conflict Management, School Safety, Workplace Violence Prevention, and Personal Protection. The markets I serve include corporations, government, law enforcement, school systems, small business, children, and families.

One Suggestion for Speakers' Success: Involve your audience to keep the pressure on them, not you. The more occupied and engaged they are, the less likely they are to be looking at their watch (and nitpicking you, the speaker).

Goals for the Future: Upon the completion of several books which are in progress, I would like to travel throughout the world, speaking and training in order to make a positive and lasting difference in the lives of others.

Check out Andy online at www.terrificspeakers.com/html/andrew_edelman.html.

Richard Q. Fowler

Character Portrayals of Benjamin Franklin: Humorous, Interactive, Educational, Modern-Day Applications

Background: As a member of the Sons of the American Revolution, I found that young people are not learning history today, especially American Revolution history. People often told me I looked like Benjamin Franklin, so I bought a costume and started doing character portrayals of Benjamin Franklin. That is helping to achieve my goal of teaching young people about the heroes of the American Revolution who fought and won our freedom.

Mentor: My mentor was Douglas North. Ten (or so) years ago, we traveled together to different schools to teach American Revolution history to young people. He had so much energy and got the kids so excited about history, and that is what I have tried to do. He is still going strong at age 92. He even broke a leg a few years ago on his way to work with young people, and yet he still keeps going. I hope to emulate him.

Greatest Success as a Speaker (So Far): My greatest success was teaching American History to over 500 fourth-grade students (in one day!) at Battle Days in Point Pleasant, West Virginia, last October. Later that evening, I also gave my presentation to more than 500 people, mostly adults, at a candlelight tour. I received many heartfelt thanks for my presentations as I have learned how to provide applications for life today.

Biggest Career Mistake: My greatest failure was a very poor turnout of only seven people at a local library. I learned that it is very important to work hard to ensure getting better turnouts.

Niche Topics and Markets: I have been niched mostly in schools and local organizations as I have developed into a better speaker during my first year. With the experience I have gained, I am ready to expand my horizons, and now serve adults, too.

One Suggestion for Speakers' Success: My suggestion for speakers would be to speak *with*, not *to*, people. It is good to move around among the people and let them know you are interested in them (more than yourself). Never speak down to them, and always liven up your presentation with humor. Ben was a great example of that!

Goals for the Future: My objective is to present myself as "Benjamin Franklin" to as many people as possible and tell them about the real Mr. Franklin and the American Revolution. As Benjamin Franklin, I hope to better capture their attention and help build in them a desire to learn more about the American Revolution and its heroes who gave us our freedom. And also, when and where appropriate, I want to provide Franklin's wisdom toward solving modern-day problems—he is a hero for all ages, and a very fascinating and unique speaker to engage.

Check out Richard online at www.terrificspeakers.com/html/richard_fowler.html.

Arlene Taylor, Ph.D.

Risk Manager and Director of Hospital Infection Control

Background: It was my first job after graduating from college—school nurse for a large high school in Utah. The students were so much fun and I loved interacting with them. Over time I began to realize that many students asked me similar questions and I replied to them over and over again. It occurred to me that it would be so much more efficient if I got a group of them together and answered the questions once. However, in terms of prioritization of fear, public speaking was number one in my book; consequently I continued to answer questions one at a time. Later that first year, the school principal asked me to speak at a general assembly about some aspect of health. Because the principal had given me a directive, my options were either to find a way to make the presentation or look for a different job (or so it seemed to me).

Mentor: At the time, my direct supervisor was a public health nurse, a woman in her late 50s who (although not a public speaker herself) was one of the most gifted communicators I have ever met. In a nutshell, she told me that people who fear public speaking usually do so because they get caught up in thinking about how others will perceive them and whether or not they will meet the expectations of the listeners (to say nothing of themselves). If you can't get past that, I later learned, you'll never be a sought-after, successful dynamic speaker, especially one that is paid to speak.

Greatest Success as a Speaker (So Far): I had been asked to present a Friday-night keynote for a weekend women's retreat for which approximately 800 women had registered. Arriving at the venue early, I discovered that more than 1,200 women had already shown up! The program schedule was in disarray and the planner was almost prostrate from stress. The dining room could not accommodate 1,200 women, nor could the meeting room that had been booked. Unexpectedly, I heard myself proposing to the host that we simply divide the women into two groups. I offered to present a keynote for the first group while the second group ate in the dining room, then we would simply exchange places and I would do it all over again. Within 30 minutes, we had everything arranged. Everything went unbelievably smoothly, I did a credible job with the keynote, and basically the weekend was saved. My greatest contribution was not in my presentation, but in being willing to brainstorm a last-minute solution with the program planner.

Biggest Career Mistake: I arrived to make a presentation to a large parent-teacher group. The venue turned out to be a huge gymnasium. Spotlights were focused in such a way that I could not see the audience or my presentation across the teleprompter. Sound through the public address system echoed and bounced around the room so that I could hardly hear what I was saying myself. I was too distracted to concentrate on what I wanted to convey and heard myself pausing repeatedly and using fillers (e.g., "Ummm … ahhh …"), all of which did not meet my standard of excellence. The audience was restless (of course!) and everyone was relieved when the long evening ground to a halt. I learned to always show up early at the speaking venue, even going the day before when feasible, to work with the planning crew and problem-solve in advance to offer the best presentation possible within available resources.

Niche Topics and Markets: *Harvard Business Journal* recently published an article entitled "Manage Your Energy, Not Your Time." That represents my passion! Brain function research has advanced to the point that we now know how the brain learns best (although not how it learns) and how individuals in every walk of life can be successful by design—as they understand more about brain function and practically apply that information on a daily basis. It is life-changing and so much fun!

One Suggestion for Speakers' Success: Identify your passion in life and then find a way to share that with others in exciting, practical, and meaningful ways. Do your own personal and professional work with the goal of having every person with whom you come into contact be better off because you touched their lives.

Goals for the Future: In collaboration with another speaker, I have developed a 21-course program entitled "Build Your Business by Design." This incorporates many of the strategies I speak about in my presentations but allows individuals to move through the information at their own pace via Internet or hard copy. It is so exciting to be able to take brain-function research and package it in easy-to-understand language so everyone can benefit from it! I intend to continue speaking regularly and to balance that with more writing.

Check out Arlene online at www.terrificspeakers.com/html/arlene_taylor.html.

Chris McIntyre

Owner, Be! Everywhere You Are!

Background: I was a Captain in the Air Force and volunteered to speak in a local prison. I just wanted to give back to a population I could have easily been a part of. Growing up, I got into a lot of trouble and saw the dreams of too many of my friends lost. Time seemed to disappear while speaking! It felt effortless! I knew instantly it was my calling in life.

Mentor: Sadly, my experience has been that speakers aren't extremely kind to newcomers. Most speakers represent a one-person show. Genuinely committed mentors, for a rookie speaker, are rare for fear of competition or conversely, lack of belief in your legitimacy! I've had much better luck finding willing mentors in the management-consulting arena. I ultimately connected with Jennifer Sedlock, who's been an amazing resource! And Dr. Lisk has been helpful to me, too.

Greatest Success as a Speaker (So Far): A few months after I moved to San Diego, I volunteered to deliver the keynote for a church's Men's Day event. It was the first time I was announced as a professional speaker. I spent a ton of time with the prep for that 20-minute talk and was never more nervous in my life! No one really knew me, so the event planners were terrified about how my performance might be. The event was a huge success, earning a standing ovation. For me, it was confirmation that I'd chosen the right line of work.

Biggest Career Mistake: Quitting my day job! I found my God-given purpose; I was a successful military officer; I was (a bit too) high on confidence! Naïveté led me to believe I'd move to a city—one I'd never been in before—start a successful business, and be rich in six months. Instead, I went broke! I spent all of the money I'd saved and went 40K into debt on credit cards. I never considered I'd have to actually prove myself before being taken seriously. Three years later, I'm still proving myself and am just now starting to earn professional keynote fees. I'd suggest not quitting your day job until it costs you to *not* speak full time. In other words, speak part time and keep your regular job as Dr. Lisk recommends in this book.

Niche Topics and Markets: Be present! My focus is simple: show up—wherever you go! I've seen far too many people miss opportunity in the moment by fearing the future … based on failures of their past. I'm most interested in working with the Fortune 500 groups. I make corporate money so I can offer discounted services to the Christian and nonprofit communities I also love to serve.

One Suggestion for Speakers' Success: Develop seminars to augment your speaking topics and have others find the work for you! I connected with every local organization doing any type of leadership development training. I took every independent contracting opportunity I could get and soon established myself as a "go-to" trainer. I backed into my speaking topics based on the needs I saw during the trainings. I get several calls every month now to deliver training to Fortune 1000 organizations! One more thing here: check your ego at the door! Not every organization's going to call you back. I wasn't used to being blown off—some only have one need for one event. Get used to it—it happens!

Goals for the Future: I want to be published in the book you're reading right now! If you're reading this, YAY ME! I plan to speak internationally on leadership and resilience. I want my mom to see me speaking on TV … in the new house that I bought her!

Check out Chris online at www.terrificspeakers.com/html/chris_mcintyre.html.

David Hart

Jump Institute (Motivational Skydiver!)

Background: Like many things in life, a fork in the road led me to speaking. I was working in sales for a pre-employment background check company and participating on the skydiving team they sponsored. The cold call sales process wasn't working for me, so I went out and booked myself as a guest speaker at human resource manager functions, their target market. Speaking like this allowed me to directly market my employer's services to their target market and ultimately close new business. In a short period of time I spoke at 60 to 70 events and realized I enjoyed public speaking and had a gift for engaging the audience.

Mentor: On a warm Ohio spring day, ironically Friday the 13th, I took Howard Putnam, former CEO of Southwest Airlines, tandem skydiving. Howard invited me to be part of a cover story in *USA Today*. Since then, Howard has gone out of his way to network me into the "right" circles within the speaking industry. I am deeply grateful for his support and friendship.

Greatest Success as a Speaker (So Far): One client in particular stands out in my mind—the Ohio Bureaus of Workers Compensation, Safety Division. They implemented most of my ideas that would take their event to a higher altitude. It is or should be every speaker's goal to create as much meaningful and relevant value as possible for the client. In the case of the safety division, they themed the conference under the title "Extreme Safety," then they had me give the opening keynote, which included an actual exhibition, skydiving into the IX Center in Cleveland. After my keynote address to 1,200 people, they all filed out of the auditorium and received a custom poster of me and my team skydiving off Lower Manhattan with the Statue of Liberty in the foreground and the event theme on the poster. It all came together to make the event memorable for the audience well after the convention. This has also been my single highest revenue-producing event.

Biggest Career Mistake: At times I lose focus on feeding my own sales process. I love to speak, teach, and write about my niche subject matter, so I tend to gravitate toward those activities. I'm learning to discipline myself to be more consistent in feeding my business, by consistent marketing (as described in this book). Fortunately, active speaking generates more speaking opportunities and corporate training, which generates sales.

Niche Topics and Markets: I love my niche topic of leadership and teamwork. Because I have lived on high performance teams as an elite Army Ranger, competitive skydiver, and business professional, I can draw from first-hand experience to convey key lessons through stories. My material is relevant to all ages and industries.

One Suggestion for Speakers' Success: Focus on the niche you enjoy and have first-hand experience with—everything good will flow from that.

Goals for the Future: My future goals are to increase the quality of my message and the quantity of people I deliver it to. These goals may never change.

Check out David online at www.terrificspeakers.com/html/david_hart.html.

John Eckberg

Journalist, Author, Storyteller, and Speaker

Background: Most people see a newspaper and think information. I see a newspaper and think stories. A life-changing moment for me came when I heard Tami Longaberger, chairman of the Longaberger Company, detail in her own words some of the lessons of her father, Dave Longaberger, who created a basket company that at one time had close to $1 billion in revenues. The sales came because associates in his company always told the story of his family. And that set me to thinking. Take about 50 conversations I have had with American moguls, cultural icons, innovators, and trailblazers; put them in a book; and then talk about the lessons of their ambition from a podium. My book, *The Success Effect: Uncommon Conversations with America's Business Trailblazers* (Sterling & Ross; a trade paperback is planned for 2008), was born and so, too, was a new career direction.

Biggest Career Mistake: My biggest failure, I think, came early on when I spoke at a breakfast meeting of a local service club. When I launched into my speech with a hearty "Thanks for having me here today," I could see the eyes of the audience go flat. I knew the next 20 minutes would be me staggering through my speech with most of the men in the audience glued to their BlackBerries or their wrist watches. I lost them from the beginning.

One Suggestion for Speakers' Success: The event illustrates the biggest challenge for speakers, which is, I think, summed up best by the character Walter in the comedy classic *The Big Lebowski*. In the movie, Walter marks a gutter ball as a big zero for bug-eyed Smokey, and when Smokey complains, Walter replies, "This is bowling, Smokey. This isn't 'Nam. There are rules!"

So, too, with public speaking … there are rules. And one of the rules, I now understand, is that the opening 10 seconds of the speech are critical to the success of the rest of the presentation. The opening line, like any decent newspaper story, needs to entertain and grab the audience. As a result, I have one strategy that never fails to work. It starts with *not* thanking folks for inviting you. That opener is so commonplace, so tired, it is guaranteed to dull the eyes and kill the appetite for whatever else you have to say. I always thank the sponsor or group, but never in the opening line. I work it in toward the end of my presentation, thereby leaving a lasting impression that I am somebody who is grateful, considerate, and likeable. I launch my speeches with an anecdote—a story.

Niche Topics and Markets: Stories have immense power to entertain, and I sprinkle them liberally throughout my speeches. One of my better tales of American commerce is about failure. It involves the Bald Men's Gardening Club of Westwood. This group of pals gardened together in the mid-1980s in Cincinnati and decided that they should create a business based on a mold that could be clamped upon a growing eggplant. So far so good. Millions of eggplants are produced by backyard gardeners each year in America. That niche would surely be huge. Their chosen mold—Elvis—would soon bring about the demise of their notion, because, well, Elvis was already claimed. The trio went ahead with their plans anyhow, created a clear plastic mold out of a bust of Elvis, and when they clamped it over an eggplant, that vegetable grew into the spitting image of Elvis, right down to the sneering lip. Everybody was going to be rich, they thought. The Elvis Presley estate had other plans, and this idea soon withered on the vine because 90 percent of the revenues would have to be directed to the Presley estate. I think this story resonates so well with listeners because it's funny, everybody knows what an eggplant and what Elvis looks like, and it taps into the dream that everybody has of achieving wealth and riches in America beyond imagination. Copyright law often brings dreams back to Earth.

Goals for the Future: As I move through my career, I plan on targeting my public speaking initiatives exclusively to after-dinner events and business-oriented audiences. For one thing, you get a free meal, and it's usually a good one, too. I also plan to continue to tell stories I know and lessons I've learned by standing on the shore of the river of American commerce. Those tales are always going to be interesting and insightful for my business audiences. What's more? There's a boatload of them, too.

Check out John online at www.terrificspeakers.com/html/john_eckberg.html.

Rodger B. Price

Primal Marketing, Expert Speaker

Background: When a recession hit my printing business, I almost lost my business. I began an intensive education program on marketing, customer service, and psychology.

I created a new way of marketing my business from what I learned based on emotion. I executed an action plan to implement this strategy. Within two years, I had doubled my sales and increased my profits by 500 percent. I bought my closest competitor's company, then sold my company for appreciably more than I could have before. I knew that I was on to something new and exciting and wanted to help other entrepreneurs like me.

Mentor: Though I have never been a mentor-seeking person, colleagues from the National Speakers Association as well as Dr. Thom Lisk, author of this book and the CEO of a speakers bureau, have been valuable resources for information, ideas, and support. The best thing I ever did was hire my professional speech coach, Alexandra Sagerman. She helped me "walk my talk." With her help, I was able to create a memorable and valuable brand.

Greatest Success as a Speaker (So Far): My greatest success came after I rebranded my company and myself. I threw out thousands of dollars of marketing material and videos and started over. Within months, my sales tripled and my fee doubled. This has lead to better referrals, better engagements, my own radio show, and countless other opportunities. The other big success is the relationships I have made with other speakers who have not only become sources of information, ideas, and support, but have become lifelong friends. After a while, relationships are what it's all about.

Biggest Career Mistake: My biggest mistake was becoming a "student" of speaking instead of a "practitioner." What this means is that my love of learning stopped me from doing. I learned so much that I couldn't implement anything because I felt overwhelmed. You don't have to implement everything every time you hear (or read) someone say, "You should do this." It is better to pick and choose what fits your own unique benchmark, not try to do it all.

Niche Topics and Markets: I have a very niche brand of Primal Marketing®, Primal Customer Service, Primal Sales, and Primal Branding. They all revolve around how we use emotion in our purchasing behavior and how emotion breaks through marketing noise and causes clients to remember you and your product. The markets I serve are associations of business owners, manufacturers, distributors, corporations with distributor channels, and franchise organizations. I do also work with speakers' bureaus like Professional Speakers Bureau Int'l and TerrificSpeakers.com.

One Suggestion for Speakers' Success: Do not try to be all things to all people. Be an expert in one area as your foundation and work from there. Unless you are famous or have done something amazing, it is better to market your topics a "name brand" than try to make it with using your name.

Goals for the Future: Release my book, *Primal Marketing*, in conjunction with a video/CD/workbook collection. I also plan to do public seminars for business owners on marketing. My next book is a humorous take on fatherhood.

Check out Rodger online at www.terrificspeakers.com/html/rodger_price.html.

ZaLonya Allen, Ph.D.

Personal Development, Leadership and Motivation Trainer, Poet, and Speaker

Background: When I was a college student, an advisor told me I had to take Speech 101. I was terrified but determined to get my degree, so I did it. I quickly learned that public speaking was the number-one fear in the world and that there were people who were more afraid of it than I was. My classmates thought I was good and encouraged me to do more. I later began volunteering to speak for schools and community groups. People from the audience would come up to me afterward and tell me how much my speech inspired them. Children would write letters explaining how my speech helped them increase their self-esteem. It was rewarding to hear people say that my words made a difference in their lives. I started to believe speaking was my calling and that I had to become a speaker to share my experiences and help those who wanted to change their lives for the better.

Mentor: A few years ago, I attended a seminar on how to become a successful speaker. That speaker had such passion for training speakers and really tried to deliver valuable and useful information. I learned more about the speaking business at that seminar than from anything I had done previous to that. I wish this book by Dr. Thom Lisk had been available to me when I started!

Greatest Success as a Speaker (So Far): One of my greatest successes was when I spoke at Detroit Edison. It was my first paid speaking engagement. I had been speaking for free and to have someone pay me to do something that I loved so much was unbelievable. It opened the door to possibilities.

Biggest Career Mistake: My biggest mistake as a speaker was when I was in front of an audience and in the middle of the speech I forgot what I was going to say. Thanks to my training, I knew how to keep the audience from realizing what was happening, but I was disappointed that my presentation didn't have the impact that I wanted it to have. From that experience, I learned how to think on my feet and became a better speaker because of it. I stopped writing such canned speeches and spoke more from the heart and was better received as a result.

Niche Topics and Markets: Although I speak on other topics, my niche topics are motivation and leadership. I studied organizational psychology in college and have always been fascinated by the study of human behavior at work. Organizational psychologists focus a great deal of attention and research on motivation and leadership, and this is an area where I felt I could really make a difference.

One Suggestion for Speakers' Success: The one piece of advice I would give other speakers is to speak all over the world, but if you do not know how to market your services, you will not have any success as a speaker anywhere.

Goals for the Future: My goal as a speaker and author is to continue to grow and deliver the most content-rich, entertaining presentations that I possibly can. I want to help people all over the world achieve more harmony in their personal and professional lives through the spoken and written word.

Check out Dr. Allen online at www.terrificspeakers.com/html/zalonya_allen.html.

Rosalie Moscoe

RNCP and Professional Speaker

Background: I was a singer/performer/recording artist for hundreds of thousands of children. It truly was an exciting career, but it became exhausting. I began to seek ways to achieve stress relief, healthier eating habits, and work/life balance for increased well-being; when I found methods that worked well, my physical health and outlook improved, and my family's health was also boosted. I decided to change careers and become a professional speaker, as I had a burning desire to tell the world what I had learned about the journey to balanced living and general wellness.

Mentor: Meeting professional speaker Burt Dubin at a conference in Atlanta some years ago was the chance of a lifetime. I sat down beside him at a table, and since that time he has helped me become a speaker with spirit and passion. He has also helped me with marketing and sales skills. His extensive learning packages and speakers' boot camps helped give me the tools to do my job at a higher level than I dreamed possible.

Greatest Success as a Speaker (So Far): The talk I recently gave for palliative care nurses and other palliative care workers wasn't my highest-paid speech by far, but I feel it was one of my greatest successes. To be able to lift people out of the depths of working with dying people is a feeling like no other. Using my stories, songs, and strategies, they said I gave to them skills, tools, strength, and joy to continue their difficult jobs. I felt I was doing God's work.

Biggest Career Mistake: Learning that giving video/teleseminars needs to be approached differently than a live talk. On my first try at a teleseminar, the lighting was poor and the audience couldn't see my face well. The medium I used with a 15-second delay was not good for interaction. Not seeing the audience was difficult for me. I learned that I needed more coaching on this front (and plan to get it to make this medium more of a success)!

Niche Topics and Markets: Health and wellness, specifically stress reduction, nutrition improvement, and finding a healthy balance in life. I feel that in order for people to become healthy in mind and body and spirit, they need to assess and work on the areas on their wellness wheel: mental, physical, emotional, vocational, spiritual, social, and financial. I study and try to live and breathe a health-and-wellness life, and these topics are for me passions of the greatest magnitude that I love to share with others.

One Suggestion for Speakers' Success: Find ways to stay calm, centered, and confident and know that you are a child of the universe. Bring into your heart the truth that you have chosen—and perhaps have been chosen to—speak your truth to help make this planet a better place through your significant messages and life.

Goals for the Future: My goal is to continue speaking and writing on issues surrounding health and well-being. I'll be applying for a government grant to help teach students in high schools and universities about "Nutrition for Good Mental Health" (the name of my proposed material), as this information can help others achieve their goals. I also plan to have my own TV show on these vital subjects. I also plan to release my upcoming e-book entitled *The Hurried Woman Transformed! From Surviving To Thriving.*

Check out Rosalie online at www.terrificspeakers.com/html/rosalie_moscoe.html.

Tad Kallini, CSP

Certified Professional Speaker, Management/Leadership Niche

Background: Some say that speakers are born, not made. Others say that speakers are made, not born. My experience would indicate that many speakers just fall into it. As early as my first high school speech course, I found that I had a certain comfort level and a connection with my audience. Twenty years of corporate experience (and a few years in the military) found me speaking to (or training) groups of people in virtually every position I held. I enjoyed it so much that, at the 20 year point, I simply made the leap to speaking professionally full time—certainly a case of blind faith!

And in 2002, I earned the designation of Certified Speaking Professional (CSP) from the National Speakers Association. Forty-eight states, six foreign countries and over 750 presentations later, I still love it!

Mentor: I would like to say that there was one person who led the way for me in terms of mentoring. I can't. I owe most of the success I've had to the professional men and women of the National Speakers Association, and specifically, the Washington, D.C. chapter. Through involvement in the chapter's Board (six years, including one year as President), I did not learn how to speak—I learned the business of speaking! And to them, I am truly grateful.

Greatest Success as a Speaker (So Far): I feel that every program that is well-received by the audience, and that makes a difference in someone's life, is a huge success. With that said, my short program delivered to an international audience at the United States Embassy in Athens, Greece, ranks as *the* success. However, it will never eliminate the horrible feeling I had for weeks after failing to show up for a pro bono speech at a local Toastmasters meeting. Lesson learned: to eliminate confusion, *always* confirm both the *day* and the *date* for every program, both well before and the day before.

Biggest Career Mistake: One of the first, and hardest, lessons to be learned is that those who are successful are "marketers who speak." There's no question that we have to have something to say and that our content must be credible. I am sure Thom Lisk confirms these facts in this great new book. But some of the best speakers on the planet are starving because they never get in front of enough audiences. And sadly, there are some fantastic marketers who are financially secure despite their content. I can't suggest that one is more important than the other. Both must be a central focus of your business and marketing plan, from my experience.

Niche Topics and Markets: My focus has always been management and leadership. I did just a bit of motivational speaking, but decided to go with my strength and my years of experience, from hourly paid worker to Corporate VP for Learning & Development. My ability to connect with all levels, but specifically with first- and second-level management, became a natural transition for speaking to that type of audience. Most of my programs are based on proven experience, with a little bit of book learning thrown in for good measure.

Check out Tad online at www.terrificspeakers.com/html/tad_kallini.html.

Dr. Maurice A. Ramirez

Renaissance Man, Business Man, Physician, and Masterful Speaker

Note to my readers: Dr. Ramirez and I are both auto-diadactic polymath thinkers, so I thought you would find the following material helpful. When Dr. Ramirez kindly responded to my request for speaker information, his focus was mostly on "One Suggestion for Speakers' Success." He has a lot of valuable information to share, and so I included as much as possible for your assimilation and application.

One Suggestion for Speakers' Success: When I was offered the honor of contributing my "ONE Thing" to guide professional speakers, I knew what to say.

"Feed your business and your business will feed you!"

The trick is what to feed your business. Many authors, speakers, and consultants will tell you to feed your business money—lots of money. While money is needed to start a new business and make a business grow, undirected money is *not* the food your business needs. In a career spanning over a quarter century, I learned that you feed your business a balanced diet from the four business food groups: education, public relations, marketing, and advertising.

Education: The concept of the highly educated professional speaker is not new. "Education through Eloquence—Eloquence through Education" is my company's catch phrase, but education is so much more than course work and technical expertise. Education includes investing in mentoring for you and being a mentor to others. It also includes becoming a member of your professional associations, like Professional Speakers Bureau Int'l, an association that markets speakers, as well as others.

Public Relations/Marketing/Advertising: When it comes to public relations (PR), marketing, and advertising, the situation becomes a little more complex. The first problem is that in most small business owner's minds, these are synonymous terms. *They are not.* My take on it is as follows:

"Public Relations" is the establishment of you and your company as *the* recognized expert within a specific demographic, geographic, and/or professional group. This is also known as "branding." Thus public relations is the process of branding. At this stage, it is almost irrelevant what your PR says as long as it positions you as the expert's expert.

"Marketing" is association of your established brand with products and or services in the mind of a particular person, demographic, geographic, and/or professional group.

A "market" is that identifiable person, demographic, geographic, and/or professional (or other) group or groups in one or more niches. While public relations is the process of "branding," marketing is the process of "establishing the brand," thus helping to create clients (as Dr. Lisk points out in this book).

"Advertising" is the establishment of a sense of need for a product or service in the mind of your market. Even if your market knows your name (brand) and your products/services, if they do not know that they need your products or services, they will never buy! On the other hand, if they "feel the need," they will seek you out.

What Comes First: Applying business triage principles, you can identify and concentrate on what you need to do most. The first step in each of these triage techniques is to identify and categorize your desired outcomes:

◆ Critical/Essential Outcomes: Those that must occur to meet the overall financial or service mission.

◆ Urgent/Important Outcomes: Those that facilitate the overall financial or service mission, but are not essential to that mission.

◆ Supportive/Optional Outcomes: Those that facilitate the overall financial or service mission, but are ancillary and thus not necessary to the mission.

Once the outcomes are classified into these categories, identify the processes that support the desired outcomes. Once the processes are identified, they, too, must be categorized:

◆ Critical/Essential Processes: Those that must be supported to meet the desired outcome.

◆ Urgent/Important Processes: Those that facilitate the desired outcome, but are not essential to meeting the desired outcome.

◆ Supportive/Optional Processes: Those that facilitate the desired outcome, but are ancillary and thus not necessary to meeting the desired mission.

Essential/Critical Outcomes are fully supported first with all available resources; then Urgent/Important, and finally Supportive/Optional. Anyone who wants to increase their profits will get great results if the just remember: feed your business and your business will feed you!

Check out Dr. Ramirez online at www.terrificspeakers.com/html/maurice_ramirez. html.

Index

C

Q-R

Great gifts for *any* occasion!

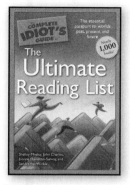

ISBN: 978-1-59257-645-6

ISBN: 978-1-59257-617-3

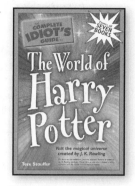

ISBN: 978-1-59257-599-2

ISBN: 978-1-59257-749-1

ISBN: 978-1-59257-557-2

ISBN: 978-1-59257-538-1

ISBN: 978-1-59257-631-9

ISBN: 978-1-59257-715-6

ISBN: 978-1-59257-567-1

ALPHA

idiotsguides.com

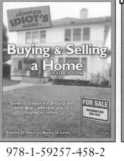
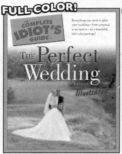
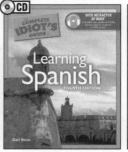